IBM'S REPOSITORY MANAGER/MVS

Books from QED

Database

Migrating to DB2
DB2: The Complete Guide to Implementation and Use
DB2 Design Review Guidelines
DB2: Maximizing Performance of Online Production Systems
Embedded SQL for DB2: Application Design and Programming
SQL for DB2 and SQL/DS Application Developers
Using DB2 to Build Decision Support Systems
The Data Dictionary: Concepts and Uses
Logical Data Base Design
Entity-Relationship Approach to Logical Data Base Design
Database Management Systems: Understanding and Applying Database Technology
Database Machines and Decision Support Systems: Third Wave Processing
IMS Design and Implementation Techniques
Repository Manager/MVS: Concepts, Facilities and Capabilities
How to Use ORACLE SQL*PLUS
ORACLE: Building High Performance of Online Systems
ORACLE Design Review Guidelines
Using ORACLE to Build Decision Support Systems
Understanding Data Pattern Processing: The Key to Competitive Advantage
Developing Client/Server Aplications in an Architected Environment

Systems Engineering

Quality Assurance for Information Systems: Methods, Tools, and Techniques
Handbook of Screen Format Design
Managing Software Projects: Selecting and Using PC-Based Project Management Systems
The Complete Guide to Software Testing
A User's Guide for Defining Software Requirements
A Structured Approach to Systems Testing
Storyboard Prototyping: A New Approach to User Requirements Analysis
The Software Factory: Managing Software Development and Maintenance
Data Architecture: The Information Paradigm
Advanced Topics in Information Engineering
Software Engineering with Formal Metrics

Management

Introduction to Data Security and Controls
CASE: The Potential and the Pitfalls

Management (cont'd)

Strategic and Operational Planning for Information Services
Information Systems Planning for Competitive Advantage
How to Automate Your Computer Center: Achieving Unattended Operations
Ethical Conflicts in Information and Computer Science, Technology, and Business
Mind Your Business: Managing the Impact of End-User Computing
Controlling the Future: Managing Technology-Driven Change
The UNIX Industry: Evolution, Concepts, Architecture, Applications, and Standards

Data Communications

Designing and Implementing Ethernet Networks
Network Concepts and Architectures
Open Systems: The Guide to OSI and its Implementation

IBM Mainframe Series

CSP: Mastering Cross System Product
CICS/VS: A Guide to Application Debugging
MVS COBOL II Power Programmer's Desk Reference
VSE COBOL II Power Programmer's Desk Reference
CICS Application and System Programming: Tools and Techniques
QMF: How to Use Query Management Facility with DB2 and SQL/DS
DOS/VSE: Introduction to the Operating System
DOS/VSE: CICS Systems Programming
DOS/VSE/SP Guide for Systems Programming: Concepts, Programs, Macros, Subroutines
Advanced VSE System Programming Techniques
Systems Programmer's Problem Solver
VSAM: Guide to Optimization and Design
MVS/JCL: Mastering Job Control Language
MVS/TSO: Mastering CLISTS
MVS/TSO: Mastering Native Mode and ISPF
REXX in the TSO Environment

Programming

C Language for Programmers
VAX/VMS: Mastering DCL Commands and Utilities
The PC Data Handbook: Specifications for Maintenance, Repair, and Upgrade of the IBM/PC, PS/2 and Compatibles
UNIX C Shell Desk Reference

QED books are available at special quantity discounts for educational uses, premiums, and sales promotions. Special books, book excerpts, and instructive materials can be created to meet specific needs.

This is Only a Partial Listing. For Additional Information or a Free Catalog contact
QED Information Sciences, Inc. • P. O. Box 82-181 • Wellesley, MA 02181
Telephone: 800-343-4848 or 617-237-5656 or fax 617-235-0826

IBM'S REPOSITORY MANAGER/MVS
Concepts, Facilities, and Capabilities

Dr. Henry C. Lefkovits

QED Technical Publishing Group
Boston • Toronto • London

© 1991 QED Information Sciences, Inc.
P.O. Box 82-181
Wellesley, MA 02181

QED Technical Publishing Group is a division of QED Information Sciences, Inc.

Library of Congress Catalog Number: 91-16704
International Standard Book Number: 0-89435-349-7

Printed in the United States of America
91 92 93 10 9 8 7 6 5 4 3 2 1

Library of Congress Cataloging-In-Publication Data

Lefkovtis, Henry C.
    IBM's repository manager/MVS : concepts, facilities, and
    capabilities / Henry C. Lefkovits
                p.   cm.
    Includes index.
    ISBN 0-89435-349-7
    1. IBM Systems Application Architecture. 2. Repository
    manager/MVS. 3. MVS (Computer system) I. Title.
QA76.9.A73L43   1991
005.74--dc20   91-16704
                                                       CIP

Tortoise: Go ahead, Achilles, take the first wish.

Achilles: Wow! But what should I wish? Oh, I know! It's what I thought of the first time I read the *Arabian Nights* (that collection of silly (and nested) tales) — I wish I had a HUNDRED wishes, instead of just three! Pretty clever, eh, Mr. T? I bet YOU never would have thought about that trick. I always wondered why those dopey people in the stories never tried it themselves.

Tortoise: Maybe you'll find out the answer.

Genie: I am sorry, Achilles, but I don't grant meta-wishes.

Achilles: I wish you'd tell me what a "meta-wish" is!

Genie: But THAT is a meta-meta-wish, Achilles — and I don't grant them, either.

Excerpt from *GÖDEL, ESCHER, BACH: An Eternal Golden Braid* by Douglas R. Hofstadter. Copyright ©1979 by Basic Books, Inc. Reprinted by permission of Basic Books, Inc., a division of HarperCollins Publishers.

CONTENTS

FOREWORD

Data dictionary systems, and the "information resource" control systems that succeeded them, have been available and in use for about a decade and a half. They provide an infrastructure upon which an integrated data environment may be built, yet there is no real consensus as to how these systems should be used. They are primarily used for Data Administration (DA) or Data Base Administration (DBA) information sources. Many Information Systems (IS) shops have a dictionary installed for only one application, or they think of it as an "after the fact" documentation chore. Those who have seen the benefits of data dictionary systems have demanded more functionality and proposed new uses for these types of systems.

During the same period of time, several interesting realities have been accepted as "conventional wisdom":

1. The need for new systems has far outstripped the ability of existing Application Development (AD) shops to deliver them, driving the application backlog to five or ten years in some extreme cases.

2.   The lack of new applications has restricted the delivery of new products and services from the enterprise of which the IS organization is a small part, and has had a profound effect on the enterprise's competitiveness. This has been felt very strongly in information-intensive industries such as banking and airlines.

3.   High-level languages (i.e. COBOL and FORTRAN) as well as application generators (i.e. IBM's Cross System Product) have become accepted tools of the development business. There is now a high degree of comfort that these generators will reliably translate the "source" code or rule statements into a proper result.

4.   Most IS shops currently claim that 60 to 80 percent of their budget is spent on maintenance of existing systems and that the quality problems inherent in those old (legacy) systems prevent redirection of resources to create new systems.

5.   The enterprise is demanding a shift to a new paradigm wherein the business is to be defined and driven by the business decision makers, not by IS.

Computer Aided Software Engineering (CASE) is a response to these realities.

On September 19, 1989, IBM announced its entrance into the CASE marketplace with its AD/Cycle architecture for application development and its Repository Manager/MVS product, which serves as the common data store for a set of cooperative and complementary application development tools.

Repository Manager is at once both a subset and a superset of a data dictionary. It provides a more comprehensive data store capability and a new way of accessing data via templates, but it lacks the product-specific tools that defined the dictionary . . . thereby limiting its usefulness. This allows an entire marketplace of AD tools to participate in a grand new scheme — cooperation and sharing of information to solve users' problems.

The grand vision of AD/Cycle is one of defining business goals and rules and having the applications produced automatically from them. I envision a shift in attention of the enterprise and the IS staff from traditional source code to the business rules and goals, once the translation of these into results is accepted as reliable. At that point, the new systems will be defined by "business-oriented people" rather than by "programming-" or "data-oriented people," and if a flaw is found in the results, the business goals and rules will be restated without a thought to changing the program that resulted from the prior attempt.

Several goals must be achieved before this vision can become a reality:

- There must be a robust repository available for this architecture to be built upon (IBM's Repository Manager product takes a large step toward achieving this).

- There must be a critical mass of tools available for users to choose from in creating their own, highly productive development environment. No two enterprises will have the same suite of tools because their development methodologies and preferences will be different.

- The tools must be willing to share their most precious asset, their data, by means of a repository.

- The tools must be willing to cooperate with each other and not knowingly interfere with the operation of other tools.

AD/Cycle is addressing this vision, and IBM is working with a large number of tool vendors to make this vision a reality.

There has been much discussion among IBM users regarding how this vision might be achieved. The consensus is that it must not only be done carefully, but that it must be started immediately. The first step on this journey is the organization of the enterprise data in a central data store — a repository — consequently the surge of interest in IBM Repository Manager.

This book provides the reader with an insight into the scope of Repository Manager, and its position within IBM's SAA and AD/Cycle strategic initiatives. It discusses the structure of Repository Manager, its key elements, and their relationships to each other. It brings together the information from a number of sources in a convenient, comprehensive form. It will provide readers with all of the information necessary to make an informed decision on the future of their application development efforts.

The author is a well-known and internationally respected authority on dictionary systems, and principal architect of the Information Resource Dictionary System (IRDS) Standard. In addition to discussing the main features and motivation behind Repository Manager, Dr. Lefkovits brings a unique perspective to the task of explaining repository concepts. This book is a welcome and valuable addition to the literature on repository systems.

Dana M. Marks, CDP
IBM Corporation
Santa Teresa Laboratory
San Jose, California

PREFACE

For a long time, the use of a data dictionary system has offered great promise to bring order into the sometimes chaotic world of information processing. However, this promise rarely came to fruition. There are many reasons for this. Among the more prominent was the high cost of creating and maintaining a dictionary, but more important was the lack of a good way to enforce the use of the dictionary, even if properly maintained.

Most dictionary systems were used in a strictly passive mode — they were good sources of information for those who wanted to access them. They could be used to generate file definitions and database definitions, but again, the decision to use them for this purpose was up to the user.

During the last few years, the effect of a major new direction in information systems development has begun to be felt. Systems engineering technology has started to come of age, and with it the availability of tools that were aimed at better methods for developing and maintaining information systems. The basic data used by such tools — referred to as CASE tools — could theoretically be found in a dictionary, but the passive nature of dictionary systems and the lack of standardized interfaces to dictionaries has led most developers of CASE tools to incorporate some form of dictionary or repository capability into their tools.

This book was motivated by the importance of the availability of IBM's Repository Manager, which can be viewed as having the potential to solve both the problem of the availability of an active dictionary and that of providing a robust base for the maintenance of meta-data for CASE tools in the IBM environment. The programmatic interface available in Repository Manager provides the environment required to allow CASE tools developed by different vendors to work cooperatively by sharing meta-data.

Writing this book has been a rewarding experience for me and has taught me a great deal about Repository Manager. I hope that it will provide readers with a better understanding of the concepts of Repository Manager and the facilities it offers.

Will Repository Manager fail as other dictionary systems have failed? Most assuredly not — not only is IBM committed to make it a successful product, but its positioning in SAA and AD/Cycle makes Repository Manager a critical element of IBM's long-range strategy.

The contents of this book is based to a large extent on material that has been made available to me by IBM, some of which is held to be IBM Confidential. For this reason, it has been reviewed by IBM to ensure that it is technically accurate, and that no material of a confidential nature is included.

I would like to acknowledge the support, help, and constructive criticism given to me by Mr. Dana M. Marks of IBM's Santa Teresa Laboratory, who was also responsible for the review required by IBM. The help of Mr. Larry G. Talbot of the Santa Teresa Laboratory in reviewing two chapters for technical accuracy is also acknowledged.

An acknowledgment is also due to Mr. William H. Campbell, Jr., who helped with an early version of some parts of the book, and to Ms. Sandra L. Lefkovits for her help with the graphics and editing of the text.

I would also like to express my thanks to Mr. David L. Stone of Digital Equipment Corporation for his help on one section of the book, and to Dr. A. J. Winkler of CTA, INCORPORATED and Ms. Sandra K. Perez of Concept Technology, Inc., for their advice on standards activities.

My deep thanks also go to Mr. Edwin F. Kerr, President/Publisher of QED Publishing Group for his support and encouragement, and to other QED Information Sciences, Inc. personnel, namely Ms. Beth A. Roberts, for her assistance and patience and Ms. Dianne C. Wood, for the copy editing.

This book was produced using WordPerfect® 5.1 and DrawPerfect® 1.1. I would like to thank WordPerfect Corporation's Customer Support Department for their assistance.

Henry C. Lefkovits
AOG Systems Corporation
Harvard, MA

TRADEMARKS

The following terms are registered trademarks of the IBM Corporation in the United States and/or other countries.

AIX
Application System/400
AS/400
IBM
Operating System/2 Extended Edition
Operating System/400
OS/2 EE
OS/400
Personal System/2
PS/2
SQL/400
Systems Application Architecture

The following terms are trademarks of the IBM Corporation in the United States and/or other countries.

AD/Cycle
CICS/MVS

Common User Access
DATABASE 2
DB2
DevelopMate
Enterprise Systems Architecture/370
ESA/370
KnowledgeTool
MVS/DFP
MVS/ESA
MVS/XA
OfficeVision
Presentation Manager
QMF
Repository Manager
Repository Manager/MVS
RPG
SAA
SQL/DS
System/370
The Integrated Reasoning Shell
TIRS
VM/ESA
VM/KA
VM/XA

BACHMAN Re-Engineering Product Set is a trademark of Bachman Information Systems

Excelerator is a registered trademark of INTERSOLV (formerly Index Technology Corporation)

PC Prism is a trademark of INTERSOLV (formerly Index Technology Corporation)

Information Engineering Workbench is a registered trademark of KnowledgeWare, Inc.

UNIX is a registered trademark of Bell Laboratories

1 REPOSITORY MANAGER — WHAT IS IT?

Repository Manager/MVS, or Repository Manager, as we shall refer to it, is a large and extremely sophisticated IBM software program product, which is very likely to have a very significant influence on how IBM users, as well as others, go about their information processing.

This book will describe the technical features and capabilities of Repository Manager/MVS; the main emphasis will be on communicating what Repository Manager/MVS can do and how it does it. We will also attempt to describe how Repository Manager/MVS is positioned within other IBM efforts and in other developments outside IBM.

The full impact of Repository Manager is based not only on its technical features and capabilities but on the fact that it is a part of Systems Application Architecture® (SAA), an overview of which will be given in the next chapter. SAA represents the strategic blueprint that is to direct IBM's product development in the years to come; it is IBM's major thrust to unify its various platforms in order to make applications transportable across these platforms, and it is key to IBM's long-term strategy. An important element of SAA is Application Development/Cycle (AD/Cycle), which will be discussed in Chapter 3. AD/Cycle represents the approach to application systems development in SAA and defines the tools to be used and how tools will communicate with each other. Repository Manager is the key element in this strategy.

A *repository* is a database of specifications — it contains what is commonly referred to as *meta-data* and the meaning of this meta-data. A repository system contains the necessary functionality to manage this database, whose physical structure can vary substantially from one repository system to another. In general, however, the interface to the database perceived by the user is that of an Entity-Relationship (ER) model. Repository Manager/MVS contains a database and can be thought of as the database management system that is used to access and maintain this repository

The paragraph above states that we are dealing here with "meta-data," but what does that really mean? The formal definition is "data about data," but in reality, what data is and what meta-data is tends to be application-dependent, or as the saying goes, "One person's data is another person's meta-data." A simple example that can be used to illustrate that point is a programmer's name and phone number. When viewed in the context of a personnel file, these are clearly data. However, when they are included in a data dictionary for purposes of designating the person responsible for a certain program, and how to contact that person in case of program malfunction, they have suddenly become meta-data.

It might be helpful to look at repository systems briefly from a historical perspective. The idea of a "repository" for meta-data is not new — it has been around by one name or another for a long time. There have always been people who thought that this was one of the most important areas in data processing, but except in rare instances, the concept has had little major impact.

1.1   DICTIONARY SYSTEMS

Efforts in the area of repositories have been in existence since the early 1960s. These earlier repositories were generally known by the name "Data Dictionary" or "Data Directory", and the reasons for their existence were to a large extent efforts, in Data Administration and Database Administration. To briefly recapitulate the history of these efforts we have:

- *Data Element Dictionary*. These efforts, taking place mainly in federal government agencies, were aimed at the standardization of data elements. Some software existed to manipulate such a repository, but it tended to be very rudimentary.

- *DBMS Support Tool*. The DBMS was intended to solve the total data management problem by creating a central pool of data instead of having file definitions embedded in programs. In theory, all applications could access this central pool of data and share it, which could have solved the data management problem, but in practice, it created a meta-data management problem in the sense that no control over data definitions existed. Generally, any one dictionary system was applicable only to a single DBMS, but exceptions did exist.

- *Data and Process Dictionary System*. These dictionary systems attempted to bridge the gap between DBMS support tools and the non-database environment. A number of problems existed that were not solved in a satisfactory manner. Among the most important of these was that, initially, each developer defined the types that were thought to be most important in the environment into which the implementation was to be placed. Unfortunately, the developer's idea of which types were important to the user were not necessarily correct. Various techniques were developed to deal with this problem, but they were not totally satisfactory.

- *Information Resource Dictionary System*. Based on recognized needs in the federal and private sectors, an effort aimed at the development of a standard was initiated. The approach taken was to attempt to benefit from the mistakes perceived to be existent in commercially available dictionary systems. This effort, resulting in an American National Standard and a Federal Information Processing Standard, will be discussed more fully in Chapter 11, and the results will be compared with Repository Manager.

Dictionary systems have always had the potential of offering substantial benefits to their users. Realistically, however, the impact they have had has been very low compared to these potential benefits. One must ask what the causes were for this state of affairs. The most likely answer is that the use of a data dictionary system never became part of the mainstream of an organization's information processing activities. It was generally viewed as an interesting exercise, but always suffered from being downgraded whenever priorities had to be reassigned. In most organizations, the dictionary system never had a fair chance to demonstrate the benefits it could produce.

1.2   CASE TOOLS

We are seeing a change in how application systems development is done. Economics and the existence of major backlogs, requiring applications to be brought to production faster, have caused development procedures to be reexamined. The result of this reexamination has been the increased use of software engineering techniques and tools, such as CASE tools. Repository Manager is a key element in IBM's recognition of this trend.

Meta-data repositories are elements of CASE tools. In general, the purpose of a repository is to support a particular CASE tool, and generally, no major effort was made to provide facilities that would be of interest to users other than those of the CASE tool that contains the repository. This has generated some problems. In general, a single CASE tool addresses only a specific part of a system's life cycle; it then becomes desirable, as well as necessary, to be able to transfer the meta-data from one CASE tool's repository to another CASE tool's repository. Of course, this problem does not exist for a set of CASE tools produced by a single software vendor referred to as an "integrated set,". but the disadvantage of an integrated set is that, in the main, it does not allow a user to introduce a tool produced by the user or by a different software vendor.

The transfer of meta-data from one CASE tool to another can take place in three ways:

1.   Building interfaces between pairs of CASE tools. This solution obviously tends not to be cost-effective, as the number of required interfaces increases geometrically with the number of tools for which interfaces are required.

2.   Specifying a generalized standard description of a transfer file to which all conformant CASE tools will adhere. Unfortunately, a general bridge for such transfers is currently not available, even though efforts exist in the CASE tool builder community to specify a transfer format that would allow meta-data to be moved from one CASE

tool specific repository to another. Such a format has been specified in the standard Information Resource Dictionary System, but its use is limited to moving meta-data from one IRDS to another.

3. Use a repository as a container that different CASE tools will access and thereby be able to exchange meta-data. Unlike the first solution, the number of interfaces required increases only linearly with the number of CASE tools involved. IBM's Repository Manager is intended to play this role, which, in fact, many of the facilities available in Repository Manager specifically address.

1.3   REPOSITORY MANAGER

In a certain sense, Repository Manager can be viewed as a dictionary system. However, as we have pointed out, it is much more than that. The role Repository Manager plays in supporting AD/Cycle is central to enabling the tasks required to support all phases of application system life cycle. An extensive set of services is provided that allows tools to interface with the repository. Information contained in the repository may then be accessed by any tool and manipulated in the format presented by Repository Manager. This information is thus sharable between tools. A tool may specify a view of the repository information that it desires.

Comparing Repository Manager to a dictionary system points out many very powerful facilities present in Repository Manager, which are usually not found in a dictionary system. Repository Manager uses an extended Entity-Relationship (ER) model that contains a number of features not usually present in a dictionary data model. The effect of these features is that more complex structures can be modeled in a natural manner and that a number of logical and integrity constraints can be specified. The user interface commonly associated with a dictionary system is not available in Repository Manager *per se*; rather, this interface is intended to be a tool.

It is intended that Repository Manager, as an element of SAA, will be available on all the platforms supported by SAA. The current release of Repository Manager/MVS is the first step not only in what may be expected to be a long series of further releases, each containing additional functionality, but also in additional implementations of Repository Manager on other platforms.

1.4   STRUCTURE OF THIS BOOK

Subsequent chapters will discuss Repository Manager/MVS, Version 1, Release 1, and will also, where appropriate, discuss Repository Manager in the more general SAA environment.

Chapter 2 will present an overview of the structure and facilities specified in Systems Application Architecture®. It will also point out the scope of the effort and show its strategic importance to IBM.

Chapter 3 is a discussion of AD/Cycle. It will present the components of AD/Cycle and the tools available for each component. The discussion will then point out the key position that Repository Manager occupies in this structure.

Chapter 4 is an overview of Repository Manager/MVS and is intended to provide a setting within which the various facilities of Repository Manager are positioned.

Chapters 5 through *10* present the description of Repository Manager/MVS. Care is taken to point out which of these features have been determined to be part of the more general SAA Repository Manager and which exist solely in Repository Manager/MVS.

- *Chapter 5* describes the Entity-Relationship and Object constructs that are in the repository, and the manner in which real-world concepts can be mapped to them.

- *Chapter 6* discusses the IBM-Supplied Entity-Relationship Model, which is a key mechanism enabling CASE tools to interchange information through the use of Repository Manager functionality.

- *Chapter 7* describes templates and the services associated with them. Templates are structured record buffers and represent the primary means of communication and units of data transfer between an application and the repository.

- *Chapters 8* and *9* are somewhat parallel. Chapter 8 presents a description of Repository Manager functions, and Chapter 9 describes the interactive panels and dialogs that can be used with Repository Manager/MVS.

- *Chapter 10* presents the Repository Manager/MVS Batch Command Language that allows repository maintenance to be carried out in a batch mode.

Chapter 11 discusses the Information Resource Dictionary System (IRDS) and the proposal of a standard for an IRDS Services Interface that has been submitted by IBM, which is based on Repository Manager facilities. A brief comparison of IRDS and Repository Manager features is also given.

Chapter 12 presents a discussion of repository technology in general and the requirements for repository technology in an Open Systems Architecture environment. Various initiatives in this area are discussed.

2 SYSTEMS APPLICATION ARCHITECTURE®

2.1 INTRODUCTION TO SYSTEMS APPLICATION ARCHITECTURE®

In March 1987, IBM introduced the Systems Application Architecture® (SAA) as a blueprint of the future direction of IBM platform-based system support and application software development. Central to this architecture is the elimination of incompatibilities among the various IBM system platforms, at least from the application development perspective. This chapter will present an overview of this architecture and will position Repository Manager/MVS within it.

From an applications point of view, the objectives of SAA are to provide:

- Ease of application transportation across systems

- Applications that span systems

- Applications with consistent user interfaces

For these objectives to be achieved, applications must be developed using SAA implementing products (as provided by IBM and various software vendors).

In actuality, SAA is an evolving collection of published software interfaces, conventions, and protocols. These specifications form the framework for developing consistent, integrated applications across some existing and future major IBM operating environments. The interfaces, conventions, and protocols are designed to provide consistency and connectivity in the following general areas:

- Programming interfaces — the languages and services available to application builders for software development.

- User Access — the design and use of screen panels and user interaction techniques leading to consistent behavior.

- Communications support — the connectivity of systems and programs.

- Applications — the software developed and supplied by IBM and other vendors.

The goal of SAA is to provide a consistent set of protocols, services, and behaviors with which applications may be developed and may interconnect across multiple participating systems. Consistency benefits developers and users. Users may interact with multiple applications that conform to similar input device procedures and that present panels with consistent information presentation areas and techniques. With common or similar appearance and interaction behaviors across applications, users may more readily move across applications, thus increasing business efficiency. This may be viewed as interacting with a common and consistent application and device personalities. From one application to the next, similar interactions yield similar results.

Under this architecture, the potential exists to also improve the productivity of development personnel. Skills learned in one environment are transferable to other environments, lessening the need for retraining and for system specialists. With common protocols, services, and presentation techniques, the movement of programmers among differing development environments can be accomplished with minimal loss of productive time. Additionally, this consistency can facilitate the portability of applications to other system environments. The development of applications for future system or multisystem environments becomes easier and faster.

SAA's connectivity is directed towards the creation of applications that span systems. The distribution of an application can permit its various functions to be processed where it is most desirable to maximize the efficiency and effectiveness of an enterprise's existing capabilities and systems. Cooperative processing is a term used in SAA publications to mean the distribution of an application's functional processing across multiple system environments. For example, an application can be developed so that much of its processing logic and data access is run on a larger host with more powerful processing features and fast access to large databases, and its human interaction is performed on a workstation with its more attractive graphics features. An additional advantage to the development of cooperative processing applications under SAA is that parts of developed applications can be more readily moved to other IBM system environments in response to changes in computing resources, data volume, and geographical distribution of users.

For each major element of SAA, IBM has established a set of definitions or specifications. In some cases, existing IBM products are already aligned to varying degrees with the specifications. For a number of the specifications, conforming products are still in the planning or development stage. In all cases, each specification is used within IBM to promote and control software development and enhance the consistency of future products within the SAA framework. Additionally, recognizing that SAA is a global plan or framework, its parts are subject to enhancement and augmentation as new requirements are addressed and existing requirements become better understood.

2.2   SAA-SUPPORTED SYSTEM ENVIRONMENTS

IBM has selected several combinations of system hardware and software as SAA environments. These are the environments for which IBM is managing the conformance to specification and providing support for SAA elements. The selected environments are:

- TSO/E in Enterprise Systems Architecture/370

- CMS in VM/System Product or VM/Extended Architecture

- Operating System/400® (OS/400®)

- Operating System/2® (OS/2®) Extended Edition

- CICS/MVS in Enterprise Systems Architecture/370

•   IMS/VS Data Communications (IMS/VS-DC) in Enterprise
     Systems Architecture/370

•   AIX® in RS/6000 RISC workstation product family

A full breadth of the SAA will be implemented in the TSO/E, CMS,
OS/400®, and OS/2® environments. Within the CICS/MVS and IMS/VS-
DC, SAA implementation will focus on these environments as hosts
where user access is accomplished via attached independent workstations. Within the AIX® environment (IBM's version of UNIX®),
limited SAA support is to be provided.

Each supported environment is being provided with software that is
unique to the characteristics of the environment and provides the
foundation for the common components of the SAA as shown in
Figure 2-1.

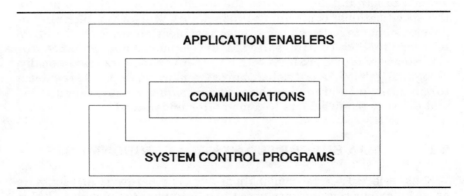

Figure 2-1   Software foundation for the SAA environment.

The SAA framework encompasses the software foundation provided
with all SAA environments. The software foundation consists of:

•   Application enablers — programs needed by application
     programs such as compilers and database programs.

•   Communications — programs that provide the means for
     the specific system to communicate with its attached devices
     or with other systems in a telecommunications network.

- System control programs — the set of programs that comprise the operating system and its extensions for a given hardware environment.

The detailed content of software foundations will vary from machine to machine, depending on the specific hardware type and configuration.

2.3   SAA ELEMENTS

In addition to the foundation software, the SAA consists of three major elements providing interfaces to application programs, users, and other systems. These elements are:

- Common Programming Interface (CPI)

- Common User Access (CUA)

- Common Communications Support (CCS)

As shown in Figure 2-2, it is through the use of these major SAA elements that applications programs obtain access to the services and features provided by the software foundation.

Common Programming Interface (CPI) defines languages and services that allow programmers to write applications that can execute in all SAA environments with little or no change.

Common User Access (CUA) defines conventions for developing consistent end-user interface for SAA applications. Applications developed using the CUA guidelines will present a common personality regardless of the particular SAA environment(s) on which they are executing.

Common Communications Support (CCS) defines architectures and protocols that interconnect SAA devices and systems and allow data to be interchanged among the devices and systems.

Common applications are programs written using elements of the CPI, and they conform to the CUA conventions. As such, they execute and present a consistent user interface in all SAA environments.

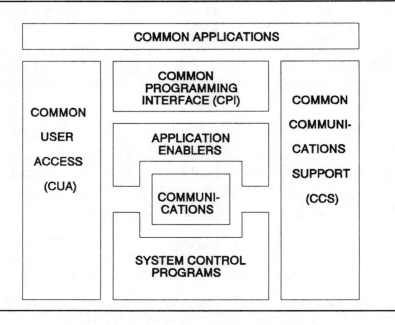

Figure 2-2 SAA major interface components.

2.3.1 Common Programming Interface (CPI)

The SAA Common Programming Interface (CPI) defines the languages, commands, and service calls that programmers employ in building applications. More than one such interface exists, and they may be grouped into two general categories:

1. Languages — the programming languages used to develop applications.

2. Services — services invoked by programs to facilitate data communications, database access, data presentation and user interaction.

There exists a specification for each component of the CPI. As with all major SAA components, existing IBM products are already aligned to varying degrees with some of the specifications, and for many of the specifications, conforming products are still in the planning or development stage.

Figure 2-3 presents the relative position of the CPI within the SAA.

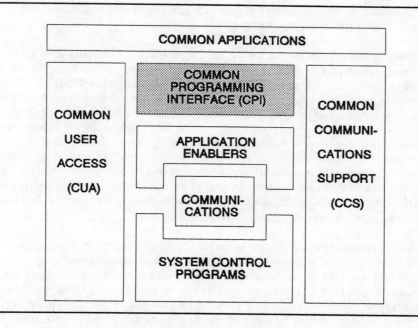

Figure 2-3   The CPI within SAA.

2.3.1.1   CPI Languages

The languages supported within the SAA are:

- Application Generator
- C
- COBOL
- FORTRAN
- PL/I
- Procedures Language
- RPG

Of particular interest to the Repository Manager is the Procedures Language CPI. IBM's Procedures Language is used for the specification of policies. The language is designed primarily for character string manipulation. Current implementations of the Procedures Language processors are interpretative (that is, as each expression is encountered by the language processor, it is evaluated and, as appropriate, submitted to the current environment as a command for execution, and no object form of the program is generated.)

Within SAA environments, use of the language is principally as a system procedure language and as an application macro processor. Use as a system procedure language is characterized by the specification of the operating system's command line interface as the environment to which the Procedures Language residual text is sent for further interpretation. The procedure takes an external view of the application it selectively starts and (in some cases) communicates with during execution. Because the command languages of the various SAA operating systems are not compatible, special features are available to determine the current execution environment and to select system-dependent paths within the procedure. These features enable the generation of portable system procedures across SAA environments.

Use of Procedures Language as an application macro processor entails the generation of procedures that pass information to and respond to applications' command line interfaces. For example, a procedure may be generated that acts as a surrogate for an end user of the application interface. Such use of the Procedures Language enables users and application programs to expand an application's command language through macros or composite commands without modifying the application.

The SAA CPI specification for the Procedures Language is based on the REXX (REstructured eXtended eXecutor) language, extensions to the language to expand its use within other application support facilities (e.g. Double Byte Character String (DBCS) handling, special Repository Manager requirements, etc.), and for environmental interfaces such as variable pool.

The implementing product in the TSO/E environment is integrated into TSO/E. It is known as TSO/E REXX. In the CMS environment, the implementing product is the System Product Interpreter (also known as REXX) and is integrated in both VM/SP and VM/XA SP. The SAA Procedures Language is not supported in the CICS/MVS or the

IMS/VS-DC environments. To date no implementations have been provided for the OS/400® and OS/2® environments.

2.3.1.2   *CPI for Services*

The services specified as part of the SAA CPI enhance the ability to develop environment-independent applications, therefore enhancing program portability across SAA environments. Use of the services buffers programmers, applications, and the user from device dependent considerations. Since the services are slated to be consistent for all SAA environments, programmers will have similar development tools across operating environments.

2.3.1.2.1   Communications Services CPI

The *SAA Communication Services* provide a consistent means for program-to-program intercommunication. These program service calls fall into two categories:

- Starter Set provides services to initiate and terminate conversations and services to send and receive data.

- Advanced Function provides services to synchronize and control conversations and to interrogate and modify conversation characteristics.

The purpose of this CPI is to facilitate the use of the communications architectures supported within the SAA Common Communications Services, while allowing programmatic independence from any particular communications architecture.

The CPI for communications services is based on the program callable communications services provided within the VM/SP operating system for System/370 CMS environments.

2.3.1.2.2   Database Services CPI

The *SAA Database Services* have the form of SQL (Structured Query Language), a nonprocedural language for the relational data model, with which users and programs may define, retrieve, and manipulate data within a relational database. Since SQL is nonprocedural, it is used by specifying what is to be done, without concern for how it is done. SQL also provides built-in functions and arithmetic operations so users can perform immediate mathematical operations on data without having to write traditional programs. In addition to the direct use of SQL, SQL statements can be embedded in traditional application programs, written in an SAA programming language and then precompiled.

The use of SQL within application programs does not require any accompanying description of how data is stored or managed. Consequently, storage and management of data can be optimized to particular environments without hindering application development processes or impacting the portability of the applications.

The CPI for database services is based on the American National Standard Database Language — SQL (ANSI X3.135-1986). The specification is almost identical to the language in DATABASE 2 (DB2) and SQL/DS available within the System/370 environments.

In the TSO/E, CICS/MVS, and IMS/VS-DC environments, the implementing product is DB2. In the CMS environment, SQL/DS is the implementing product. In the OS/400® environment the implementing product is the OS/400® Database Manager with SQL/400®. In the OS/2® environment, the OS/2® Extended Edition Database Manager is the implementing product.

2.3.1.2.3   Dialog Services CPI

Dialog Services are used for the display and control of user interaction with panels on a screen-type device and for the transfer of user-provided data and function requests from the device to the application. The dialog interface also includes the dialog tag language — an application development language for the specification of dialog objects such as application panels, help panels, messages, keylists, and application commands. As specified at the source level, dialog objects are independent of operating system and specific device type. A dialog tag language compiler converts these source specifications to run time objects for execution in the target computing environment.

From the application developer's perspective, dialog services appear as an extension of the operating system services. They facilitate the generation of interactive applications, which communicate with users to present application results or to request and accept user input. Both the dialog interface and the dialog tag language enforce the Common

User Access (CUA) rules on information presentation and user interaction.

The CPI specification for dialog services is based on parts of the ISPF and EZ-VU product interfaces.

2.3.1.2.4   Presentation Services CPI

Presentation Services are a comprehensive set of functions to allow information to be displayed or printed in an effective and standardized fashion. The major services facilities are:

- A windowing system that can be used to tailor the displays of selected information.

- Presentation and interaction presentation and control support for both keyboard and pointer devices in conformance with the CUA of the SAA.

- Fonts, including support for DBCS.

- Limited image support.

- Saving and restoring graphics images.

- Support for various types of display terminals, printers and plotters.

The use of these services simplifies application development and buffer programmers and the applications they develop from device-dependent considerations. Applications developed with these services have enhanced portability across SAA environments and conform more closely to the rules and guidelines of the SAA CUA.

The CPI specification for presentation services is based on System/370 and OS/400® GDDM products and on the OS/2® Presentation Manager. In particular, the graphics portion of the specification is based on a combination of the GDDM products and the OS/2® Presentation Manager. All other parts of the specification are based on the OS/2® Presentation Manager.

2.3.1.2.5 Query Services CPI

Query Services provide the simplified means to compose relational database queries and to create reports of query results. Application programs can invoke query services through a program-to-program call interface or through query objects. Query objects are files that contain records of query, procedure, and form. Such objects can be built and manipulated by applications and then used with query services to produce the desired data and reports. Since query objects can be defined outside the application and are stored outside the application code as files, an application can be updated by changing query objects without any modification to code or program recompilation.

The approach minimizes the need for an application to handle database manager protocols or to have extensive SQL error handling and interpretation. By using query services, an application can pass fewer commands to allow access to data in an exported format.

The common programming interface specification for query services is based on an extension of the interface in the System/370's **Query Management Facility (QMF)**.

In the TSO/E and CMS environments, the implementing product is the Query Management Facility, with the exception of the callable interface elements. On OS/400®, the implementation will be provided by the OS/400® Query Manager. In the OS/2® environment, the implementation is provided by the **Query Manager** component of the OS/2® Extended Edition.

2.3.1.2.6 Repository Services CPI

Repository Services are a comprehensive set of program callable functions to perform query and update of a repository of enterprise-wide information and to perform related utility and service functions on the repository. These services include:

- Definition of the information to be stored in the repository

- Description of the information views available to repository applications

- Definition of controls and constraints applied to the use of repository information

- Information query and modification

- Special utility and service functions

Within SAA, a repository is a special-purpose relational database containing information on an enterprise's business activities, organization, and goals; information about the data needed to run the business; and information about the procedures, applications, and systems that support the business.

The implementing product for the S/370 environment is Repository Manager/MVS. As will be discussed in more detail later, this product implements the Repository Manager CPI and also contains extensions, which are referred to as the Repository Manager/MVS Applications Programming Interface (API). It can be expected that many of these extensions will be incorporated in some manner into the Repository Manager CPI.

2.3.2   Common User Access

The second major element of the System Application Architecture is the Common User Access (CUA), shown in Figure 2-4. CUA specifications establish the framework and definitions of user interface components that are to be the same across all applications. CUA's purpose is to provide high degrees of usability and consistency within each application and to facilitate the presentation of common presentation and interaction characteristics across applications.

The SAA CUA specifications contain definitions, rules, and guidelines on the presentation components, user interaction with presentation components, action implementation, and the overall process sequence of communication between users and computers. At the lowest level, the CUA specifies what keys on what type of keyboards are reserved for the user to request what action, and, where applicable, it defines the basic uses of mouse movement and buttons. At the highest level, it describes principles and goals to guide the design of an application's user interface.

Due to the extensive disparity between commonly available user interface devices, the specifications provide two distinct user interface models: *entry* and *graphical*. The provision of two distinct models allows the exploitation of graphical capabilities in programmable workstation or stand-alone personal computers far beyond that

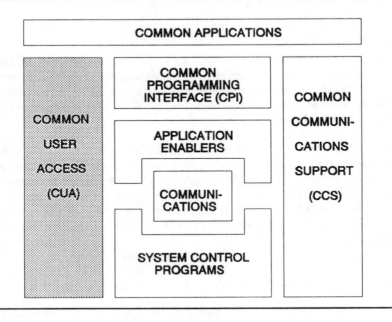

Figure 2-4   CUA within SAA.

achievable within the constraints of non-programmable terminal capabilities.   To maximize consistency between implementations employing either model, similar interface characteristics are specified wherever practical.

The *entry model* is for applications that interact with panels presenting menus and prompts. It is most suitable for data-entry-intensive applications on non-programmable terminals; however, it may be applied to similar applications on a programmable workstation.

The *graphical model* is intended for all programmable workstation applications operating on the OS/2® platform. It incorporates windows, action bars with associated pull-downs, parallel dialogs for the support of additional or supplemental user services such as "help," and graphical cues such as check boxes. The specification for this model emphasizes the implementation of user-driven interfaces. Within the graphical model a *text subset* is defined that is appropriate for decision-intensive applications on non-programmable terminals. The text subset defines the use of standard graphical cues such as check boxes.

The CUA does not establish a basic set of services that will be made available through an SAA-compliant product. As specified, it cannot be fully satisfied by an implementation providing lower-level services to be invoked by application programs. The use of the CUA involves application development following the specified rules and guidelines and the use of various SAA-conformant products implementing CPI for the development language(s), presentation services, dialog services, and any other SAA-provided services (e.g., database access or communications) as applicable.

2.3.3   Common Communications Support

The third major element of the SAA is the Common Communications Support (CCS), as shown in Figure 2-5. CCS specifications define the interfaces and protocols that allow communication among devices, applications, systems, and networks.

The CCS implementation provides services to the CPI implementation or to application programs that allow the applications to interact with data or devices on the same or different systems within a network configuration, as reflected in Figure 2-6.

CCS is based on parts of IBM's Systems Network Architecture (SNA), as well as selected standards published by the following organizations:

- International Telegraph and Telephone Consultative Committee (CCITT)

- Institute of Electrical and Electronics Engineers (IEEE)

- International Standards Organization (ISO)

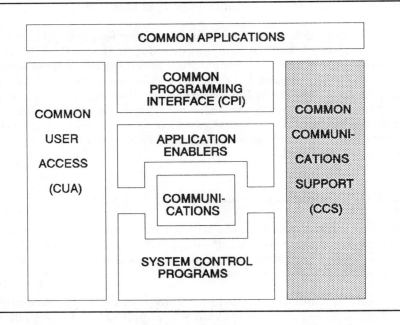

Figure 2-5   CCS within SAA.

The CCS may be viewed as items that address one of the following six general categories:

- Objects — the contiguous grouping of data of a single type occurring within a single document may be considered an object. Within this CCS architecture, an object must have a description of both its structure and its content. Objects, of two types can be associated with a document: (1) data objects such as text objects, graphics objects and image objects; and (2) resource objects, such as font objects, which are referenced by the data objects. Object content architectures currently included in CCS are:

    - Presentation Text Object Content Architecture (PTOCA)

    - Image Object Content Architecture (IOCA)

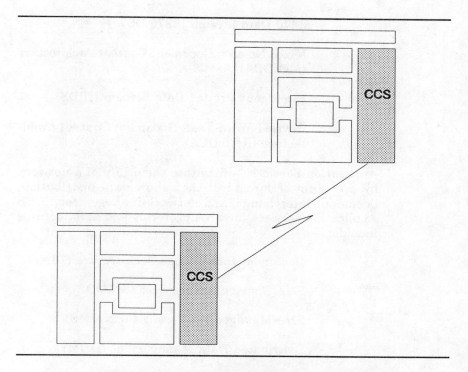

Figure 2-6   System-to-system CCS interface.

–   Graphics Object Content Architecture (GOCA)

–   Font Object Content Architecture (FOCA)

Objects may be transmitted in data streams and can be stored in libraries by applications and system components of the network.

• Data Streams — continuous ordered streams of data elements conforming to a proscribed format. Applications can generate data streams destined for printers, workstations, or other application programs. Data stream architectures currently included in CCS are:

- 3270 Data Stream (3270 DS)

- Mixed Objects: Document Content Architecture (MO:DCA)

- Intelligent Printer Data Stream (IPDS)

- Revised-Form-Text: Document Content Architecture (RFT:DCA)

- Application Services — facilitate the utility of a network by providing architectures that allow data distribution, document interchange, and network management. CCS Application services for SNA protocols and architectures include:

  - Document Interchange Architecture (DIA)

  - SNA/Distribution Services (SNA/DS)

  - SNA/Management Services (SNA/MS)

  - Distributed Data Management (DDM)

CCS application services for OSI protocols and architectures include:

  - File Transfer, Access, and Management (FTAM)

  - X.400 Message Handling System

  - OSI Association Control Service Element (ACSE)

- Session services — establish communication between two application programs, transfer data between application programs, and terminate communications between application programs.   Session service architectures currently included in CCS are:

  - SNA Logical Unit Type 6.2 (LU 6.2) program-to-program protocol

  - OSI Presentation Layer — Kernel and ASN.1

- OSI Session Layer — Versions 1 and 2

- OSI Transport Layer — Classes 0, 2, and 4

- Network services — facilitate connectivity between systems. CCS network service architectures for SNA include:

    - SNA Type 2.1 Node architecture provides peer-to-peer low level networking)

CCS network service architectures for OSI include:

    - Connectionless-Mode Network Services (CLNS) using Internet

    - Connection-Oriented Network Services (CONS) using Subnetwork Interface to X.25

- Data Link Control — A data link consists of connections between two link stations within separate data terminal equipment (DTE) configurations. The link stations are each connected to data circuit-terminating equipment (DCE) devices, and the DCEs are interconnected by transmission medium. The transmission medium is used as a communications channel within a network. Data link control protocols define how control data is interpreted and how data is transmitted across a link. CCS includes data link controls that allow data to be transmitted in packet-switched networks, wide-area networks, and local area networks. CCS data link control architecture for SNA support includes:

    - Synchronous Data Link Control (SDLC)

CCS data link control architecture for OSI includes:

    - X.25 in Packet-Switched Data Networks (PSDN)

    - IBM Token-Ring (IEEE 802.2/IEEE 802.5 and ISO 8802-2/ISO 8802-5)

2.3.4   Common Applications

As shown in Figure 2-7, common applications run on top of the three major SAA components; that is, they consist of programs written in conformance with CPI-defined language(s), use CPI-defined services, and have user presentation and interaction characteristics consistent with the CUA guidelines. In brief, a common SAA application is any suite of software programs that is SAA compliant.

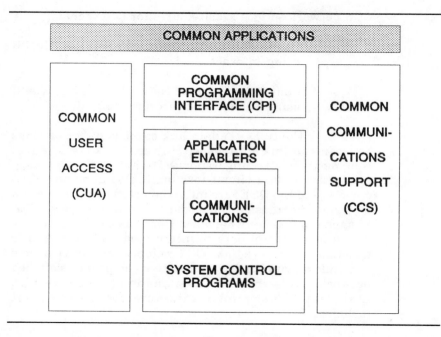

Figure 2-7   Common applications within SAA.

Common applications may take the form of office support, business management, systems management, manufacturing control, development support, or personal recreation. A good example of an SAA application is IBM's OfficeVision suite of office automation products. This multifaceted package works across most of IBM's major environments and includes a number of office support functions such as electronic mail and scheduling.

Currently, there exists no formally recognized form of compliance testing for Common SAA applications. IBM has provided a checklist and various test suites for developers and users as an aid for ensuring SAA compliance in software products.

Of particular interest are Applications Development/Cycle (AD/Cycle) applications or tools. The AD/Cycle strategy is a framework to support application development and maintenance across the entire application life cycle. Central to the architecture is the role of Repository Manager/MVS as the single central source and control point for application development information. The repository is structured to contain an application development model suitable for AD/Cycle tools sharing information across the life cycle. AD/Cycle will be discussed in the following chapter.

3 AD/CYCLE

Application Development/Cycle (AD/Cycle), announced by IBM in September of 1989, is a framework designed to support application development and maintenance. The original announcement specified that the strategy's objective is to improve application development by:

- Supporting development and maintenance across the entire life cycle of applications.

- Providing a single application development information control point.

- Providing a framework that is open and extensible by users and software vendors.

- Providing a total customer solution via a complementary collection of software tools developed by IBM and selected tool vendors.

- Having an ongoing series of strategy conferences to assist software vendors in having their products interface with the AD/Cycle framework.

- Protecting investments in existing IBM application development tools, skills, and data.

- Providing flexibility to facilitate the adoption of new application development technologies and methodologies.

The announcement stated that AD/Cycle is evolving to include a comprehensive set of application development life cycle tools. AD/Cycle is central to the SAA, and a key element of AD/Cycle is Repository Manager. It is also intended that AD/Cycle should complement and extend SAA.

The overall structure of the AD/Cycle architecture and strategy is based on a substantial number of approaches and prototypes, within both IBM and other locations, to improve the systems development process. In this sense, AD/Cycle represents the evolutionary product of a number of different technologies. A substantial amount of input to AD/Cycle requirements was received from the GUIDE and SHARE user groups.

AD/Cycle has its roots in the need to provide support for the efficient development of application software and to help reduce the backlog of needed applications through advanced automation techniques. An additional problem being faced today is the high cost of maintaining existing, older-generation application systems.

A conceptual representation of AD/Cycle is shown in Figure 3-1. As can be seen in this figure, AD/Cycle recognizes activities that go across life cycles as well as those that are concerned primarily with a single life cycle.

In this manner, AD/Cycle avoids some of the problems that other tools have faced in the past. Among these problems:

- Tools that address different phases of the life cycle are unable to share data.

- Tools are either not integrated or are integrated in such a fashion that it is difficult to add other tools that incorporate different technologies.

- The development process itself is not integrated, and no centralized controls can be put in place.

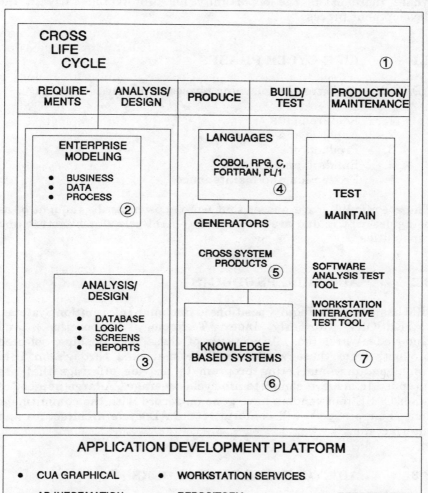

Figure 3-1   Model of AD/Cycle.

An aid to achieving these objectives is the architecture of AD/Cycle where there exists the opportunity for prototyping early in the development process.

3.1   LIFE CYCLE PHASES

AD/Cycle recognizes the following phases of a system's life cycle:

1.   Requirements
2.   Analysis and design
3.   Production
4.   Building and testing
5.   Production and maintenance

The specific life cycle phases that were chosen can be thought of as being descriptive and are not central to AD/Cycle's architecture and capabilities.

3.2   AD/CYCLE PRODUCTS

IBM has established equity positions in Bachman Information Systems, INTERSOLV (formerly Index Technology Corporation,) and KnowledgeWare, Inc. As a result of these relationships, selected products from these vendors will be marketed through an IBM complementary marketing program to provide offerings that are intended to achieve complete life cycle coverage. A large number of other CASE tool vendors have gone on record with the commitment that their products will conform to the AD/Cycle architecture and interfaces.

3.3   AD/CYCLE BUILDING BLOCKS

In Figure 3-1, for the purpose of classifying tools and methodologies, eight blocks are shown representing specific activities that take place in AD/Cycle. These are:

1.   Cross Life Cycle Activities
2.   Enterprise Modeling
3.   Analysis and Design
4.   Languages
5.   Generators

6.   Knowledge Based Systems
7.   Test and Maintenance
8.   Application Development Platform

The AD/Cycle strategy is to provide tools and methodologies in each one of these blocks, so that:

- There exists centralized control and management of all application development data.

- AD/Cycle tools will conform to SAA standards, thereby achieving a simplified transition from one tool to another for the user.

- The AD/Cycle environment represents an Open Systems architecture to which tools and methodologies based on new technologies can be added in the future.

- Individual tools can be IBM products, vendor-supplied, or user-written.

Each one of these components will now be discussed.

3.3.1   Cross Life Cycle Activities

Tools in this category are concerned with the broad activities that span essentially, the entire life cycle. Among these are:

- Process Management
- Project Management
- Documentation
- Performance Monitoring
- Query and Reporting
- Prototyping
- Reusability Management
- Impact Analysis

Among products announced in this area are Application Development Project Support/Process Mechanism (ADPS/P) and Application Development Project Support/Application Development Model (ADPS/M). These are tools designed to improve productivity by providing support in the management and control of application development processes. In the MVS environment, ISPF/PDF support is provided. Users of PWS tools can adapt an ADPS-provided tool interface in such a manner as to be able to access PWS tools from the ADPS host session.

It is important to be able to identify and locate components that are common across different phases of the system life cycle, such as models, designs, programs, and so forth.

3.3.2   Enterprise Modeling

Activities covered in this block are in the area of modeling:

- The business of the enterprise
- Data
- Processes

Product offerings for these purposes are the following:

- IBM's DevelopMate, which focuses on the definition, refinement, and validation of an enterprise model through prototyping.

- Information Engineering Workbench®/Planning Workstation from KnowledgeWare, Inc., which can be used to capture, model, and analyze data about an enterprise and its use of information.

- PC Prism from INTERSOLV (formerly Index Technology Corporation,) which is intended to help an enterprise develop and analyze enterprise and other business models.

3.3.3   Analysis and Design

The selection of tools for these activities is dependent on the design methodology chosen by an enterprise. The AD/Cycle framework will support the integration of analysis and design tools based on current software methodologies. AD/Cycle product offerings in this area are:

- Information Engineering Workbench®/Analysis Workstation and Design Workstation products from KnowledgeWare, Inc., which are designed for refining and analyzing end user requirements and for the logical design of information systems based on these requirements.

- Excelerator® from INTERSOLV (formerly Index Technology Corporation,) which is intended to be used for developing process and data models, validating design information, prototyping screens and reports, and generating system documentation.

- The BACHMAN Re-Engineering Product Set from Bachman Information Systems, which includes tools for advanced data modeling and database design.

3.3.4   Languages

This component consists of the third-generation language (3GL) compilers, editors, and debuggers, as well as fourth-generation language (4GL) generators. SAA-supported languages, as mentioned in the previous chapter, are:

- C
- COBOL
- FORTRAN
- PL/I
- Procedures Language
- RPG

A significant aspect of this AD/Cycle constituent deals with the heavy reliance of third-generation development projects on library management systems to control source code versions. Improved Library Service facilities under AD/Cycle are planned to provide the function of library management as well as configuration management that automatically keeps track of interdependencies and synchronizes compilations and link edits.

3.3.5   Generators

An Application Generator is a generalized application development tool that facilitates the development of some types of programs without resorting to coding with a traditional high-level language or excessive involvement with system details. The SAA Application Generator Cross System Product is designed to support the portability of applications across system environments. Its has a two-part structure:

- The application development portion, CSP/AD, is used to generate an application maintaining relative independence on operating system and hardware considerations.

- The application execution portion, CSP/AE, is used for the implementation and adaptation of the code for the specific system on which the application is to run.

It is planned that CSP/AD will be able to be used in conjunction with other application development tools. It is also planned that integration of, and communication between, different programming languages will take place, allowing different parts of application systems to be written in different programming languages.

Product offerings providing Cross System Product facilities for cooperative development on the Personal System/2® operating under OS/2® Extended Edition are very important.

3.3.6   Knowledge Based Systems

It is important that knowledge based systems should be able to participate as tools in the AD/Cycle architecture. The usefulness of these techniques is becoming more recognized, and it is important that an enabling mechanism exist in AD/Cycle to allow procedural and knowledge based code applications to be used in the applications development process.

Current IBM products in this area are The Integrated Reasoning Shell, Expert System Environment, and Knowledge Tool.

3.3.7   Test and Maintenance

These activities are key ones in the systems development process. It can be expected that IBM will provide a number of new product offerings in this area. The products discussed below are among the current offerings:

Software Analysis Test Tool supports an application developer in the testing and maintenance of software applications. This collection of integrated tools provides support in the COBOL and PL/I programming language environments and works in conjunction with debugging facilities. Both "bottom-up" and "top-down" testing is supported, as well as structured methodologies based on the logical structure of the application. Metrics expressing the testing adequacy are produced. Software Analysis Test Tool complies with the SAA CUA graphical model and is available for operation under OS/2® Extended Edition.

Workstation Interactive Test Tool is an OS/2® Presentation Manager application that complies with the CUA graphical model specified in SAA. The tool saves recorded terminal sessions in IBM Programmable Workstation disk files that can be replayed at a later time. Comparisons of a current session from a previous one can be made, and reports of mismatches can be produced.

Support for program testing and debugging is also provided by IBM's INSPECT for C and PL/I programs. This tool allows a developer to control the execution of a C or PL/I program by inspecting and modifying variables during execution. INSPECT runs either in an interactive mode, with multiple windows and extensive on-line help, or in a batch mode.

3.3.8   Application Development Platform

It is this component that is of most interest, as it contains the Repository Manager, Repository services, and the IBM Supplied ER Model, which will be discussed in detail in the rest of this book. In addition to these, the Application Development Platform also contains the SAA-compliant user interface, workstation services, and the Dictionary Model Transformer.

The Dictionary Model Transformer provides migration of information from the DB/DC Dictionary System to the repository. This migration can be either in online mode or through the batch interface of Dictionary Model Transformer. The result of extraction is a set of records formatted for the Repository Manager/MVS Batch Command Language, and this facility is used to update the repository. User exits have been provided to allow the customization of the extraction.

3.4   AD/CYCLE TECHNOLOGY

A number of significant technologies are introduced into the AD/Cycle environment, particularly in the Application Development Platform. In addition to the services available that enable the integration of tools (all of which are discussed later in this book), important component technologies of the Application Development Platform are the following two related elements:

- User interface components defined by CUA

- Workstation services

The main objective of user interface services is to implement an integrated environment for AD/Cycle tools based on OS/2® Extended Edition. In this sense, "integrated" is intended to denote that the workplace model is not to be segmented along tool boundaries. The resultant model can also serve as a guideline for future SAA applications and their concomitant user services.

In current technology, the management of the window of a workstation is largely the responsibility of the programmer. Since this is not desirable, a secondary objective of the user interface services is to increase the separation of the management of the window from the tools that operate in the window. This should lead to increased productivity and smaller size of tools.

The Application Development Platform model of a customized workplace is based on an object paradigm. where an object is the fundamental unit of manipulation on the screen. When an object has been opened, functions on the object can be carried out by the object handler. This allows a user to concentrate on the data objects and the actions associated with them, rather than selecting an AD/Cycle tool and specifying the data to be processed by the tool. A window is a container holding one or more objects, which limits the context in which the user works.

An important aspect of this interaction is that the objects with which a user is concerned may be highly complex. In this mode of operation, it will then be possible for the user to specify the level of abstraction at which an object will be worked with at a specific time, and the actions appropriate to that level of abstraction. Visual presentation at different levels of abstraction can be presented as an integrated part of the workplace managed by workplace services.

In summary, user interface services play a dual role in the Application Development Platform supporting AD/Cycle:

- The services simplify the structure of the content of the tools that are enabled on the workstation.

- The services facilitate building the AD/Cycle workplace by providing simplified management for the application developer.

4 OVERVIEW OF REPOSITORY MANAGER/MVS

Repository Manager, as Repository Manager/MVS will be referred to in this chapter, was announced in September 1989 and first released in June 1990. It forms the basis for the administration of system development in SAA environments for the foreseeable future. It is conceivable and entirely possible that the use of an enterprise's repository could become so extensive that virtually all major areas of the firm's business activities would be impacted.

The objective of Repository Manager is to provide the means for an enterprise to maintain information about:

- The enterprise's business activities, organization, and goals

- The data needed to run the business

- The automated applications systems that support the business

- The systems that support the applications

- The relationships among the above

Repository Manager is a full-featured information system, providing both program-callable and interactive panel interface services to support a repository of enterprise-wide information. These services provide means for the following:

- Definition of the information to be stored in the repository.

- Specification of what information types particular repository applications can access.

- Specification of the way repository information is stored.

- Definition of the global, application-specific, and user-specific controls and constraints to be in effect when the repository is accessed.

- Query and maintenance of repository information.

- Performance of supporting utility and service functions (e.g., data importing and exporting, system maintenance and tuning, etc.).

Repository Manager supports three different kinds of perspectives from which repository data may be accessed. These perspectives address a repository-wide view (the *Conceptual View*), application or tool-specific views (*Logical Views*), and views oriented toward how information is physically stored (*Storage Views*).

An integral part of Repository Manager is a supplied model that defines information types common to many uses and supports current and future repository-based applications or tools within IBM's AD/Cycle application development environment.

This chapter presents an overview of these features. Subsequent chapters will examine them in more detail.

4.1   APPROACH TO REPOSITORY MANAGER USE

As shown in Figure 4-1, use of the repository falls into two distinct categories:

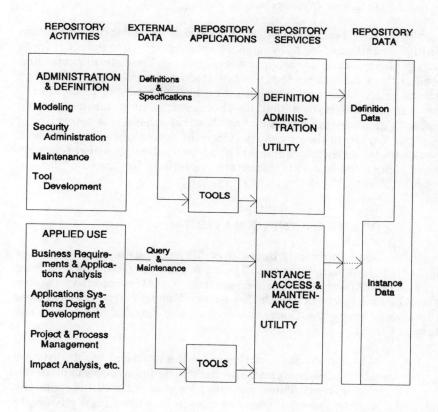

Figure 4-1   Use of the repository.

1.   *Specification* — consisting of definitional activities and
     the administration of these definitions stored in the
     repository, including how the definitions stored in the
     repository are to be used.

2. *Run-time services* — consisting of the invocation by tools for access to Repository Manager-managed data (data services), dialog management (user services), and system facilities (system services).

A major part of repository administration is establishing and maintaining definitions of data models, repository functions, storage arrangements, and security constraints. These definitions and specifications dictate what kinds of data may be collected, what can be done to the data and by whom, and how the data is to be stored. The information is provided by those responsible for supporting Repository Manager installation and those responsible for determining the particular use of the repository. Once the definitions are established, the day-to-day users may employ repository applications or repository-provided services to create, maintain, and query instances of data in accordance with the definitions.

4.2   VIEWS OF INFORMATION

As previously mentioned, Repository Manager uses three views of information that enable the specification of both data and function from three perspectives: a global perspective, a tool perspective, and a physical storage perspective. In Repository Manager, these perspectives are referred to as the *Conceptual View*, the *Logical View*, and the *Storage View*.

- The *conceptual view* describes the repository-wide data for the entire organization and is intended to be a model of the enterprise. The conceptual view is entirely independent of how the data is used by tools or how the data is physically stored.

- The *logical view* identifies a subset of the conceptual view data, which is used by a particular tool. It also specifies how the tool processes the data and interacts with the tool user. Each tool consists of one or more repository functions that operate on the data in a logical view. In the same manner that the conceptual view is repository-wide, the logical view is tool-specific.

- The *storage view* defines the physical storage for the contents of the repository, i.e., how the repository data is mapped to physical storage.

As shown in Figure 4-2, these views interrelate to define the kinds of information that can be stored in the repository, how and what information can be accessed under what conditions, and how the information is stored and accessed by the underlying database management system or file management system.

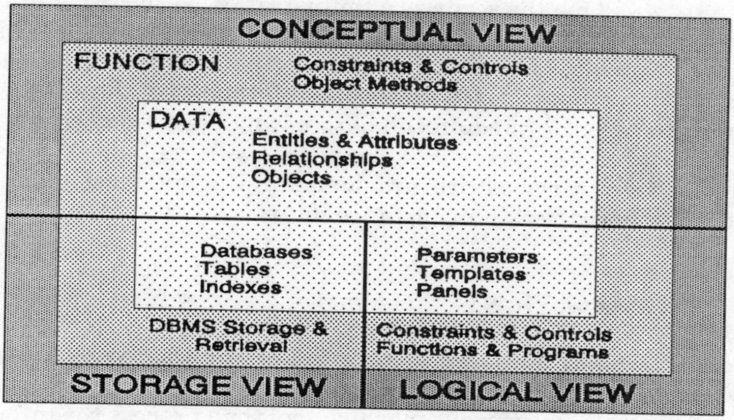

Figure 4-2   Repository Manager's views architecture.

Each of the views provide access to selected repository features, functionality, and data. This architecture promotes view independence, in that one view of information may be used with no prerequisite knowledge of others. Additionally, the architecture facilitates the ability to modify views without necessarily forcing the modification of others.

4.2.1   Conceptual View

The conceptual view is a perspective of information common across the repository. It addresses the definitions of the data and all corresponding instances of these definitions. Since the definitions of the data form the model(s) of the information (to be) instantiated, whenever values are associated with definitions, instance data (in the form of entities and their attributes, relationships, aggregations, and/or objects) are created in the repository.

Conceptual view specification services are provided to allow the creation and maintenance of models in the repository. Models are expressed by relationship types associating entity types and with entity types having attribute types. Additional controls may be defined to maintain integrity, compute data values, and perform processing upon the change of information states. These controls are specified in the form of policies and are associated with the components of a defined model. (Security conditions to be enforced for components of the conceptual view are specified via the security administration services.) Additionally, definition services are provided to establish and maintain object-oriented constructs. Object types may be defined as collections of entities along with associated methods. (Methods are the authorized operations to be performed on the data of an object.)

Conceptual view services are provided for the retrieval, addition, modification, and deletion of instance data.

4.2.2   Logical View

A logical view is a perspective of a subset of repository instance information accessible by a repository application or tool, and it may also carry controls on the ways in which tools can process the information. As such, it addresses logical definition data and the corresponding instance data. Many logical views can exist, but only one at a time can be effective for a repository tool or user.

Each repository function has its own logical data view. A logical data view consists of structured record buffers called templates, which can be combined into hierarchical data structures called template trees. Data is carried within fields of templates.

Logical view specification services are provided to define functions, template types, and template type trees, which include the specification of subsets of repository definition information required for specific repository applications to access corresponding instance information. Additionally, parameters may be defined to be passed among tools, and panels may be defined that a tool uses to interact with tool users. Like the conceptual view, policies may also be defined to insure integrity, compute data values, and perform special processing upon changes in information states. Logical view policies are effective only for the particular logical view for which they are defined. (Security conditions to be enforced for components of a logical view are specified via the security administration services.)

Logical views are the basis for the creation of repository applications or tools. This facility also allows the sharing of data views, policies, display panels, and parameters among various sets of tool processing logic.

4.2.3   Storage View

A storage view provides a perspective of the physical representation of repository data based on a subset of storage specification data. As such, it reflects the way repository instance data is physically represented for some subset of conceptual view constructs, and it includes the procedural logic for accessing the database or files. Repository Manager allows one and only one public storage view to be in effect at a time. To support development and testing activities, private storage views may be generated from conceptual view definitions and be accessed exclusively by a repository user. Note that Repository Manager/MVS uses DB2 for the storage of instance data in its public storage view and MVS data sets for the storage of instance data in private storage views.

Storage view specification services are provided for defining storage views and for mapping conceptual view constructs to either the DB2 storage view or a private storage view. Extensive services are provided for the maintenance of DB2 object definitions. (Such objects include storage groups, databases, table spaces, tables, and indexes.) Storage view definition activities generate SQL data definition language statements. These SQL statements are subjected to a DB2 bind resulting in an application plan that is used by DB2 to store and retrieve from the repository. The services also generate assembly language programs with embedded SQL for use by Repository Manager in the establishment and maintenance of repository data. These programs are subjected to precompilation, compilation, and linkedits to generate load modules for Repository Manager invocation in the addition, retrieval, modification, and deletion of repository instance data.

4.2.4   Use of Views

The type of activity to be performed with the repository dictates the type of repository view to be used. For model definition activities, the conceptual view is used. In the execution of repository functions, logical views are used. Access and storage of repository information, whether based on the use of the conceptual view or a logical view, always entails the use of a storage view. In general, the use of a storage view is transparent to repository applications and users. This transparency results in the independence of application data from considerations of actual internal storage organization and database management system access techniques.

4.3   DATA MODELING

Repository Manager contains an extensive data modeling capability. Two interfaces to this data model are provided:

1.   An Entity-Relationship interface

2.   An Object interface

The Entity-Relationship interface consists of entity types, relationship types, entity type attributes, and aggregation types. Relationship types are binary, and each member of a relationship type can be either an entity type or a relationship type.

Attributes on relationship types can be modeled as dependent entity types. The following semantic constraints on relationship types can be defined:

- Cardinality
- Mandatory
- Controlling
- Ordered

In the object interface, object types, subtypes, and supertypes can be defined. Each instance of an object type is an instance of an aggregation type, and methods and method implementations, which will be discussed later, are defined for object types.

Repository Manager also provides repository services that allow instances of aggregation types to be *locked* and *unlocked*. The purpose of these services is to provide control for referencing and altering such instances in an environment where there exists concurrent access by several users. It should be noted that these services are available only for instances of aggregation types. Hence, if a user is dealing with instances of a particular entity type over which such control is to be exercised, an aggregation type of which the entity type is a constituent must be the subject of the locking and unlocking services.

The control provided by locking over the constituent entity type instances of an aggregation type instance may persist for a long time, spanning multiple commits, multiple terminal interactions, or even multiple repository sessions. Locks are maintained based on a registered user Id. Four hierarchical levels of locking are provided, which will be discussed in detail in Chapter 8.

An important aspect of the data modeling facility is the concept of *policies*, which are discussed in the next section.

4.4   POLICIES

At the conceptual view and the logical view levels, controls may be defined and specified to enforce rules of entity and relationship integrity, attribute and field value assignment standards, and data access authority. Additionally, controls may be assigned to invoke functions when predefined events are detected. These kinds of controls are defined to the repository as policies and are implemented in the form of nonprocedural logic using REXX. There are four types of policies:

- *Derivation policies* that assign values to attributes or template fields based on the existence of specified conditions or the occurrence of certain events.

- *Integrity policies* that define and enforce criteria for valid entity and relationship instances or template fields whenever a write action (add or update) or delete is attempted on the instances of specified construct types.

- *Trigger policies* that invoke repository functions whenever selected maintenance or retrieval actions are performed on instances of specified entity types, relationship types, or template types, or whenever selected events occur associated with specified repository functions.

- *Security policies* that associate access levels and access conditions on selected repository definition and instance constructs for the determination of processing authorization.

Conceptual and logical view specification services are provided to define derivation, integrity, and trigger policies. Repository Manager security administration services are provided for the definition of security policies.

Policies will be discussed in greater detail in Chapter 5.

4.5   THE SUPPLIED ENTITY-RELATIONSHIP MODEL

An element of Repository Manager/MVS is the Supplied Entity-Relationship Model. This model contains a number of ER model definitions and also provides definitions of information that can be used to describe aspects of an enterprise's organization. The Supplied ER Model consists of a set of definitions of entity types, relationship types, attributes, and aggregation types, and the intent is that it be shared among tools and users, as well as adapted to the particular needs of an enterprise. Also included are definitions of information in support of IBM language and database products. This model will be discussed in detail in Chapter 6.

4.6   REPOSITORY DEFINITION ACTIVITIES

Repository definitions and associated specifications are established and maintained by several interrelated and ongoing activities (See Figure 4-3.) These are:

- Model definition — the specification of ER model constructs and object oriented constructs.

- Function definition — the specification of repository function constructs.

- Storage specification — the mapping of model definitions to storage structures.

- Security administration — the explicit specification of access and update permissions on model and function constructs addressing both definition and instance data.

Each of these activities is dependent on definitions established by other activities. Model definition provides the ER model constructs required

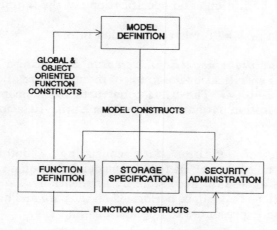

Figure 4-3   Repository definition activities.

for function definition, storage specification, and security administration activities. However, globally invoked functions and object-oriented functions cannot be fully incorporated into model definitions until the functions have been specified within the function definition activities. Since security can be enforced at the function level as well as the model level, function definitions must be established before associated security conditions for functions and function data constructs can be specified within security administration activities.

4.7   DEFINITION AND INSTANCE DATA

At the highest level, data in the repository may be characterized as:

1.   *Definition data*, consisting of definitions and specifications of the kinds of data that may be stored in the repository; the conditions under which the data may be accessed, created, modified or deleted; and specifications of the organization of the data by the underlying storage management software system.

2. *Instance data*, stored in the repository in accordance with the definitions and specifications of the definition data.

Definition data may be further subdivided into:

- *Conceptual model definition data*, consisting of definitions and specifications of kinds of instance data allowed in the repository. The basic constructs for conceptual model definition data are used to form Entity-Relationship (ER) models.

- *Logical definition data*, consisting of definitions and specifications of the types of model definition and associated instance data accessible by applications, as well as the actions that can be performed on the data and how information is presented to applications and users.

- *Storage specification data*, consisting of mapping specifications of conceptual model definitions to the storage constructs employed by the underlying storage management software.

- *Security administration data*, consisting of associations of access and update permissions with the constructs of the conceptual model, and logical definition data with user identifiers.

4.7.1   Model Definition Data

Model definition data is established in the repository to reflect Entity-Relationship models of the applied information to be maintained within the repository. Models are represented with the following basic constructs:

- Entity types reflecting classes of things (e.g., people, places, events, programs, files, etc.) about which information is (to be) stored in the repository.

- Attribute types associated with each entity type representing the kinds of characteristics (to be) stored in the repository as data for each instance of an entity type.

- Relationship types that associate instances of entity types with entity types, entity types with relationship types, and relationship types with relationship types

The definition of entity and relationship types includes the specification of semantic constraints and conditions for their instantiation.

More complex model definition construct types are formed from the basic constructs. These include:

- Aggregation types that are collections of interrelated entity types.

- Object types that are aggregation types combined with the predefined operations that are allowed to be performed on instances of the types.

Model definition data also includes special rules specified as actions to be performed surrounding the creation, access, and modification of entity, attribute, and relationship type instances.

Model definitions must be established in the repository before logical definitions, storage specifications, security administration data, and instance data can be added.

4.7.2   Logical Definition Data

Logical definitions are established based on existing model definition data. These include definitions and specifications of repository functions that operate on instances of the model definitions. The definition of a function includes specification of the following:

- Construct types that define the repository data types that are accessible and that are the means of information exchange with Repository Manager and other repository functions. These constructs are called templates.

- Panels that may be invoked by the functions.

- Special rules specified as actions to be performed surrounding the execution of the function and access to the repository data.

4.7.3   Storage Specification Data

Storage specifications are established to reflect the way repository instance data is physically represented. The specifications define the mapping of conceptual view constructs to the space allocation and data grouping mechanisms of the database management system or file management system under which the repository information is stored. They include the procedural logic for accessing the database or files.

4.7.4   Security Administration Data

Security administration data is established to control access and update authorizations for definition data, instance data, and functions within the repository. This data reflects the kinds of repository data users may access, whether or not they may update this data, and what repository functions they may use.

4.8   REPOSITORY TOOLS

A repository tool is a program or set of interrelated programs that invokes one or more repository functions. Tool programs have the procedural logic to invoke repository functions and perform editing, calculation, and formatting operations on data intended for or obtained from the repository. They may interface with a source of data (e.g., panel presentations to users) to obtain control, query, and update information. In essence, tool programs are the applications for users to query and maintain data within the repository. The terms "repository tool" and "repository application" are synonymous. Tool programs can be coded in any of the repository-supported languages, i.e., C, COBOL, PL/I, or REstructured eXtended eXecutor (REXX). They may be obtained from IBM or other software vendors, or they may be developed in-house.

4.9   TOOL GROUPS

Within the repository, a tool group is a packaging mechanism that facilitates the exporting, importing, reporting, and access to collections of repository data. A tool group's members consist of conceptual view definitions (entity types, relationship types, aggregation types, and object types), logical view definitions of repository functions, and messages. Each definition and message established within the repository must belong to at least one tool group and can belong to many tool groups. Additionally, there is no limit to the number of tool groups defined within the repository. Tool groups are defined and members assigned to satisfy the requirements of logically related repository functionality and data access.

A tool group serves two purposes:

- It provides easy access to the definitions with which a specific user is working at one time and thus eliminates having to search through long lists of definitions.

- It establishes boundaries around the repository information that pertains to a given tool or group of tools. Reports on the facilities used by the tool group can be generated.

4.10   TEMPLATES

Templates are the means of information exchange between repository functions, between repository functions and Repository Manager, and between repository functions and repository tools or applications. At execution time, a template becomes a block of structured storage, containing data fields and control information.

Control information that is carried in a template includes identification of the action requested of Repository Manager, status on return of the action request, status of data fields, and, in some cases, characteristics of the template and its content relative to similar related templates.

Template types, established as part of function definitions for logical views, are defined to facilitate some data requirement of functions. To provide access to repository information, a template type may be defined as mapped to an entity type, in which case its data fields will correspond to some or all of the attributes of the entity type. Fields corresponding to entity attributes can have characteristics that differ from the attribute type. Template types not mapped to entity types may be defined to pass parameters between repository functions, hold panel display variables, or provide local main storage for the function.

Hierarchical arrangements of template types, called *template type trees*, may be defined for cases where a function requires access to multiple entity types and instances of those types are connected by relationships. Tree definitions are provided by specifying connections between template types, where each connection corresponds to one relationship type that connects the entity types in the conceptual view.

4.11   REPOSITORY FUNCTION TYPES

Repository functions provide access to Repository Manager-supplied services and to repository data. When repository functions are defined using the logical view specification services, the following are specified as applicable:

- Data constructs (template types and template type trees) defining a *logical data view*

- Panels and messages to be displayed

- Nonprocedural logic (*policies*)

- Procedural logic to be executed

Repository Manager recognizes four types of repository functions:

- *Fully integrated functions* are associated with a specific tool program. By calling the repository function, the tool program is invoked. The tool program can then directly access the repository services and data.

- *Non-fully integrated functions* are invoked by a program first invoking a built-in Repository Manager OPEN service to obtain addressability to the functions' templates and to access repository services and data. These type of functions are not tied to a specific tool program, and they cannot be invoked directly. Any repository tool program can use one or more non-fully integrated functions to access repository data and services.

- *Method functions* define the operations that may be invoked on instances of object types. When a method is invoked for a specific object instance, Repository Manager selects and invokes a method implementation function based on the method and object type of the specific object instance.

- *Method implementation functions* are functions that are associated with methods of object types and that define which operations are performed on object instances of a particular object type for a particular method. Method implementations are invoked when a method is called for an object of a specified type.

Table 4-1 shows, for each repository function type, which definition components (listed left to right) are applicable to that type.

Table 4-1   Applicability of repository function components.

Function Type	Logical Data View	Panels & Messages	Nonprocedural Logic	Procedural Logic
Fully Integrated	required	optional	optional	required
Non-fully Integrated	required	optional	optional	not applicable
Method	parameter only	not applicable	optional	not applicable
Method Implementation	required	optional	optional	optional

Each of the function types is applicable for certain conditions, as follows:

- Fully integrated functions are associated with specific tool programs and execute the logic that directly accesses repository data and services. Functions of this type are directly invoked.

- Non-fully integrated functions are used by fully integrated functions and method implementations to access repository data and services. Functions of this type are invoked after being opened by the calling program and are closed by the calling program whenever the function's use or the function's logical data view is no longer required.

- Methods are associated with object types and are directly invoked by programs for a specified object instance.

- Method implementations perform operations on object instances. They are associated with object types, and, like fully integrated functions, each has a logical data view; tool program; and optional panels, messages, and policies. A function of this type is invoked by a method that has been invoked for a specified object instance.

4.12   REPOSITORY MANAGER SERVICES AND SUPPLIED FUNCTIONS

A full set of services and built-in functions is provided by Repository Manager. These services and functions may be used by other repository functions, including those built by an installation. Additionally, some of the supplied functions may be used directly by users.

4.12.1   Repository Services

Repository Manager provides a set of services that may be invoked by repository functions. The services are used to:

- Access and manipulate repository data.

- Access services of the underlying operating system.

- Facilitate user interaction with repository tools.

These services are classified as template services or actions and system call actions.

Template services are invoked on one or two templates. The procedural logic for their invocation involves assigning the value for the desired action and any associated data values to appropriate template fields.

Template actions invoked on one template are oriented toward actions on entity types. Functions are available for the following:

- Add entity instances.

- Delete entity instances along with any immediate relationships.

- Retrieve and update the values of entity attributes.

- Map and unmap entity types to and from templates.

- Display template data and messages on panels.

- Interrogate and control panel cursor positions.

- Issue commands to Interactive System Productivity Facility (ISPF).

- Set to null all template fields that map to input panel fields.

- Move message text to templates.

- Log messages in a diagnostic trace file.

- Commit and restore (rollback) repository updates, in Repository Manager/MVS only (See 4.12.2).

- Call other fully integrated repository functions.

Template actions invoked on two templates are oriented toward actions on relationship types. Functions are available for the following:

- Add and delete relationship instances.

- Connect and disconnect templates in a template tree.

Low-level system services are obtained via system call actions. These service invocations are characterized by the use of individual parameters instead of template fields. System call actions are available to:

- Open and close non-fully integrated repository functions.

- Obtain information on the Repository Manager environment and current state.

- Call a procedural program written in one of the Repository Manager-supported compiled languages from REXX.

- Control diagnostic trace recording.

- Control and access system timers.

4.12.2   Repository Manager Supplied Functions

Repository Manager/MVS provides an extensive set of functions that may be invoked by a tool program or a repository function. Two kinds of functions, which differ in terms of their position in the Repository Manager component of SAA, are made available:

1. The first kind is functions defined for the Repository Manager *Common Programming Interface* (CPI).

2. Others exist specifically for Repository Manager/MVS. These latter functions are said to belong to the Repository Manager/MVS *Application Programming Interface* (API), and it can be expected that these functions, or a close parallel to them, will eventually be incorporated into the Repository Manager CPI.

This distinction is not significant for users who are strictly interested in Repository Manager/MVS, but it is meaningful in terms of future releases of Repository Manager for other SAA platforms. It can be expected that the CPI version of these functions will be made available on these platforms. In the detailed discussion of the functions, the distinction as to whether a function is a CPI function or a Repository Manager/MVS API function will be noted.

All repository functions related to a storage view are part of the Repository Manager/MVS API.

Functions are classified by their form of interaction with the calling source. Two types of functions exist:

1. *Directly invocable interactive functions.* These functions interface with users exclusively via Repository Manager panels. They are directly invocable with no programmatic parameter exchange.

2.   *Built-in functions.* Built-in functions may be categorized by the two ways in which they interact with the user. These are:

a.   Those that can be executed either interactively or non-interactively

b.   Those that can be executed only non-interactively

Regardless of type, a built-in function is invoked by a program using a parameter template. For a built-in function that can execute interactively, a parameter field in its invocation template is assigned a value to specify whether interactive or non-interactive execution mode is desired. If the interactive mode is selected, a built-in function will use its associated panel(s) to interface with the repository user. For built-in functions that can only execute non-interactively and for built-in functions that are invoked in their non-interactive mode, all data exchange with the invoking program is accomplished via template fields.

A large number of directly invocable interactive functions are available in Repository Manager/MVS. Following is a list of the major categories of these functions, more details of which will be given in Chapter 8.

- Tool group query, selection, and maintenance

- Conceptual view query and maintenance

- Logical view query and maintenance

- Storage view query and maintenance

- Import and export of repository data

- Batch processing of repository commands

- Repository Manager system maintenance actions on system tables, security, tuning parameters, and PTF installation

- Access to special Repository Manager facilities, including trace and timer facilities and security profile selection

Built-in functions are provided for the following purposes:

- Tool group built-in function to query the members of a tool group

- ER modeling built-in functions

- Logical view built-in functions

- Security administration built-in function to bind security profiles.

- Storage view administration built-in functions

- Utility built-in functions

- Repository data query built-in functions

- ER model Program Temporary Fix (PTF) maintenance built-in functions

- Repository data services built-in functions

- System services built-in function to set to null all template fields that map to entity attributes

4.13   REPOSITORY MANAGER DIALOGS

An interactive function and associated panels establish an interactive session with a terminal user, referred to as a *dialog*. The interactive function prompts the user to type information on a panel that is appropriate to the function requested and then displays the result.

A dialog is associated, in general, with a hierarchy of panels. The user navigates these panels by indicating an option on one panel, which then causes a subsequent panel to be displayed. Different interactive functions have different hierarchies.

Repository functions that are interactive can be developed by creating panels for them using SDF II or the SDF/PDF text editor.

After a panel has been defined, Repository Manager can be made to map the panel input and output field to a logical data view. Code to

move data from one buffer to another does not have to be written.
Figure 4-4 shows an example of mappings between panels, templates
and repository data.

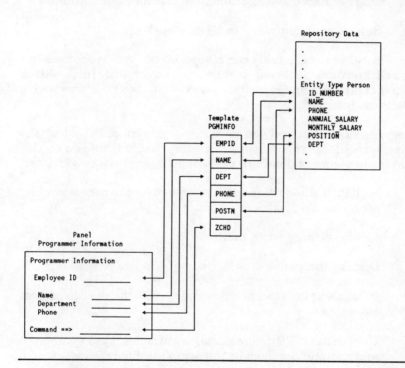

Figure 4-4   Mappings of repository data between panels and templates.

Repository Manager/MVS Version 1 Release 1, makes these dialogs
available only by interaction with a mainframe. It is likely, however,
that IBM will develop interfaces to make this capability available on
Work Station platforms.

Two types of panels exist within the repository:

- Interactive panels
- Message help panels

Many of different kinds of operations can be performed with *interactive panels*, such as:

- Input, display, and output of logical view data

- Display and update of function control information

- Selection of functions to be executed

With repository services, panels can be displayed, user responses can be processed, and data displayed on panels can be scrolled. Information between a tool program and repository services can be transferred using a user services template.

Repository services that provide user services perform most of the interactive panel processing. When a repository function issues a display request, the following actions are performed by repository services:

- Map ISPF dialog manager variables over the corresponding template field values.

- Invoke display write policies.

- Display the panel.

- Invoke display read policies and permit the user to correct any errors.

- Unmap the ISPF dialog manager variables, leaving any new template field values in the template fields.

When interacting with a panel, a user can issue a variety of commands, by employing the program function (PF) keys or inserting a command on the command or selection line. These commands can be ISPF commands or commands defined for the repository function. The ISPF Command Table intercepts certain commands before they are passed to the repository function.

Commands that do not appear in the ISPF Command Table or that are not intercepted are passed through to the tool program for processing. The list of commands in the ISPF Command Table can be modified. Certain restrictions on modifications apply.

A panel can have a scrollable *panel window* to display the elements in a template array. If a template array maps to an entity type, the elements in the current domain of the template can be scrolled through in the panel window. The concepts of an arrayed template and the domain of a template will be discussed in Chapter 7. A template array can also be an array of working storage templates. Only one panel window can be defined on a panel. The panel window can refer to several template arrays that have exactly the same extent.

Repository services can be used to scroll a panel window forward and backward in the template array without tool program assistance, unless a scrolling request would take the panel window beyond the last entry or before the first. In this case, the tool program performs part of the scrolling operation; it refills the template array from a different part of the domain, first saving any changed data.

A repository function interacts with a panel via one or more *user services templates*. The user services template communicates information about terminal usage in both directions between repository services and the tool program. There is no relationship between the number of user services templates in a repository function and the number of panels in that function. A single user services template can be used in several panels, or several user services templates can be used for a single panel. A user services template can be an arrayed template.

When a repository function is created, Repository Manager automatically provides a user services template that contains all the possible panel control fields. Fields that are unnecessary can be deleted; the automatically created template can be copied if additional user service templates are required. A user services template can have any name and can be any type of template, including the function's parameter template.

Repository Manager maintains a set of *system messages* that it uses, and any repository function is allowed to use these messages. Additional messages and message help panels can be defined within the repository and displayed from repository functions.

When a message is defined, it must contain a long form of the message, the explanation of the message, the system action that should be taken, and the user response text. A short form of the message is optional.

A message must be *bound* before it can be used. Binding consists of converting the message definition stored in the repository (in the form of an ER model) into an ISPF message library entry and ISPF message help panels. A message can belong to more than one tool group, but must be bound to each tool group in which it belongs.

There are several ways messages can be used from a repository function:

- Displaying a message directly on a panel

- Placing a long message in a template field for further processing

- Writing the message ID and long message text to a diagnostic trace file

4.14   SECURITY CONCEPTS

The Repository Manager security facility allows site control of access and updating to features and data of the repository. The administration of security consists of using the provided security services to indicate which users can and cannot retrieve, update, and delete repository definitions and data, and which users can and cannot access repository functions.

In general, security administration consists of using Repository Manager services to:

- Define security profiles of what can be accessed to what degree and what cannot be accessed.

- Define a list of user identifications to which security profiles can be assigned (called the Authorized User List).

- Assign security profiles to users identified on the Authorized User List.

This facility allows the assignment of multiple security profiles to multiple users to accommodate situations where a group of users perform the same or similar repository tasks and consequently require the same security profile. Since users can be assigned multiple profiles, cases where some users perform differing repository tasks that merit different security profiles can also be satisfied. Note that a repository user can have only one currently effective security profile at a time.

Security profiles are files created with Repository Manager that define exactly what repository information a user or group of users can access. Each security profile contains:

- Identifiers of groups and individual items of repository definition data. The groups are called security object groups, and the individual items are called security objects.

- Levels of access assigned to the security objects, defining if a user can delete, add, update, retrieve, or call individual items as applicable.

- Optional conditions for access at each given level.

Security objects are feature and data types that can be subject to security control. The following kinds of features and data constructs may be security objects:

- Entity type definitions

- Entity instances

- Entity attributes

- Relationship type definitions

- Relationship instances

- Template fields

- Repository functions

Security for entity type definitions, entity instances, entity attributes, and relationship type definitions is enforced at the entity attribute level. Security enforcement on the other types occurs at the level of the type (i.e., relationship instance security is enforced at the relationship instance level, template field security is enforced at the template field level, and repository function security is enforced at the repository function level). Consequently, Repository Manager recognizes four types of security objects:

- EA (Entity Attribute) consisting of entity type definitions, entity instances, entity attributes, and relationship type definitions.

- R (Relationships) consisting of relationship instances.

- TF (Template Fields) consisting of template fields.

- F (Repository Functions) consisting of repository functions.

More specifically, security profiles consist of:

- Default access levels by security object type

- Security object group names with assigned

  - Security object identifiers

  - Security object access levels

  - Access level conditions

Table 4-2 presents the allowable security object access levels in order of precedence.

Table 4-2   Security object access level precedence.

Access Level	Allowed Access
Delete	Delete, Add, Update, Retrieve
Add	Add, Update, Retrieve
Update	Update, Retrieve
Retrieve	Retrieve
Call	Invoke
Noaccess	none

Access level conditions are optional REXX functions that

- State a special requirement for access.

- Retrieve or evaluate the values of security objects.

- Yield a true (1) or false (2) result. If true, access is allowed; if false, access is denied.

Since a security policy consists of a security object associated with an access level and, optionally, a condition, a security profile may be viewed as a collection of security policies.

The Authorized User List consists of the identifiers of users who can use specific security profiles (not a list of identifiers of users permitted to invoke and use Repository Manager). Identifiers on this list can be assigned one or more security profiles. All users (whether identified on this list or not) can use a default profile (DWKPUB) provided with Repository Manager.

The recommended minimum level of security includes controlling access to the following repository information:

- The Supplied Entity-Relationship Model definitions (see Chapter 6)

- The security administration functions of Repository Manager

This level of security can be achieved by adding the security object groups DWKDEF and DWKSEC to the default profile DWKPUB. After these security object groups are added to the unbound security profile, DWKPUB must be bound in order to be effective.

Repository Manager also contains a special security profile named ZZZADMIN, which provides maximum access to Repository Manager. This security profile is intended to be restricted to users responsible for:

- Administration of the repository

- Administration of repository security

- Installation of Repository Manager maintenance

As a security administration aid, various levels of reports can be generated on the specified security conditions. Additionally, Repository Manager provides an individualized log of access denials for each user. Entries are made of the dates and times of a user's unsuccessful attempts to add or delete protected entity instances, add or delete protected relationship instances, and call protected repository functions. Requests to access protected template fields, entity attributes, or entity or relationship type definitions are not logged.

4.15   BATCH COMMAND LANGUAGE

A *Batch Command Language* is provided in Repository Manager/MVS that allows maintenance on the repository to be performed through commands that can be executed in batch mode. Separate commands exist for operating on types and instances. Maintenance on repository-wide derivation, integrity, and trigger policies can also be performed.

This facility is important when large amounts of information are to be added to, deleted from, or updated in the repository, and it is more efficient from an operational view to run these operations in batch mode.

This facility is also used by the Dictionary Migration Tool (DMT) to provide migration facilities for the contents of an IBM DB/DC Data Dictionary to the repository.

The commands will be discussed in more detail in Chapter 10.

4.16   REPOSITORY EXPORT AND IMPORT

A facility exists in Repository Manager that allows repository definitions and aggregate instances to be exported from one repository and subsequently imported into another (or the same) repository.

4.16.1   Exporting and Importing Definitions

The following definitions can be exported and imported:

- Entity types
- Relationship types
- Aggregation types

- Object types
- Functions
- Messages
- Security profiles

Additionally, individual definitions, definitions contained in a tool group, or all definitions in a repository can be exported and imported.

This facility is accessed through the panel DWKUMN1, which is the same panel that is used to process batch commands (See Chapter 10). When definitions are imported, the following options exist:

- Perform a *Trial Run*, i.e., compare the definitions to be imported with those existing in the repository, but not make any changes. This option is useful in that it allows potential problems to be identified prior to the definitions being imported.

- The *Add* option, where new definitions to be imported are added to the repository, but where, in case a definition exists in the repository with the same name as the one imported, the existing one is to be left as is and the new definition is not imported.

- The *Update* option, where new definitions are added to the Repository and existing definitions are replaced with new definitions with the same name.

Definitions imported to a repository are not automatically bound by Repository Manager, and a bind must be issued for each new entity type, relationship type, and object type.

4.16.2   Instances of Aggregation Types

As discussed previously, an instance of an aggregation type consists of one instance of the root entity type together with all instances of the entity types subordinate to the root entity type in the definition of the aggregation type. The following instances can be exported and imported:

- All instances of a given aggregation type
- All instances that match a specified key pattern
- A specific instance

When importing aggregation instances, the options *trial run*, *add*, and *update* are available and have the same meaning as for the import of definitions. Additionally, processing options related to locking of aggregation instances can be specified.

4.17   QUERY MANAGEMENT FACILITY

Query Management Facility (QMF) is normally thought of as being used to access relational data using the QMF query methods SQL, Prompted Query, and Query-By-Example (QBE).

However, QMF ER Prompted Query can be used to access Entity-Relationship data in the repository; it does not access the underlying relational databases directly.

ER Prompted Query operates by prompting the user for the Entity-Relationship data that is to be retrieved . The user is guided through a series of *dialog panels* where this data is specified. The dialog panels are displayed on the right side of the screen, and as the query is built, it is displayed in the *echo area* on the right side of the screen.

The Help function key can be used to obtain online help at any time. Help information is presented in a window that overlays a portion of the panel from which it is requested.

To begin a query, a *view* is selected on the *Show View* dialog panel by the user, this view designating either an entity type or an aggregation type. The user can enter this entity type or aggregation type directly or can request a list of all of these in a specified tool group. A list of tool groups available can also be requested. To narrow the search in such a list, the "wild-card" characters can be used:

    _   substituting a single unspecified character
    %   substituting zero, one, or more unspecified characters

When an aggregation type is requested, the view displayed represents the template tree that is used to access the repository instances that are to be queried. In place of the template names, the entity types are listed, followed in parentheses by the parent relationship type. It is possible that the same entity type may appear more than once in the view being displayed; in that case, it is necessary for the user to know the underlying template names to distinguish these occurrences. A function key is available for this purpose.

A query can be executed by means of the RUN key; for queries where the response to the query does not fit on a screen, scrolling is available.

The Show View dialog panel is also used to build the query that is to be executed. These actions take place by combining positioning of the cursor with pressing of a selected function key. The following actions can be specified:

- Attributes for any of the represented entity types can be selected.

- Instances of entity types can be qualified.

- Parts of the view, not including a root entity type, can be deleted from the View.

- A *QMF variable attribute name* can be used. This can be any name chosen, prefixed with a "&", which does not have to be named until the query is executed.

- Conditions for attributes can be specified.

These conditions for attributes use the basic form

```
< entity type attribute > <comparison operator> <value>
```

The rules for comparison operators and for combining basic forms are very much the same as those for the *selection expression* in *keyed retrievals* (See section 7.1.5).

The *value* that can be specified has a more general form than in the above selection expression; the following options for this value are provided:

1. A constant (character string or numeric value)

2. A *QMF substitution variable*, which must be specified prior to the query being executed

3. A template field name equivalent to some entity type attribute name

A QMF Prompted Query can be *saved* with a user-supplied name not exceeding 18 characters in length. It can be retrieved at a later time for execution.

The variable attribute name and substitution variables provide substantial flexibility in reusing the same query at different times.

Facilities are provided for formatting the response to a query; these will not be discussed here.

EXPORT and IMPORT commands are provided for the following purposes:

- EXPORT allows external applications to use repository information retrieved by a QMF Prompted Query.

- IMPORT provides the capability of bringing an externalized object back to QMF's work area.

The format of the externalized object is specified and is not discussed in detail here.

5 ENTITY-RELATIONSHIP AND OBJECT INTERFACES

Repository Manager uses an *Entity-Relationship* data model formalism as a means for modeling conceptual view constructs in the repository. Understanding of this data model formalism is important for comprehension of the modeling capabilities of Repository Manager. This model, and the manner in which it is used, will be discussed in this chapter. At the end of this chapter, the topic of *Object constructs* in the repository will also be discussed. Later chapters will discuss the *services* provided by Repository Manager to define and manipulate both Entity-Relationship and Object constructs.

Since the principal purpose of these constructs is to represent the real world in the repository, a data modeling formalism to represent the real world will be discussed.

5.1   THE REAL WORLD

The purpose of the repository is to contain a model of the enterprise, or at least, initially, a part of the enterprise. The usefulness of the repository, and the tools that will operate on it, are directly related to how good this model is, i.e., how accurately it represents the real world as seen by the enterprise.

Building a model of the enterprise in the repository requires a good understanding of what the real world is like. Hence, this section will deal with how the real world is described in order to be represented in the repository. It must be pointed out that there exist many such schemes. The one described here has proved useful in terms of the Repository Manager environment, and later sections will describe how this representation is translated into repository terms.

This section will define the constructs that are used in establishing the model of the real world. These constructs are not identical to the ones used to represent this model in the repository, but there is a close analogy between the two sets of constructs, and, wherever possible, the terminology used for the real-world model and its representation in the repository are quite similar.

5.1.1   Real-World Entities

The term *real-world entity instance* is intended to denote any "thing" or event that can be identified. Typical of such instances of interest in the repository environment are programs, modules, files, databases, departments, employees, etc.

Real-world entity instances have properties, which are termed real-world attributes, and values are assigned to these. It is these values that distinguish one real-world entity instance from another. For example, attributes of employee might be the employee number, grade level, etc. For the employee John Smith, the values of these might be 123456 and 8, and for the employee George Brown, the values of these might be 246891 and 9.

5.1.1.1   *Real-World Entity Types*

A collection of real-world entity instances can usually be grouped into one or more sets, where the instances in one set satisfy a certain membership criterion. For example, employees are people who work for a certain enterprise. This membership criterion defines what is called a *real-world entity type*. The instances of a real-world entity type tend to have a more or less common set of attributes.

5.1.1.2   *Supertypes and Subtypes*

A real-world entity instance may be a member of more than one real-world entity type. Consider the case of a programmer named John Smith, where *programmer* is a real-world entity type. At the same time, we may also look at John Smith as being simply an employee. Then John Smith is also a member of the real-world entity type *employee*. Since the real-world entity type *employee* has a broader membership criterion than the real-world entity type *programmer* — i.e., there are employees who are not programmers — we refer to the entity type *employee* as being a *supertype* of the entity type *programmer*. In a like manner, the entity type *programmer* is said to be a *subtype* of the entity type *employee*.

In general, if an entity type is a supertype, it will have not only one but many subtypes. The issue of attributes of supertypes and subtypes needs to be discussed. In the above example, the real-world entity type *employee* might have the real-world attributes employee number, grade level, and date of hire. For the employee John Smith, these might be 123456, 8, and December 14, 1987. George Brown is also an employee, but he is a member of the accounting department and, hence, not an instance of the entity-type *programmer*. We can assume that there is a subtype of *employee* named *accountant*, of which George Brown is an instance. Since both *programmer* and *accountant* are subtypes of *employee*, all attributes of *employee* are also attributes of its subtypes. On the other hand, there can also be attributes of the subtypes that do not apply to the supertype. For example, *programmer* might have attributes recording the person's preferred programming language, system skill, etc., which would not apply to accountants. The manner in which attributes are passed from a supertype to its subtypes is commonly referred to as *inheritance*.

The subtyping mechanism can reach any desired depth; for example, *programmer* may have subtypes *exempt programmer* and *nonexempt programmer*. The former might have the attribute *salary*, whereas the latter might have the attribute *hourly wage*. For each subclassification, there are presumably attributes that are relevant to each subtype that are not relevant to the others. In general, subclassification only makes sense when this is true.

5.1.1.3   *Simple and Composite Real-World Entities*

Depending on the context and level of detail the definer of a real-world entity has in mind, this entity can be a simple "thing," or it can be a combination of other "things." An example might be one person thinking of a house as an entity, whereas another person thinks of an apartment in the house an entity, and a third person thinks of a room in an apartment as an entity.

All of these points of view are valid. In order to introduce a better structure among them, two terms should be introduced. A *simple* real-world entity instance is one that is characterized solely by a list of its attributes and their values. On the other hand, a *composite* real-world entity instance is one that is characterized by one or more constituent entity instances, and possibly a list of attributes of the composite real-world instance and their values.

The constituent entity instances of a composite real-world entity instance may be ordered. For example, in the above, the apartments in the house might be ordered by the apartment number, and the rooms in an apartment might be ordered by their square footage.

The constituent entity instances of a composite real-world entity instance can have different degrees of dependence on the composite entity instance. In some cases, a constituent entity instance cannot meaningfully exist independently of the composite entity instance. In this case, the constituent entity instance is said to be *existence-dependent* on the composite entity instance. Such entity instances are also called *local* entity instances. Other cases exist where a constituent entity instance is not existence-dependent.

In the same manner that simple real-world entity instances have an entity type, such types can be established for composite real-world entity instances. In order for these types to be meaningful, their instances tend to have the same attributes and constituents from the same set of entity types.

5.1.2   Real-World Relationships

The term *real-world relationship instance* is intended to denote an association of two or more real-world entity instances. An example of such an association is the fact that a house contains an apartment.

Real-world relationship instances can be classified according to the number of entity instances that participate in the association, as follows:

- When only two real-world entity instances participate in the association, the relationship instance is said to be *binary*.

- An association of three real-world instances is said to be a *3-ary*, or *ternary*, relationship instance.

- An association of n entity instances, where n is greater than 2, is said to be an *n-ary* relationship instance.

Each real-world entity instance that participates in a relationship instance is said to have a *position* in the relationship instance. For example, in the binary relationship instance between a programmer instance and program instance that denotes that a programmer has done maintenance on a program, the programmer instance is in the first position and the program instance is in the second position.

Real-world relationship instances are generally identified by the real-world entities that participate in them. However, it is also sometimes necessary to associate real-world attributes and their values to them. For example, in an association between a programmer, a program, and a test case representing a test, it may be desirable to associate the real-world attributes *status*, *date*, etc., to the association.

Sometimes there can be multiple real-world relationship instances between the same set of entity instances. This may occur in the association of a programmer and a program intending to denote that the programmer has done maintenance on the program. Since this may occur a number of times, it is necessary to assign a value of a real-world attribute, in this case, *date of maintenance*, to each association.

5.1.2.1   *Real-World Relationship Types*

In the same manner that real-world entity types have been defined, a *real-world relationship type* is a set of real-world relationship instances that satisfy a certain membership criterion.

The following characteristics of the members of a real-world relationship type are not required, but they tend to make the relationship type more useful.

- They have the same number of positions.

- A given position is occupied by instances of the same real-world entity type.

- The have the same real-world attributes.

5.1.2.2   *Naming of Real-World Relationship Types*

The two most common ways of naming a real-world relationship type are:

- The *Verb form*.

  In this case, the name of the relationship type is composed of a clause containing the names of the constituent entity types, separated by verbs or prepositions that express the role played by the participant.

  For example, a real-world relationship type between the real-world entity types *programmer* and *program*, intending to denote that a programmer wrote a program, can be referred to by the clause "programmer writes program," and the real-world relationship type can be named *programmer writes program*.

  In the case of an n-ary real-world relationship type, as for example, one defined by the criterion "is a relationship instance between a programmer, a program, and a test case, representing a program test," it can be referred to by the clause "programmer tests program using test case," and the relationship can then be named *programmer tests program using test case*.

- The *Noun form*.

  In this form, the real-world relationship type is given a noun or noun phrase as its name. In this form, the relationship types of the preceding paragraphs might be named *program development* and *program test*.

5.1.2.3   *Real-World Relationship Cardinality*

The term *cardinality* denotes a set of integers that specify a constraint on the maximum number of instances of an entity type in a given position that can exist in instances of a given relationship type for one instance each of the remaining entity type. This concept can best be explained by examples.

- It may be desirable to express the fact that each program can be written by, at most, one programmer. In the relationship type *programmer writes program*, this constraint is expressed by the cardinality *(1,m)*. Here, m is an integer that may be as large as desired.

- It may be found necessary to further constrain m, the number of occurrences. This might be the case in the real-world relationship type *department has section*, instances of which are intended to denote the organizational structure of departments. In addition to the fact that each section can only belong to one department, there may be an internal policy that states that no department may have more than seven sections. This policy would translate then into assigning the cardinality *(1,7)* to this relationship type.

- In the case of a real-world relationship type, *program accesses file*, the cardinality would normally be *(m,m)*, meaning that a program may access many files and, conversely, that a file may be accessed by many programs. Again, should it be desirable to limit the number of instances in a relationship type with cardinality *(m,n)* to some maximum or minimum, either integer, or both, can be replaced with that maximum or minimum, respectively.

5.1.2.4   *Ordered Real-World Relationship Types*

A real-world relationship type is said to be *ordered*, which indicates how the instances of the type are to be ordered. For example, in the real-world relationship type *programmer writes program*, it might be desirable to have all the relationship instances for a given programmer grouped together and, perhaps, all these instances ordered in ascending sequence of the program's name.

5.1.2.5   *Recursive Real-World Relationship Types*

In a real-world relationship type, it is not required that the real-world entity types that appear in different positions be distinct. Whenever two such entity types are the same, the relationship type is said to be *recursive*. In such a case, it is desirable to number or label the positions of the relationship type and to distinguish the participants by their position number or label. In the case of a recursive relationship type, it is also not required that the entity instances that are members of a relationship instance be distinct. For example, an instance of the relationship type *procedure calls procedure* could have the same instance of the entity type *procedure* in both first and second position. This would mean that this procedure instance calls itself.

5.1.2.6   *Viewing Composite Real-World Entities as Real-World Relationships*

An alternative view of a composite real-world entity instance is as real-world relationship instances. A composite real-world entity instance is one that is characterized by one or more constituent entity instances, and the constituent entity instances can be thought of as being separate from the composite entity instance and associated with it by means of binary relationship instances. Using this alternative view is equivalent to breaking up the composite entity instance into its constituent entity instances. This view of a composite real-world entity instance is particularly useful whenever the constituent entity instances are not existence-dependent on the composite.

5.1.2.7   *Viewing Real-World Relationships as Real-World Entities*

A real-world relationship instance may always be viewed as a real-world entity instance. In fact, some modeling methodologies require that a relationship instance with attributes always be considered an entity instance.

5.1.3   Real-World Attributes

As previously stated, real-world entity instances have properties or characteristics, termed real-world attributes, and values are assigned to these. It is these values that distinguish one real-world entity instance from another. For example, attributes of employee might be the employee number, grade level, etc. Similarly, real-world relationships can also have real-world attributes.

5.1.3.1   *Single-valued and Multivalued Attributes*

A real-world attribute may have zero, one, or more values for a given real-world entity or relationship instance.

If a real-world attribute has no value for a given real-world entity or relationship instance, this denotes that either the value does not exist or is not known.

A real-world attribute that can have, at most, one value for a given real-world instance is said to be a *single-valued attribute*. For example, the attribute *date of birth* for an employee is a single-valued attribute. There exist other real-world attributes that can have more than one value for a given real-world instance; such an attribute is said to be a *multivalued attribute*. For example, the attribute *date of compilation* for a program can have multiple values, as the program may have been compiled many times.

5.1.3.2   *Attribute Groups*

Sometimes a real-world entity or relationship instance has multiple attributes, and it is convenient or logically meaningful to be able to collect them into a named grouping called an *attribute group*. For example, the attributes *first name*, *middle initial*, and *last name* could be grouped into an attribute group called *name*. Along different lines, the attributes *state name*, *state abbreviation*, and *state capital* could be combined into the attribute group *state*.

5.1.3.3   *Repeating and Non-repeating Attribute Groups*

In a manner similar to single-valued and multivalued attributes, attribute groups can have either, at most, a single set of values for a real-world instance, or more than one set. In the former case the attribute group is said to be *non-repeating*, and in the latter case it is said to be *repeating*.

In the case of a repeating attribute group, it is convenient that the group should contain one or more attributes whose value can be used to distinguish one repetition from the other.

5.1.3.4   *Real-World Identifier Attributes*

A real-world attribute can be used to refer to an instance of a real-world entity or relationship; such an attribute is referred to as an *identifier attribute*. In order for a real-world identifier attribute to be useful, it is desirable that each one of its values uniquely identify an instance, as in the case with the attribute *social security number*. If an identifier does not have this property, it is necessary to qualify its values with an appropriate context. For example, the value of *name* is generally not unique for a set of programmers; if *name* were used as an identifier attribute, its values would have to be qualified by a phrase such as "John Smith who works in Department 105" in order to refer to a specific programmer.

5.1.3.5   *Real-World Versions*

The concept of a version is very important in the description of the real world in a repository. In the real world, many things progress through certain stages, and it is important to be able to track this progression. Typically, we then deal with a group of things that are very much alike, and it is possible to think of them as "versions" of each other. Such a group is called a *version set*. In this manner, composite real-world entities, e.g., systems, databases, etc., can be thought of as existing in different versions.

This concept allows all members of a version set to be given a common name, and each member can be distinguished from another member by its *version identifier*.

5.2   DATA LAYERS

As an introduction, it must be noted that the repository, like databases of other repository systems such as dictionary systems, can be viewed as being logically composed of a set of "layers" of data. Note should be taken that there is no implication of physical storage in the definition of these layers — i.e., when an implementor develops the system and designs the databases and files that contain the information contained in these layers, the identity of these databases and files may well disappear.

Three data layers can be identified:

1. The *Repository Meta-Model* layer provides the (allowable) contents of the Repository Information Model layer (see below). It is accessible only to IBM, and its contents and definition are not made available to Repository Manager users. It is the equivalent of what in the Information Resource Dictionary System is called the IRD Schema Definition layer.

2. The *Repository Information Model* layer holds definitions and generic descriptions of the allowable content of the Repository Information layer (see below). The contents of this layer are provided in two ways:

    a. It contains the *Supplied Entity-Relationship Model definition*, which is provided by IBM (and which will be discussed in the next chapter). This model cannot be modified by a site.

    b. The contents of this layer can be extended by the use of Repository Manager facilities. These facilities are described in a later chapter. The consequences of making such extensions will be discussed in Chapter 6.

    This layer is analogous to the IRD Schema layer in the Information Resource Dictionary System.

3. The third layer is the *Repository Information*. It contains instantiations of the definitions contained in the Repository Information Model layer and, hence, contains the actual data of the enterprise being modeled. Repository tools are used to populate this layer, which is analogous to the dictionary in a dictionary system.

The term *repository* will be used to denote the database consisting jointly of the Repository Information Model and Repository Information layers.

The definition of these layers provides a recursive definition of the repository database. It provides the power to specify structures as complex as desired and required. The concept of these layers will serve as a context for the following sections. To be remembered is that Repository Manager services and functions that deal with types address the Repository Information Model layer, whereas those services and functions that deal with instances address the Repository Information layer.

An exception to this layer structure will be discussed in Chapter 6, which deals with the Repository Manager/MVS Supplied ER Model. The use of modeling facilities in this model involves defining both types and their instances in the Repository Information layer.

5.3   ENTITY-RELATIONSHIP CONSTRUCTS

In this section, we will present the Entity-Relationship repository constructs into which real-world constructs will be mapped.

The two concepts used to model an organization's data are *entity types* and *relationship types*. This section will discuss how these are used in order that the Repository Information Model contain a single description of an organization's data.

5.3.1   Entity Type

An entity type represents a class of persons, places, or things that are significant to the organization. An entity type has an *entity type name* that must be unique in the set of all entity types.

An entity type has one or more descriptive attributes. Each *entity attribute* has an *entity attribute name* that must be unique within the entity type. Each entity attribute has a default data type, a length, and for decimal data types, a scaling factor.

One, and only one, attribute for each entity type serves as the *key attribute*, which uniquely identifies each *instance* of the entity type. An instance of an entity type consists of the actual values for its attributes.

The key attribute of an entity type can be either *user-assigned*, like an ID_NUMBER, or *system assigned*. For a user-assigned key attribute, users are responsible for assigning all values; for a system-assigned key attribute, Repository Manager automatically assigns a unique value for each instance of the entity type. A system-assigned key is advantageous when it is difficult to guarantee that all values of any attribute of an entity type will be unique.

An entity attribute can be defined as being *derived* from one or more entity attributes. A derived attribute is created by defining a repository-wide *derivation policy*, which defines the condition and algorithm for deriving an attribute. All attributes, including derived attributes, need to be mapped to physical storage. Policies will be covered in a later section of this chapter.

Additionally, *integrity policies* can be optionally specified for the entity attributes. These are global constraints on entity attributes of the entity type, enforced by repository services at the time an instance of the entity type is used or created.

The specification of an entity type can also optionally include *trigger policies* for the entity type, which are enforced by repository services whenever an instance of the entity type is retrieved or added.

5.3.2   Relationship Type

Each Repository Manager relationship type consists of a set of relationship instances with similar characteristics. A relationship type is a binary directed association between

- two entity types or
- an entity type and a relationship type or
- two relationship types

It is possible to have multiple distinct relationship types with the same components.

Referential integrity is dynamically maintained by Repository Manager; i.e., if a source or target instance is deleted, the relationship instance existence is detected, and deleted. This is referred to as "automatic delete propagation." These dynamic deletions are, however, constrained by integrity policies. If a condition that prevents one of the controlled relationships in the propagation chain from being deleted is detected, a restore is forced and an error message generated.

Every relationship type has a *primary* relationship type name, as well as an *inverse name* for the relationship type in the opposite direction. This is to say, each relationship type in the repository is bidirectional — i.e., if there exists a relationship type between EMPLOYEE and PROGRAM named EMPLOYEE_MAINTAINS_PROGRAM, an *inverse* relationship type exists between PROGRAM and EMPLOYEE, which might be named PROGRAM_MAINTAINED_BY_EMPLOYEE.

In entity-relationship diagrams, the notation adopted is to enclose the name of an inverse relationship type in parentheses.

Every relationship type connects a *source* and a *target*. In the example above, the entity type EMPLOYEE is the source of the relationship type EMPLOYEE_MAINTAINS_PROGRAM, and the target is PROGRAM. The source of the inverse relationship type is PROGRAM, and the target is EMPLOYEE.

Relationship types, in the same way as entity types, also have *instances*. An instance of a relationship type associates an instance of the source with an instance of the target.

A relationship has a number of *semantic constraints*:

1. *Cardinality*. The source and target instances must be related as follows:

    a. *"1 to 1" (1–1)*: A given source instance must be related to zero or one target instance. Also inversely, a given target instance must be related to zero or one source instance.

    b. *"1 to many" (1–m)*: A given source instance can be related to zero, one, or more target instances. However, a given target instance must be related to zero or one source instance.

    c. *"many to 1" (m–1)*: The inverse of the above.

    d. *"many to many" (m–m)*: A given source instance can be related to zero, one, or more target instances. Inversely, a given target instance can be related to zero, one, or more source instances. This is the unconstrained case, which is the default when cardinality is not specified.

2.   *Mandatory (M)*. This constraint provides extended semantics for instance creation. The entity or relationship instance at the mandatory end of the relationship cannot be created unless the relationship instance is also created.

3.   *Controlling (C)*. This constraint provides extended semantics for instance deletion. The entity or relationship instance at the controlling end of the relationship will be deleted when the relationship instance is deleted.

4.   *Ordered (O)*. In this case, instances of the target of the relationship type will be retrieved by Repository Manager in the order defined when the instances were added to the repository. Either a primary relationship type or its inverse can be defined to be ordered, but not both. The target of the relationship defined as being ordered must be an entity type — it cannot be a relationship type.

The following optional *policies*, which act as constraints on relationship instances when a relationship instance is added or deleted, can optionally be declared:

1.   An *integrity policy* provides create, update, and delete integrity constraints to inhibit storing invalid data values.

2.   A *trigger policy* provides data-state-driven processing, which is independent of individual repository function processing logic.

5.3.3   Dependent Entity Type

A *dependent entity type* is an entity type that tends to occur naturally in a hierarchy. A dependent entity type provides a form of name scope, where the entity key value of an entity instance need only be unique within the context established by other entity key values. An example is a dependent entity type called INTERNAL_PROC with the key NAME, an owning relationship type MODULE_CONTAINS_INTERNAL_PROC, and where the parent is the entity type MODULE. It is now possible that an internal procedure in one module might have the same name as an internal procedure in another module. The composite key value (name of the instance of MODULE and name of the instance of INTERNAL_PROC) that is used for these instances as dependent entities ensures that the keys are unique.

The connecting relationship type between an entity type and a dependent entity type must not be ordered. It is called the *owning* relationship type, and the source of the owning relationship type, which can be either an entity type or a relationship type, is called the *parent*. The key of the dependent entity type is a composite key consisting of the key of the parent combined with the key of the entity type that is the dependent entity type.

The following constraints apply:

1.   A dependent entity type can occur in the set of dependent entity types only once (i.e., it cannot be its own owner).

2.   The set of dependent entity types must eventually terminate at an owner that is not a dependent entity type.

Dependent entity types can exist at several levels; for example, the parent of a dependent entity type can also be a dependent entity type.

In some other ER models it is possible to associate an attribute with a relationship type. This might be of interest, for example, in the case of entity types PROGRAMMER and MODULE and the relationship type PROGRAMMER_CODES_MODULE, where it is desirable to record the completion date of the module. The dependent entity type modeling mechanism can be used to achieve this purpose. Figure 5-1 shows these two entity types and the relationship type, and the dependent entity type DATE, whose parent is the relationship type PROGRAMMER_CODES_MODULE. The entity type DATE should have a system-assigned key attribute.

5.3.4   Aggregation Type

Repository Manager provides for the facility to group a hierarchical set of entity types and relationship types into a single named construct called an *aggregation type*. The entity type at the top of the hierarchy is termed the *root entity type* of the aggregation type.

The specification of an aggregation type consists of:

The *aggregation type name*

The *name of the root entity type*

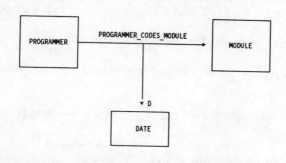

Figure 5-1   Modeling an attribute type as a dependent entity type.

The *names of the relationship types*, including their position in the hierarchy

The *names of the policies* to be enforced at specific events

Optionally there can be a *description* for documentation purposes.

This construct can be dealt with as a single unit. An instance of an aggregation type consists of an instance of the root entity type and instances of all entity and relationship types that make up the aggregation type.

5.3.5   Policies

In the preceding sections, the role of policies in the Repository Manager data model was mentioned. In this section, we will discuss *policies* in greater detail.

At the conceptual view and the logical view levels, controls may be defined and specified to enforce rules of entity and relationship integrity, attribute and field value assignment standards, and data access authority. Additionally, controls may be assigned to invoke functions when predefined events are detected. These kinds of controls are

defined to the repository as policies and are implemented in the form
of nonprocedural logic using REXX. There are four types of policies:

- *Integrity policies*, for data value standards.

- *Derivation policies*, for nonprocedural calculation of data
values.

- *Trigger policies*, for supporting data-state-driven processing.

- *Security policies*, which consist of the association of access
levels and conditions with features and components of the
repository that are subject to security control.

Conceptual and logical view specification services are provided to define
integrity, derivation, and trigger policies. Repository Manager security
administration services are provided for the definition of security
policies.

5.3.5.1 *Integrity Policies*

An integrity policy is used to insure that a requested action will result
in a valid entity attribute, relationship, or template field value,
whenever a specified event occurs and, optionally, when a specified
condition is not in effect. For example, an integrity policy can ensure
that a data value is within a valid range before it can be saved in
permanent storage.

An integrity policy may be repository-wide (i.e., defined in the
conceptual view) or may be for a specific logical view. Policies of this
type are implemented conceptually in the form of:

```
On Event, IF (Condition = FALSE) THEN DO Action
```

where

Event is a system-defined event (e.g., entity write).

Condition is a REXX expression that states the requirements that
valid data must meet.

Action is a message number to present if the condition is false, and the repository function is prevented from continuing to process.

For the *conceptual view*, integrity policies are associated with entity attributes or with relationships. The types of events that may be used to invoke a conceptual view integrity policy are:

- *Entity write* (add, update, or delete), when a policy is associated with attributes of the entity type

- *Relationship write* (add or delete), when a policy is associated with the relationship type

All repository functions are subject to conceptual view integrity policies. No action needs to be taken to cause a new repository function to enforce these integrity policies.

Logical view integrity policies are associated with template fields. The types of events that may be used to invoke a logical view integrity policy are:

- *Function initiation,* when a policy is associated with a template field defined to the function

- *Display read,* when a policy is associated with a receiving template field

5.3.5.2   *Derivation Policies*

A *derivation policy* is used to assign a value to an entity attribute or template field whenever a specified event occurs and, optionally, a specified condition is in effect. A derivation policy may be repository-wide (i.e., defined in the conceptual view) or may be for a specific logical view. Policies of this type are implemented conceptually in the form of:

```
On (Event), IF (Condition = TRUE) THEN ASSIGN
(Expression) TO ATTRIBUTE
```

where

Event is a system-defined event (e.g., template write).

Condition is a REXX expression, the results of which are used to determine whether or not to apply the derivation action

Expression is a REXX expression that produces the new value of the entity attribute

For the *conceptual view*, derivation policies are associated with entity attribute types. The types of events that may be used to invoke a conceptual view derivation policy are:

- *Entity read*, when a policy is associated with a nonkey entity attribute of the entity type

- *Entity write* (add, update), when a policy is associated with a nonkey entity attribute of the entity type

Logical view derivation policies are associated with template fields. The types of events that may be used to invoke a logical view derivation policy are:

- *Function initiation*, when a policy is associated with a template field defined to the function

- *Function termination*, when a policy is associated with a template field defined to the function

- *Template write*, when a policy is associated with a template field within the template to be written

- *Template read*, when a policy is associated with a template field within the template to be read

Specifications of template read and template write derivations are shared between repository functions that use the same templates. On the other hand, function initiation and function termination derivation policies are more dependent on the individual characteristics of the repository function's operation; hence, they are not shared between repository functions.

A template field or an entity attribute may have more than one type of derivation policy or more than one policy of the same type. Derivation policies of different types may be ordered, and the policies are applied in the order specified. Derivation policies of any one type (e.g., template write) are processed in parallel.

5.3.5.3   *Trigger Policies*

A trigger policy is used to invoke a repository function whenever a specified event occurs and, optionally, a specified condition is in effect. A trigger policy may be repository-wide and specified for the conceptual view or may be for a specific logical view. Policies of this type are of the general form:

```
On (Event), IF (Condition = TRUE) THEN DO Action
```

where

Event is a system defined event.

Condition is a REXX expression, the results of which are used to determine whether or not the function specified in the action is to be invoked.

Action is the name of a function which is to be invoked if the condition is true, followed by values for fields in the parameter template.

Conceptual view trigger policy actions are queued until a *commit* occurs. *Logical view trigger policy* actions are executed immediately.

The type of repository function called by a trigger policy may be either a fully integrated repository function or a method repository function. Trigger policies cannot directly invoke non-fully integrated repository functions, method implementation repository functions, or repository services built-in functions.

For the conceptual view, trigger policies are associated with entity types or relationship types. The types of events that may be used to invoke a conceptual view trigger policy are:

- *Entity read*, when a policy is associated with the entity type

- *Entity write* (add, update, or delete), when a policy is associated with the entity type

- *Relationship write* (add or delete), when a policy is associated with the relationship type

Logical view trigger policies are associated with repository functions or templates. The types of events that may be used to invoke a logical view trigger policy are:

- *Function initiation*, when a policy is associated with the function

- *Function termination*, when a policy is associated with the function

- *Template read*, when a policy is associated with the template

- *Template write*, when a policy is associated with the template

5.3.5.4   Security Policies

Security policies consist of the association of access levels and conditions with those features and components of the repository that are subject to security control. Policies of this type are specified as part of security profiles and are expressed in REXX as conditions. These policies may be repository-wide or tool-specific. Repository-wide security policies control access to repository data and definitions regardless of the repository function or logical view employed. Such policies always have precedence over tool-specific policies. They control access to the following:

- Entity type definitions

- Entity instances (control of access to entity key attributes)

- Entity attributes (control of access to entity nonkey attributes)

- Relationship type definitions

- Relationship instances

Security policies on entity instances grant or restrict access to the entire entity instance. If access is allowed to the key attribute of an entity type, then access is allowed to the nonkey attributes, unless additional security policies apply to the nonkey attributes. A security policy on a dependent entity type also applies to the owning relationship.

Allowable access levels for entity types, entity instances, entity attributes, and relationship types are *Delete*, *Add*, *Update*, *Retrieve*, and *NoAccess*. (Note that the preceding list of access levels is given from the least to the most restrictive.) Allowable access levels for relationship instances are *Update*, *Retrieve*, and *NoAccess*.

Tool-specific security policies control access to:

- Repository functions

- Template fields

An access level of *Call* or *NoAccess* may be granted for a function. Allowable access levels for template fields are *Update*, *Retrieve*, or *NoAccess*.

5.3.5.5   *Sequence in which Policies Are Processed*

The order in which policies are processed is important. This issue will also be referred to in Chapter 6, in connection with adding policies to constructs of the Supplied ER Model.

The following list shows, each processing point, the sequence in which policies will be processed.

Processing Point	Policy Processing Sequence
Function Initiation	1. Security policies on repository function 2. Derivation policies on template fields 3. Integrity policies on template fields 4. Trigger policies on repository function
Display Read	1. Derivation policies on template fields 2. Integrity policies on template fields 3. Trigger policies on repository function
Display Write	1. Security policies on template fields 2. Derivation policies on template fields

Processing Point	Policy Processing Sequence
	3. Trigger policies on repository function
	4. Security policies on scrollable template fields
Template Read	1. Security policies on template fields
	2. Derivation policies on template fields
	3. Trigger policies on template fields
Template Write (add, update)	1. Derivation policies on template fields
	2. Trigger policies on template fields
Template Write (delete)	1. Trigger policies on template fields
Entity Read	1. Security policies on relationship type
	2. Security policies on entity's key attributes
	3. Derivation policies on the nonkey entity attributes
	4. Security policies on the nonkey entity attributes
	5. Trigger policies on entity type
Entity Write (add, update)	1. Derivation policies on the nonkey entity attributes
	2. Security policies on all entity attributes
	3. Integrity policies on all entity attributes
	4. Trigger policies on entity type
Entity Write (delete)	1. Security policies on relationship type
	2. Security policies on all entity attributes
	3. Integrity policies on all entity attributes
	4. Trigger policies on entity type
Relationship Write	1. Security policies on relationship type
	2. Integrity policies on relationship type

Processing Point	Policy Processing Sequence
	3. Trigger policies on relationship type
Function Termination	1. Derivation policies on template fields
	2. Trigger policies on repository function

5.4   REAL-WORLD REPRESENTATION IN THE REPOSITORY

In previous sections of this chapter, we examined:

- Constructs that can be used to construct a model of the real world

- Constructs that are supported in the repository

This section will address techniques that can be used to represent these real-world constructs in the repository. The techniques used are by no means unique; in many cases, alternative methods for this representation are given, and others can be devised to handle special situations in the real-world environment. Note that the discussion on the IBM-Supplied Entity-Relationship Model definition (see Chapter 6) will discuss a set of further constraints on the mapping of real-world constraints.

The notation that generally will be used is to refer to real-world things by lower-case letters (for example, e) and the corresponding Repository Manager thing by the equivalent upper-case letters (for example, E).

5.4.1   Simple Real-World Entities

A simple real-world entity type e can be represented as a Repository Manager entity type E.

Single-valued real-world attributes of e can be represented as Repository Manager attributes of E. No special modeling is required to accommodate null values, as Repository Manager keeps track of the presence or absence of the value of a Repository Manager attribute.

Multivalued real-world attributes can be modeled in two different ways:

1.   A separate attribute of the Repository Manager entity type
     can be defined for each value of the multivalued real-world
     attribute. For example, if the real-world attribute *location*
     is used to designate where certain documentation is kept,
     and if it is known that there never are more than two
     copies, then this information can be modeled by defining
     the Repository Manager attributes LOCATION_1 and
     LOCATION_2.

     This way of modeling is most useful when the number of
     repetitions is small.

2.   A Repository Manager entity type can be defined, each
     instance of which corresponds to a value of the multivalued
     real-world attribute and which is linked to the Repository
     Manager entity type as shown in Figure 5-2. The cardi-
     nality constraint *1–m* indicates that for each instance of
     the type DOCUMENTATION, there can be *m* instances of
     DOCUMENTATION. The letters M and C denote that the manda-
     tory and controlling constraints on the target are in effect.
     This ensures that there will not exist an instance of type
     DOCUMENTATION_LOCATION without a corresponding instance
     of type DOCUMENTATION.

Figure 5-2 shows diagrams of these two alternative ways of
representing multivalued attributes.

In a manner similar to the above, *attribute groups*, whether non-
repeating or repeating, can be modeled either by an implied grouping
or as a separate attribute entity.

5.4.2   Binary Real-World Relationships

A binary real-world relationship type is represented in the repository
by a Repository Manager relationship type whose members are entity
types corresponding to the real-world entity types of the relationship
type.

Modeled as multiple attributes

Modeled as a separate attribute entity

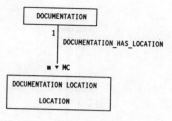

Figure 5-2   Alternative methods for representing multivalued attributes.

Figure 5-3 shows examples of both type and instance diagrams for the representation of the real-world relationship type *programmer writes program*. The instance diagram shows that the programmer John has written three programs.

Single-valued attributes of a real-world binary relationship type can be represented in a separate Repository Manager entity type, called an *attribute entity type*, linked to the Repository Manager relationship type.

This can be illustrated by the following example. Consider the real-world relationship type *program accesses file*, whose members have the attribute *access type*. This construct can be represented in the repository as shown in Figure 5-4. SYSKEY* is a system-assigned key for instances of PROGFILE_A.

The semantic constraints have the following significance:

•   Each instance of PROGFILE_A will be associated with, at most, one instance of the relationship type PROGRAM_ACCESSES_FILE, and vice versa.

Type diagram

Instance diagram

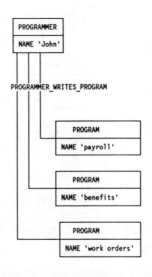

Figure 5-3   Type and instance diagrams for a relationship type.

- Attribute values in isolation are meaningless — an instance of PROGFILE_A will never exist in the absence of an associated instance of PROGRAM_ACCESSES_FILE.

- An instance of the relationship type PROGRAM_ACCESSES_FILE will never exist without an associated attribute value.

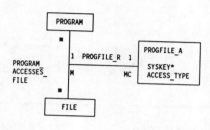

Figure 5-4 Representation of an attribute entity type.

The representation becomes somewhat more complicated if *multiple* real-world relationship instances can exist between the same two real-world entity instances. The real-world relationship type can still be represented by a Repository Manager relationship type, but each instance of this type can now potentially represent a set of real-world relationship instances, namely, the relationship instances between a pair of real-world entity instances. The individual members of such a set can then be represented by instances of an additional Repository Manager entity type associated with the Repository Manager relationship type.

Consider the example of the recursive real world relationship type *procedure calls procedure*, where the statement number in the calling program is used to distinguish the multiple calls one procedure makes to the other. Figure 5-5 shows the diagram that can be used to represent this example.

5.4.3 n-ary Real-World Relationships

An association of n real-world entity instances, where n is greater than 2, is said to be an *n-ary* relationship instance. Since all Repository Manager relationship types are binary, a representation method different from a straight mapping must be applied.

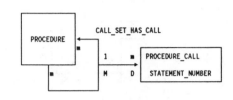

Figure 5-5   Diagram of a recursive relationship type with attributes.

Let us assume that a real-world n-ary relationship type has the real-world entity types *e1*, *e2*, . . . , *en* in positions 1, 2, . . . , n, respectively. This relationship type can then be represented by

•   A Repository Manager entity type ER

•   For each Repository Manager entity type Ei representing *ei*, a Repository Manager relationship type Ri from Ei to ER

In this case the Repository Manager entity type ER is called a *relationship entity type*. Figure 5-6 shows a diagram of this general form.

The semantic constraints on the connecting relationships R1, R2, . . . , Rn denote the following:

•   The instance control constraint 1–1 or 1–m ensures that a given instance of ER will not be associated with more than one instance of each Ei.

•   The mandatory and controlling constraints on targets will ensure that an instance of ER will never exist in the absence of an associated instance of each Ei.

The above can be modified to apply to the case where n=2 to enforce the cardinality constraints of a real-world relationship type.

To represent single-valued attributes of the members of a real-world relationship type, it is only necessary to include the equivalent Repository Manager attributes in the Repository Manager relationship entity type.

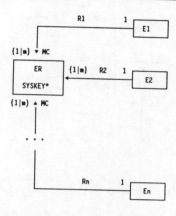

Figure 5-6   Diagram of a relationship entity type.

If multiple instances of a given real-world relationship can exist between the same two real-world entity instances, the general case is modified as shown in the diagram in Figure 5-7. Here the key of ER corresponds to the attribute of the real-world relationship instances that is used to distinguish one relationship instance from another for the same pair of entity instances. ER should be made dependent on one of the Repository Manager entity types E1, E2, . . . in order that proper qualification of A exists. Any additional single-valued attributes for the relationship type can be included in ER.

5.4.4   Real-World Identifier Attributes

As was previously stated, a real-world attribute can be used to refer to an instance of a real-world entity or relationship; such an attribute was referred to as an *identifier attribute*. In addition to the above guidelines for the representation of real-world attributes, in view of the special role played by identifier attributes, additional considerations apply.

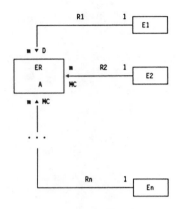

Figure 5-7   Multiple instances in an n-ary relationship type.

For real-world entity instances, it is possible that more than one attribute can serve as an identifier attribute. In order to represent such a real-world entity type in the repository, it is then necessary to assume that one of these attributes can be selected as the *primary identifier attribute*. Its values will then be used as the principal basis for identifying instances of the type and manipulating them. It is desirable that the values of this identifier attribute be unique across the instances of the type, so that no further qualification is necessary.

An identifier attribute other than the primary identifier attribute is referred to as an *alias identifier attribute*, or *alias*.

5.4.4.1   *Primary Identifier Attributes*

Desirable characteristics for the representation of primary identifier attributes are the following:

- Faithful representation of external naming schemes. This means that it should not be necessary to introduce a mapping between a real-world identifier value and its corresponding value in the repository.

- Use of Repository Manager entity instance keys whenever real-world identifier values are unique. This allows this Repository Manager feature to enforce this uniqueness.

- Use of Repository Manager entity instance keys whenever possible. This will facilitate the retrieval of real-world representations.

The above implies that, for a real-world entity type *e*, for which the values of the primary identifier attribute are unique, the attribute should be represented as the key attribute of the Repository Manager entity type E, which represents *e*.

If the values of a real-world identifier attribute are not unique for the instances of the real-world entity type *e*, then other representational techniques can be used.

1. *Identifier Attribute Prefixes*

   If the real-world identifier attributes are in the form of character strings, they can be concatenated with a prefix in order to make them unique. The combined string can then be used as a Repository Manager key value. If the prefix is of variable length, a special separator character can be used to separate it from the rest of the key value.

   This technique is most useful when the qualified external names cannot be decomposed into a fixed number of parts to be represented as Repository Manager dependent entity chains, a technique that will be described next.

2. *Repository Manager Dependent Entity Chains*

   As suggested above, this representational technique applies to the case where the properly qualified identifier attribute values can be decomposed into a *fixed* number of parts.

   This technique is based on the fact that, if a Repository Manager entity type is defined that is the target of an owning relationship type (i.e., it is a dependent entity) then it is only necessary that key values qualified by their parent key values be unique, where the key parent is the key of the source of the owning relationship type.

As an example, consider the following case, illustrated in Figure 5-8. The real-world identifier attribute *name* for the real-world entity type *procedure* does not have unique values. Nor does the real-world identifier attribute *name* for the real-world entity type *program*. However, the real-world identifier attribute *name* for the real-world entity type *library* does have unique values. Thus, a properly qualified identifier attribute for the real-world entity type *procedure* can be built by concatenating its name with the name of the library that contains the program and with the name of the program that contains the procedure.

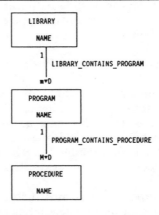

Figure 5-8   Example of an identifier attribute built by a dependent entity chain.

The Repository Manager dependent entity chains used to represent name scopes need not be linear; they may include dependencies not only on Repository Manager entity types but also on Repository Manager relationship types. In the example shown in Figure 5-9, the VERSION entity type is not a dependent, and the dependent entity chain includes the Repository Manager LIBVERS_CONTAINS_PROG, which has as its source the relationship type LIBRARY_HAS_VERSION and as its target the Repository Manager entity type PROGRAM.

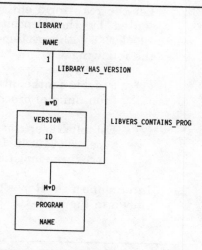

Figure 5-9   A dependent entity chain containing a relationship type.

3. *System-Assigned Keys*

A Repository Manager feature that can be used to represent non-unique real-world identifier attributes is the system-assigned key. When a Repository Manager entity type has a system-assigned key, Repository Manager assigns a unique key value to every instance of the entity type as it is added to the repository. The following example shows how this feature can be used to represent real-world instances with non-unique identifier attributes.

Assume that *procedure* is a real-world entity type whose instances have non-unique identifier values, and that *program* is a real-world entity type whose instances are the contexts within which the *procedure* identifier attribute values are unique. Then these types may be represented as follows:

a.   Let the real-world entity type *program* be represented by the Repository Manager entity type PROGRAM with key NAME.

b. Let the real-world entity type *procedure* be represented by the Repository Manager entity type PROCEDURE with a system-assigned key, and either of the following:

(1) Provide another attribute NAME to represent the (non-unique) *procedure* identifier attribute.

(2) Establish a separate Repository Manager entity type, PROCEDURE_ID, to represent the set of *procedure* identifier attribute.

c. Interconnect the Repository Manager entity types as shown in Figure 5-10.

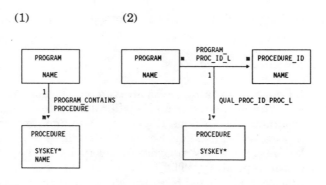

Figure 5-10   Use of system-assigned keys for identifier attributes.

There are significant differences between the two cases. In case 1, retrieval of an instance of PROCEDURE requires two pieces of information: a NAME value for PROCEDURE and a NAME value for PROGRAM. The PROCEDURE instance is retrieved that has the specified NAME value and that is related via the relationship type instance to the PROGRAM instance with the specified NAME (of the PROGRAM).

In case 2, when an instance of PROCEDURE is added to the repository, an instance of PROCEDURE_ID is also added to hold the identifier attribute value for the PROCEDURE instance, and the two are connected via appropriate instances of the relationship types. If the identifier value already exists, only the instances of the relationship types need to be added. The entity type PROCEDURE_ID will normally have no other attributes than the key and can be thought of as directly representing the identifier attribute of PROCEDURE. As in case 1, again, two pieces of information are required to retrieve an instance of PROCEDURE.

Case 2 has the advantage that it permits identifier attributes of PROCEDURE to be represented only once and shared as required.

The context of the Repository Manager entity type PROCEDURE may be a more general structure than a single Repository Manager entity type, as long as it permits navigation to a single instance of PROCEDURE with the specified PROCEDURE_ID value.

In the techniques where real-world identifier values are represented as Repository Manager key values, if an identifier attribute needs changing, it is necessary to delete the Repository Manager instance holding the old value and add an entity instance with the new identifier attribute value as its key value. Using the system-assigned key representation has the advantage that such a change can simply be handled as a change to any other attribute value.

5.4.4.2   Real-World Alias Identifier Attributes

It is possible to use a real-world alias identifier attribute to select instances in the repository in the same way that a primary identifier attribute is used.

If using an alias in this manner for a real-world entity type *e* is desired, an auxiliary Repository Manager entity type E_ALIAS can be specified and linked to the Repository Manager entity type E. Instances of E_ALIAS can be used to hold the alias values of instances of *e*.

- If the real-world alias identifier attribute values are unique, the alias identifier is made the key of E_ALIAS.

- If these values are not unique, any one of the techniques discussed in the previous sections can be used to qualify them.

If using an alias identifier attribute to select instances of a real-world entity type e is not desired, this alias can simply be made a nonkey attribute of e. Selection of instances by means of this alias is still possible, but will, in the general case, result in multiple instances of the Repository Manager entity type E being returned.

5.4.5   Real-World Text Descriptions

A text description is a real-world attribute whose representation in the repository requires special consideration. In the simplest case, one can think of such an attribute to be represented by a Repository Manager attribute. However, the strings making up the values of such an attribute may be quite long, and limitations in the underlying DBMS may inhibit the use of very long strings. Similarly, programming languages in which functions are written may have limits on the size of fields in which text descriptions are based.

An alternative is to consider a long string as being made up of "lines," and representing each such line as an instance of an ordered multivalued attribute. If this alternative is used, it may make it easier for general purpose programs, such as text editors, to more conveniently handle text description attributes.

5.4.6   Composite Real-World Entities

A composite real-world entity type ce can be represented as a Repository Manager aggregation type. The root Repository Manager entity type of the aggregation type can be used to hold the real-world attributes of ce and to serve as an anchor for the representation of any real-world relationship types in which ce participates. The constituent real-world entity types of ce can be represented by Repository Manager entity types that are included in the aggregation type representing ce.

If the instances of a given constituent entity type ei are ordered by the value of one or more of its attributes, this ordering can be represented by including these attributes in the key of the Repository Manager entity type representing *ei*, due to the default Repository Manager ordering by key value. If the ordering is not based on attribute values, the appropriate Repository Manager relationship can be defined as being ordered by target.

Whether or not a constituent real-world entity type is existence-dependent on the composite entity type it can be represented by appropriate constraints on the corresponding Repository Manager relationship type.

5.4.7   Real-World Entity Supertypes and Subtypes

A real world entity supertype p can be represented by a Repository Manager entity type P. The subtypes $p1, p2, \ldots, pn$ of p in a given subclassification can then be represented by additional Repository Manager entity types P1, P2, . . . , Pn, where there exist Repository Manager relationship types R1, R2, . . . , Rn connecting P to each one of the Pi. The cardinality of each of the Ri should be 1–1. In addition, a Repository Manager policy should be provided to ensure that only one instance of these relationship types exists for a given instance of P. This policy reflects the fact that an instance of a given real-world supertype can be a member of only one subtype in a given type subclassification. This policy will have to invoke a Repository Manager function in order to check for the existence of other Repository Manager relationship instances.

Other semantic constraints will have to be stated depending on whether or not the supertype instances have a common primary identifier attribute, as follows:

- If the supertype instances have a common primary identifier attribute, the keys of P1, P2, . . . should be system-assigned, and each Ri should be mandatory and controlling on the target. This ensures that an instance of P exists, and, hence, an identifier attribute value, at the time the associated instance of Pi is added.

- If the supertype instances do not have a common primary identifier attribute, the key of P may be system-assigned. Each Ri should be controlling on the source, and a Repository Manager policy should exist to ensure that an instance of P does not exist without an associated Pi instance.

5.5   OBJECT CONSTRUCTS

An *object* is a high-level abstraction of data; it is composed of both data and information — the latter identifying the object to the repository, — and specifies what operations can be performed on its object data.

The data of which an object is composed is real-world data and can be stored in the following ways:

- Completely within the repository as Entity-Relationship constructs in the form of aggregates.

- Some of it within the repository and some outside the repository, as, for example, in a sequential file or a VSAM data set.

- Completely outside the repository.

Object constructs provide an additional degree of flexibility in dealing with repository data. The data in an object may be an aggregate, and the object provides a single structure for common tasks shared by different, but similar, tasks. As such, groupings on existing data that have similar operations performed on them are candidates for being defined as objects. As mentioned above, the location of this data is not significant.

5.5.1   Object

An object is an abstraction of enterprise information that is usually treated as a unit during creation and use. An object has two constituents:

1. *Object Data.* This component is the data that processes normally manipulate. It may be an aggregate Entity-Relationship construct or source records of a source program that is to be manipulated by an editor or compiler.

2. *Object Control Information.* This component is the information of a control and management nature about an object.

This information is maintained by Repository Manager and stored independently of the object data in order to provide uniform descriptive information for all objects in one common pool.

The process of *creating* an object must include the creation of the object control information, which is part of the object, and the type of the object must be specified. Object data for the object may optionally be created at that time.

5.5.1.1   *Object Name*

Every object has a unique name that consists of the following four tokens:

1.   Collection
2.   Object Type
3.   Part
4.   Edition/Level

The *Collection* token is the identifier of an instance of the collection construct, which provides an application-related name. It is the highest qualifier of an object instance name and frequently represents a project or a product release. Each object has one and only one collection token.

The *Object Type* token (See 5.5.2) identifies the object as being an instance of a specified type construct. It also specifies the set of methods that can be applied against the object. Each object is named by one and only one object type token.

The *Part* token identifies a "simple" name of an object. For example, in an applications development environment where "A calls B" is used, "A" and "B" would be part tokens. In practice, it may not be possible to assign unique names to all parts, but since *part* is qualified by *collection*, the occurrence of a name in one collection can represent an object distinct from one with the same name in another collection.

The *Edition/Level* token is used to distinguish instances having the same collection, object type, and part token values that may have been defined as part of some development process. Repository Manager supports this feature to allow tracking of the application development heritage of objects by relating a newer object to an older base object.

All of these tokens are constituents of the Object Control Information for the object.

5.5.1.2   Based-on Object

Based-on Object allows the specification of the fact that a new object is related to an older one, and is imported for purposes of development heritage tracking. For example, the new object may be the result of a copy operation on an existing object. The based-on object is recorded in the repository by means of an instance of a relationship type that has object as both source and target. Instances of this relationship type can be analyzed to determine the impact of a contemplated change.

5.5.1.3   Based-on Collection

Based-on Collection provides for specification that an existing collection is related to a new collection for the purpose of grouping objects for a given purpose. The based-on collection is recorded in the repository by means of an instance of a relationship type that has collection as both source and target. Instances of this relationship type can be used to assemble groups of objects in accordance with terms understood by a using application.

5.5.1.4   Object Data

Object Data is the applications-related information that constitutes the body of an object. *Internal Object Data* refers to data that is stored in the repository in the form of Entity-Relationship constructs, and *External Object Data* refers to data stored elsewhere. The location of the data, and its format if stored externally, are options of the object type specifier.

Method implementations (See 5.5.2.2) should be the only way used to manipulate object data. It should be noted that Repository Manager Object Services that create and delete objects operate only on the Object Control Information and do not affect the object data itself. In other words, Entity-Relationship constructs that may constitute object data are not deleted if the object is deleted.

5.5.2   Object Type

Object Type is used to specify the functional environment for a set of objects having the same object type token in their name. The object type specification includes the following:

1. The names of the methods (See 5.5.2.1) applicable to the object type

2. For each method, the name of the method implementation (See 5.5.2.2) to be used

3. Optionally, the name of a super object type (See 5.5.2.3)

4. For each object type which has internal object data, the name of the aggregation type that specifies the object data

The object type must have a name that is unique in the repository.

Different object types may share a method specification. If the storage media for instances of these are different, different method implementations must be provided. If, however, the storage media for instances of two object types are identical, the same method implementation may be shared by the two object types.

5.5.2.1   *Method*

A *Method* is an abstraction of a data manipulation function that can be applied to an object. A method is a repository function, and its specification consists of the following:

• A *parameter template*

• *Derivation, integrity,* and *security policies* on the parameter template fields

• Any applicable *trigger policies* for the method

• The *method intent,* which specifies how an object instance is to be locked

When a method is called, Repository Manager uses the method's parameter template to determine what object instance is involved, as well as what method implementation to call.

The purpose of the method call interface is to insulate the caller from the specifics of the organization of the object data and from any data storage and format changes that may occur to the object data with time.

For object data stored in the repository as an Entity-Relationship construct, this data may also be accessed directly through Repository Manager Entity-Relationship services. Such an access would, however, not be considered as accessing the object, because an object can only be accessed through a method.

5.5.2.2 *Method Implementation*

A *Method Implementation* specifies the name of a repository program that implements the abstract function specified by a method for an object type. One or more method implementations can be specified for each object type and method combination. Unlike methods, method implementations can have the complete set of repository function specifications.

When repository services are called to perform a method, they convert each parameter supplied from the form specified for the method to the form required for the method implementation, if necessary. Then the method implementation is called to perform the requested function. In addition to manipulating object data, a method implementation may also manipulate the Object Control Information of an object.

Some methods are designated as *Library Methods*. This indicates that some library manager functions may be built using method implementations. Library managers typically control bulk data objects, and this control can be integrated with Repository Manager.

5.5.2.3 *Super Object Type*

In a manner similar to entity types, which may have super types, a *super object type* may be defined for a set of object types. However, different conventions for inheritance apply to a super object type. Here, subtypes inherit all the method – method implementation pairs associated with the super object type.

This object type generalization scheme provides additional tool-developed productivity, as it allows existing method implementations to be reused on objects of different object types. Extensive hierarchies can be built; however, such a hierarchy cannot contain closed loops and must be unambiguous.

Two special functions are available that can be specified as the method implementation for any method: *method implementation no-op* (DWKNOOP) and *method implementation required* (DWKMIRQ).

DWKNOOP is used in the development of an object hierarchy when it is desired that a method implementation not be inherited from the super object type. DWKMIRQ is used when it is not intended to create instances of the super object type, but it is required that all affected object types in the hierarchy are to be provided a method implementation for a certain method.

5.5.3   Object and Object Type Management

When an object type is defined, instances of entity types that are part of the Supplied Entity-Relationship Model are created. Each object type is represented as an instance of the GLO_OBJECT_TYPE entity type defined in the Global (GLO) submodel. The definition of the object type is related to instances of other entity types. Similarly, the Edition/Level of an object is also recorded in the repository.

Details of these mechanisms will be discussed in connection with the description of the Repository Manager/MVS Supplied Entity-Relationship Model in the next chapter.

6 THE SUPPLIED ENTITY-RELATIONSHIP MODEL

An element of Repository Manager/MVS is the Repository Manager Supplied Entity-Relationship Model, or the Supplied ER Model for short, which contains a number of ER model definitions. In addition to defining of the model for maintaining information about objects, the Supplied ER Model provides definitions of information that can be used to describe aspects of an enterprise's organization. It also supplies definitions of information in support of IBM language and database products, and more definitions of information supporting IBM products will be included over time. The Supplied ER Model consists of a set of definitions of entity types, relationship types, attributes, and aggregation types, and the intent is that it be shared among tools and users as well as adapted to the particular needs of an enterprise.

Repository Manager list panels (See Chapter 9) can be used to display the names and descriptions of the definitions available in the Supplied ER Model, and to obtain reports on them.

6.1   RATIONALE FOR THE SUPPLIED ER MODEL

The Supplied ER Model is very extensive and was designed to provide support for a wide range of enterprise activities in applications development, information systems management, and other similar classes of applications. The model is a formal description of data to be managed by Repository Manager. The content of the model includes enterprise definitions, application requirements, logical data definitions, process definitions, and definitions required by a set of IBM language and database products.

There are two distinct orientations in looking at this model: the tool builder's perspective and the user's perspective, which we will now discuss.

6.1.1   The Tool Builder's Perspective

This orientation requires, foremost, that the model be responsive to tool builders and contain a range of constructs that tools can use as input as well as output. This issue is important if Repository Manager is to fulfill its mission in the AD/Cycle framework: the ability for different tools to pass information to each other through the repository requires that different tools use common constructs. It is the Repository Manager strategy that the strict use of the Supplied ER Model sufficiently general to achieve this goal.

The problem being addressed here is that the Entity-Relationship data model formalism, as intuitively clear as it may be, does not lead to unique results. Two modelers, or two modeling teams, looking at the same real-world situation, may come up with totally different models, both of which may accurately describe that situation. The differences arise simply from the different points of view on the situation different modelers have.

The basic problem is that the concept of what a "thing" is cannot be defined. Consider a very simple, and somewhat simplistic, example. In a college curriculum environment, it may make sense to one modeler to consider a course to be an entity and the course's location and time period to be properties of the course. As strange and illogical as it may seem, to some other modeler (one who perhaps is concerned more with building management), the location may be considered an entity, with the course name and time period as properties of the location. A third point of view (perhaps that of a modeler concerned with traffic flow) may see the time period as an entity and the other two data items as an instance of a repeating attribute group. It is clear that if relationships were to be introduced into this model, many more different models would be opened up.

Not only is there a problem with entities and attributes, but there is also a duality between entities and relationships. An easy example is John and Mary, who are married. A straightforward way of modeling this situation is to use a relationship "is married to," that associates John and Mary. An equally straightforward way, however, is to define an entity type called "marriage" and define two relationship types to designate husband and wife. Of course, the entity/attribute and entity/relationship dualities can be combined, which gives rise to an even larger set of different models.

It must be clear that from the point of view of tools and tool users, this situation is completely untenable. If two tools use different models, it is impossible for the repository to pass information from one tool to the other.

There have been efforts in the past, and there are ongoing efforts (one of which the author is a member of), dealing with this problem in a generalized way, i.e., specifying facilities that allow a system to "unify" or "integrate" these various models, and in effect, create mappings from one model to another, or perhaps a set of mappings to a neutral model. To date, no successful solutions have been found; but even if one is found it may not be cost-effective in terms of performance.

The Supplied ER Model is attempting to solve the problem by not allowing it occur in the first place. The degree to which it will be successful will depend on how comprehensive the model is and how conscientiously tool developers will adhere to it. On the first issue, one must assume that IBM has conducted extensive tests on the completeness of the model, but it also must be assumed that additional "fine-tuning" of the model will be required. On the second issue, the answer will undoubtedly be driven by market forces: if users want tools that interface with the repository, then tool builders will produce tools that interface with the Supplied ER Model.

6.1.2   The User's Perspective

Another approach to making ER constructs useful is based on the needs of users rather than tools. A concept of interest here is a grid developed by J. A. Zachman called *A Framework for Information Systems Architecture*, or simply the *Zachman Framework* (IBM Systems Journal 26, No. 3, 276-292, 1987). This approach employs the concept of scope of information of a model, which represents an approximate idea of the information level to be represented in a model. Scope is one dimension of the grid; the other a listing of the basic categories of information that are of interest. In this architecture, it is thus easy for users to orient themselves in an existing model as well as specify new constructs when the model needs to be expanded.

The Repository Manager/MVS Supplied ER Model exhibits many characteristics indicating that its structure has been influenced heavily by the concept of the Zachman Framework. As will be seen later in this chapter, the basic idea of dividing the model into submodels not only makes it more tractable but corresponds to categories of information. Equally, the constructs within any one submodel appear to correspond reasonably to the levels of information that appear in the Zachman Framework.

If this is indeed the case, the Supplied ER Model should prove to be responsive to the needs of users. The model is large and complex, and caution should be taken not to try and absorb all of it at once, rather, the classification and level of detail the user is seeking should dictate the paths taken through it.

6.2 MODIFICATIONS OF THE SUPPLIED ER MODEL

The Supplied ER Model can be used as made available by IBM or as modified by an installation. Modifications to the model can occur in two ways:

- Addition of new constructs
- Alteration of existing constructs

Different guidelines and rules apply to these.

6.2.1 Addition of New Constructs to the Supplied ER Model

The discussion presented earlier in this chapter points to the desirability and possible longer-term advantages of using constructs existing in the Supplied ER Model. Even though extensive facilities exist in

Repository Manager for defining new constructs, these should be used judiciously. Extensions which are purely of local interest and are not likely to be used by tools would appear to be relatively safe, but it should be remembered that any extensions are potentially dangerous to the successful integration of tools. Since extensive facilities are available also for querying Repository Manager for the contents of the Supplied ER Model, these should be used to research the need for defining new types.

An exception to the above will be discussed in the procedures presented in Section 6.4. The constructs being defined there require new entity types and relationships to be defined; these, however, should be viewed as being of an auxiliary nature and not representing new types of "things" being modeled in the repository.

IBM employs certain procedures when configuring, naming, diagramming, and documenting constructs for the Supplied ER Model. It is recommended that these same procedures be followed for extensions to the model to ensure that the constructs being defined are consistent and compatible with the Supplied ER Model.

Another reason for recording extensions made to the Supplied ER Model is that it enables the identification of extensions that might be affected by Program Temporary Fixes (PTFs). Repository Manager provides the option of placing a supplied construct on hold so that notification in advance of PTFs for that construct can be issued. More detail on this subject will be found in Chapter 9.

6.2.2   Modifications of Existing Constructs in the Supplied ER Model

As might be expected from the central role the Supplied ER Model plays, a number of restrictions exist on modifications that can or should be made to the model by an installation. Whether a modification can be made or not depends on whether or not *basic security* is installed. If so, Repository Manager uses the DWKPUB *security profile* modified by the addition of the DWKDEF security object group to it, (See Chapter 4), which prohibits all users of the installation from making any change to the supplied entity and relationship types. If it is necessary to add policies to these definitions, a security profile other that DWKPUB must be used.

To ensure the integrity and consistent maintenance of the Supplied ER Model, it is recommended that all restrictions be observed even if basic security is not installed. The following restrictions should be observed.

6.2.2.1   *Naming Rules*

IBM has restricted itself to using names starting with A through I, and an underscore in the fourth position. Additionally, all constructs that are part of the Supplied ER Model, as well as supplied functions, templates, and panels, use the prefix DWK. Hence, no user-defined construct should use this prefix, and, if the first letter used in a user-defined name is in the range A through I, the fourth character should not be an underscore.

An aggregation type definition includes default names of templates that map to the entity types in the aggregation type. The option exists to have Repository Manager assign a name to them or for the user to name them, in which case the first three letters should not be DWK.

6.2.2.2   *Entity types and Relationship Types*

The following restrictions should be observed:

- The definition of a supplied entity type or relationship type should not be modified in any way other than to add policies to it. Policies that have been added can be modified at a later time.

  An exception to the above is that integrity policies for attributes of an anchor entity type should not be defined, as they could interfere with Repository Manager's processing of instances of this type.

  Any policy that is added (i.e., derivation, integrity, or trigger) to a supplied construct that already has policies of that kind should be placed in the sequence of policies in such a manner that it is processed only after the supplied policies have been processed. The order in which policies are processed is discussed in Chapter 5.

- Relationship types can be defined where one or both members are a supplied entity type or relationship type, but such relationship types should not be declared mandatory or controlling for a supplied construct that is a member.

6.2.2.3   *Attributes*

Attributes can be added to a supplied entity type, but they should be modeled as a separate entity type containing the attributes. A relationship type should be defined that connects them to the supplied entity type.

6.2.2.4   *Aggregation Types and Tool Groups*

Definitions of aggregation types and tool groups should not be changed.

6.3   DESCRIPTION OF THE SUPPLIED ER MODEL

This section will describe the Supplied ER Model that is a component of Repository Manager/MVS Version 1 Release 1. Because of the broad scope of this model, it is divided into submodels, each of which addresses particular classes of information systems objects. Each submodel is composed of Repository Manager construct types (entity types, relationship types, and aggregation types) that are relevant to the purpose of the submodel.

Submodels are connected to each other through Repository Manager relationship types, each of which is assigned to one of the submodels it connects.

The Supplied ER Model is composed of four submodels, with name and submodel code as follows:

1.   IMS/VS (code DLI)

2.   Enterprise (code ENT)

3.   Global (code GLO)

4.   High Level Languages (code HLL)

A diagram of the Supplied ER Model in Repository Manager/MVS Version 1 Release 1 is shown in Figure 6-1. In this diagram, boxes represent submodels, and lines between the boxes represent relationship types that connect constructs in one submodel to constructs in another.

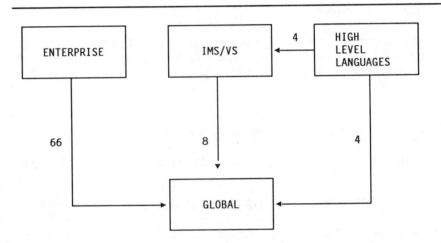

Note: Numbers on lines represent counts of interconnecting relationship types.

Figure 6-1   Map of the Supplied ER Model.

It must be emphasized again that the submodels specified in Version 1 Release 1 may not be completely stable, and that it is possible they may be slightly at variance with like submodels contained in later releases.

Equally, it can be expected that later releases will contain additional submodels with linkages to the other submodels. In particular, it must be pointed out that the current Supplied ER Model does not address support of SQL and DB2; this requirement will certainly be addressed in a future version of Repository Manager/MVS. Moreover, as additional tools are defined, it can be expected that these will require constructs that will be added to the Supplied ER Model.

The documentation of each submodel contains the following *conceptual view definitions*:

- *Entity type* definitions, including

  - *Entity type name*, short description, and long description

  - *Lock* specification

  - *Trigger policies*, including
    - Policy description
    - Policy condition
    - Policy function
    - Policy parameters

  - *Attributes*, including
    - Attribute name, short description, and long description
    - Default characteristics
    - Integrity policies, including
      - Policy description
      - Policy condition
      - Policy message identifier
    - Derivation policies, including
      - Policy description
      - Policy condition
      - Policy expression

- *Relationship type* definitions, including

  - *Relationship type name*, short description, and long description

  - *Inverse name*

  - *Source name and type*

  - *Target name and type*

  - *Semantic constraints*

  - *Integrity policies*, including
    - Policy description
    - Policy condition
    - Policy message identifier

- *Trigger policies*, including
  - ◦ Policy description
  - ◦ Policy condition
  - ◦ Policy function
  - ◦ Policy parameters

- **Aggregation type** definitions, including

  - *Aggregation type name*, short description, and long description

  - The *entity types* and *relationship types* that are the constituents of the aggregation type

  - *Aggregation element processing options*

  - *Extended definition processing specifications*

- Definition of **messages** referenced in integrity policies, including

  - Message identifier

  - Message text

  - Message description

  - Action level code

  - System action specification

  - User response specification

- Definition of **functions** invoked from policies, including

  - *Function name*, short description, and long description

  - Function header report

  - Function code (REXX)

- Specification of **instances** of defined entity types and relationship types

Additionally, for ease in understanding the existing cross-references, the following are also provided:

- For *entity types*

  – Alias
  – Referencing relationship types
  – If dependent, the owning relationship type and qualifying keys

- For *relationship types*

  – Alias
  – Reference number
  – Referencing relationship types

The four submodels will now be discussed. In view of the wide scope and substantial level of detail available, only a top-level description will be presented here. An exception will be the Global submodel, as constructs in this submodel provide extended modeling capabilities, which will be explored in more detail.

6.3.1   The IMS/VS Submodel

The IMS/VS (DLI) submodel contains 18 entity types, 45 relationship types, and 6 aggregation types. The names of all constructs defined in this submodel have the prefix DLI_.

The purpose of this submodel is to supply ER model constructs for the information content of the following, used in the execution of an IMS/VS DB/DC system:

- IMS Data Base Descriptors (DBDs)
- IMS Program Specification Blocks (PSBs)
- IMS Program Control Blocks (PCBs)

These constructs can also be used in AD/Cycle dialogs and batch functions for:

1.   Specification and maintenance of DBDs and PCBs.

2. Generation of input to the IMS/VS DBDGEN and PSBGEN utility programs, and preparation of the JCL for the execution of these.

3. Preparation of reports on DBDs and PSBs and related groups of these.

4. Various uses of DBD and PSB information in other products using repository information, such as application generators, query and report writers, etc.

As can be expected from the foregoing, the constructs existing in the submodel closely parallel the concepts required in the definition of DBDs, PSBs, and PCBs. Aggregation types are used to contain the definition of DBDs, PSBs, and PCBs. Relationship types between this submodel and the Higher Level Languages submodel (HLL) serve to make higher level language constructs available in the definition of the IMS/VS constructs. Relationship types between this submodel and the Global submodel will be discussed later.

6.3.2 The Enterprise Submodel

The Enterprise (ENT) submodel contains 66 entity types, 272 relationship types, and no aggregation types. The names of all constructs belonging to this submodel have the prefix ENT_.

The purpose of this submodel is to provide a high-level model that can be used to define the components of an enterprise and the manner in which these relate to each other. The scope is limited to those areas of the enterprise that are required for enterprise modeling.

The submodel provides for the following:

• Identification of key enterprise components as entities that can be described by attributes and association with other entities or relationships.

• Identification and decomposition of enterprise processes.

• Identification of the data components and data structures associated with processes.

• Specification of simple and complex data structures.

- Specification of attributes that provide value set and symbol set restrictions for data elements.

- Support for machine-interpretable specifications that can be used as the base for applications development automation.

- Use of concepts and terminology that are accepted in the CASE community.

The scope of the model makes unfeasible a complete description of it here. However, some of the entity types are very important in understanding how this submodel is intended to be used for enterprise modeling. Among these are the following entity types:

- Enterprise Model and Information submodel
- Entity Type
- Process
- Attribute Type
- Information Flow
- Relationship Type and Relationship Link
- Information Type

Each one of these will now be discussed, and the manner in which they are related to some other entity types will be described.

6.3.2.1   *Enterprise Model and Information Submodel*

The Enterprise Model entity type provides the means whereby two or more enterprise models can be constructed and maintained in the same repository. An instance of this entity type establishes a "name space" for model constructs, i.e., different constructs associated with different instances of this entity type can have identical names.

The Information Submodel entity type allows further partitioning of the information modeling name space. Several people or teams can work on independent projects without their work needing to be immediately synchronized.

6.3.2.2 *Entity Type*

Understanding the purpose of this entity type is key to understanding the manner in which IBM intends the Supplied ER Model to be used. *Entity type*, or to use its formal name, ENT_ENTITY_TYPE, is an entity type whose instances are themselves user-defined entity types. This option to some extent blurs the concept of the layer structure of the repository, since it causes types and instances to exist in the same layer.

This fact illustrates the duality that Repository Manager provides for modelers. If an entity type is to be defined by a user, there are two options:

1. Services are available for defining an entity type that is not part of the Supplied ER Model. Instances of the type can then be defined using appropriate services.

2. The entity type can be defined as an instance of the entity type ENT_ENTITY_TYPE. Instances of the type can be defined through structures defined in the Supplied ER Model.

It is clear, for a number of reasons, that IBM's intent is that the latter option be chosen. First and foremost, this option brings the entity type into the realm of commonality for different tool builders. A fact also to be considered is that the semantic richness built into the Supplied ER Model is substantially greater than the basic modeling constructs available in the basic Repository Manager ER model. This semantic richness translates into a more complete and more meaningful specification of the entity type. What may make the first option more attractive to some users is the fact that this option is considerably simpler and may in some cases be more efficient to process.

Facilities exist in the Supplied ER Model for subtyping and supertyping entity types and for assigning them to specific Information submodels. Attributes of ENT_ENTITY_TYPE are made available that deal with the number of instances expected over time.

6.3.2.3 *Process*

Instances of this entity type represent activities with a well-defined start and end, such as a transaction. A semantically rich set of attributes exists for this entity type, and it is integrated into other parts of the Enterprise submodel.

6.3.2.4   *Attribute Type*

An instance of this entity type represents a characteristic or property of an entity type, a data element used in a process, or a free standing data element to be assigned at a future time to an entity type or process. It should be noted that the term "attribute type" used here is synonymous with the term "attribute" used elsewhere in the description of Repository Manager.

Values of attributes (or attribute types, as used here) and instances of relationship types constitute the basic descriptions of entities. The entity type attributes available for this entity type provide for a semantically rich description of instances of the type, including a full description of policies.

Attributes can be assigned not only to the Entity Type entity type but also to, among others, entity types representing constraints, identifiers, processes, information submodels, and information flow collections.

6.3.2.5   *Information Flow*

An instance of this entity type is used to represent a set of data constituting facts about entities, attributes, relationships, and subinformation flows.   Equally, an entity of this type can be a constituent of one or more entities of type Information Flow Collection.

6.3.2.6   *Relationship Type and Relationship Link*

This entity type is used in a similar manner to the ENT_ENTITY_TYPE entity type, and an instance of this type represents a relationship type. The same discussion given earlier applies here.

An instance of this entity type provides only the information about the relationship type that is not associated with the directional nature of the relationship type. Information of a directional nature is represented by instances of the entity type Relationship Link.

6.3.2.7   *Information Type*

This entity type allows data typing; an instance of this type represents a class of values that are used and understood in the enterprise.   The entity type provides a globally reusable definition of data elements. The attributes associated with this entity type allow the specification of valid operations on the data type.

6.3.3   The Global Submodel

This submodel contains 12 entity types, 20 relationship types, and 9 aggregation types. The names of all constructs belonging to this submodel have the prefix GLO_.

This submodel is significant in the sense that it supports a set of common modeling requirements for all other submodels.   The requirements currently supported are in the following areas:

- Annotation Text
- Object Control Information
- Repository Anchor Entity Types

Additionally, this submodel contains an entity type named GLO_MANDATORY_ATTRIBUTES, which serves to specify a set of attributes that Repository Manager makes available to every entity type in the Supplied ER Model. Also included in the submodel is an entity type named GLO_VALIDATION_CHECK, an instance of which represents an internal-consistency or cross-consistency check of an object instance.

The Global submodel also provides additional modeling facilities for object types, which are discussed in Section 6.4. Further information about the structure of this submodel will be found in that section.

6.3.3.1   *Annotation Text*

Many times, text values will be too long to store as a single attribute value. The following cases are of interest:

1.   Text against which operations may be performed, e.g., source code that will be edited, can be stored as object data outside the repository.

2.   Text that represents a description of an instance of an entity type can be stored using the text annotation function DWKTEDT (which will be discussed in Chapter 8).   This function stores text using the dependent entity type chain

shown in Figure 6-2. This facility is available for all entity types in the Supplied ER Model.

6.3.3.2   *Object Control Information*

The Global submodel of the Supplied ER Model is used by Repository Manager to control information for objects. This model, or more specifically, the Global submodel, supports the definition and use of objects. Figure 6-3 shows the Supplied ER Model construct that is used for this purpose.

As described previously, an object whose data resides in the repository is an ER structure whose contents exist in the repository as an instance of an aggregation type. For an aggregation type to serve this purpose, it must be defined with the GLO_OBJECT_EDITION entity type as its root. This aggregation type must be defined before the object type can be defined. When the aggregation type is defined, Repository Manager creates an instance of the entity type GLO_AGGREGATION, which then holds the definition of the aggregation type.

In like fashion, methods and method implementations must be defined before they can be assigned to the object type. When they are defined, their definitions are stored in the repository as instances of the anchor entity type GLO_FUNCTION.

After these preliminaries, the object type can be defined. The definition of the object type is stored by Repository Manager as an instance of the entity type GLO_OBJECT_TYPE. Referring to Figure 6-3, the following relationship instances are created:

1.   An instance of GLO_OBJECT_TYPE_USES_AGGREGATION, which specifies in the repository which aggregation type the object type will use for its instances.

2.   One or more instances of GLO_OBJECT_HAS_METHOD, which associates methods with the object type.

3.   An instance of GLO_OBJECT_TYPE_METHOD_USES_MI, which specifies in the repository the association of the method – method implementation pair with the object type.

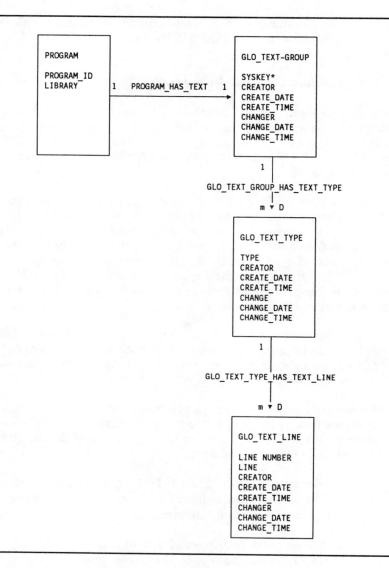

Figure 6-2 ER Model representing Programs and Text that describes them.

4. An instance of GLO_OT_HAS_SUPER_TYPE_OF_OT is used to specify a supertype for this object type.

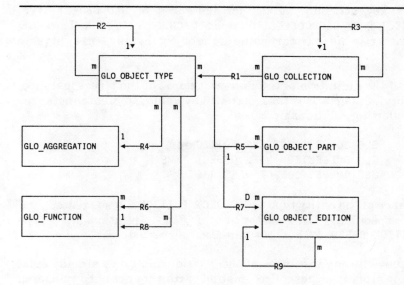

Legend: The relationships shown above have alphanumeric identifiers corresponding to the following:

R1	GLO_COLLECTION_USES_OBJECT_TYPE
R2	GLO_OT_HAS_SUPERTYPE_OF_OT
R3	GLO_COLLECTION_BASED_ON_COL
R4	GLO_OBJECT_TYPE_USES_AGGREGATION
R5	GLO_COLLECTION_OT_USES_PART
R6	GLO_OBJECT_TYPE_HAS_METHOD
R7	GLO_COL_OT_PART_HAS_EDITION
R8	GLO_OBJECT_TYPE_METHOD_USES_MI
R9	GLO_EDITION_BASED_ON_EDITION

Figure 6-3   Control information for objects in the Global submodel.

In order to create instances of the object type, instances of the entity types GLO_COLLECTION and GLO_OBJECT_PART, as discussed below, are required for the name of the object instance. If so specified, Repository Manager also creates an instance of the relationship type GLO_COLLECTION_BASED_ON_COL.

At this point, instances of the object type can be created. For each object type instance, Repository Manager creates an instance of GLO_OBJECT_EDITION. Since this entity type is a dependent entity type, it needs key attribute values for instances of GLO_OBJECT_TYPE, GLO_OBJECT_PART, GLO_COLLECTION, and GLO_OBJECT_EDITION. These key values comprise the four-part name of the object instance that uniquely identifies it.

As part of the definition of the four-part name of the object instance, Repository Manager uses these parent key values to create instances of the following relationship types:

- GLO_COL_OT_PART_HAS_EDITION
- GLO_COLLECTION_USES_OBJECT_TYPE
- GLO_COLLECTION_OT_USES_PART

An instance of the entity type GLO_OBJECT_EDITION is also created, and if so specified, an instance of the relationship type GLO_EDITION_BASED_ON_EDITION can also be created.

In the above, if any instances of the relationship types already exist in the repository for other collections and parts, they are not duplicated.

Prior to using an object, the user or tool calling the method needs to know the four-part name of the object instance on which an operation is to be performed. Also, the appropriate lock level needs to be obtained for the object instance through Repository Manager's locking facility prior to the method being called.

6.3.3.3 *Anchor Entity Types*

The Global submodel of the Supplied ER Model contains entity types, called *anchor entity types*, that can be used to model ER model constructs and repository functions in the repository. Each instance of these anchor entity types represents a defined or undefined ER construct or repository function. Values of the instance can be used to track the construct or function. The anchor entity types, which belong to the Global submodel, are given shown in Table 6-1.

The entity type attributes applying to these are as follows (other than as noted, the attributes apply to all four anchor entity types):

NAME – the key attribute, which is used to specify the name of the ER model construct or repository function the instance represents. If the instance represents a relationship type, the value of NAME is the name in the primary direction.

Table 6-1   Anchor entity types.

Anchor Entity Type	Description
GLO_ENTITY	Represents all entity types defined in the Repository and, optionally, entity types that have not yet been defined as well as those that have been deleted.
GLO_RELATIONSHIP	Represents all relationship types defined in the Repository and, optionally, relationship types that have not yet been defined as well as those that have been deleted.
GLO_AGGREGATION	Represents all aggregation types defined in the Repository and, optionally, aggregation types that have not yet been defined as well as those that have been deleted.
GLO_FUNCTION	Represents all repository functions defined in the Repository and, optionally, repository functions that have not yet been defined as well as those that have been deleted.

INVERSE_NAME (for GLO_RELATIONSHIP only) – provides the name of the inverse of the relationship the instance represents.

DESCRIPTION – provides the description of the ER model construct of the repository function represented by the instance. If the construct or function already exists in the repository, DESCRIPTION will contain the short description used in the definition.

TYPE (for GLO_FUNCTION only) – specifies the type of repository function represented by the instance.

INTENT (for GLO_FUNCTION only) – if the repository function is a method, specifies the method intent of the function represented by the instance.

DEF_EXISTS — a flag that indicates whether the ER model construct or repository function represented by the instance exists in the repository.

MEMBER_NAME — specifies the name of the partitioned data set member that contains the bound form of the definition the instance represents.

CREATOR-FUNCTION — contains the name of the repository function that created the instance.

CREATOR, CREATE_DATE, CREATE_TIME — specifies the user ID under which the instance was created and the date and time of creation.

CHANGER, CHANGE_DATE, CHANGE_TIME — specifies the user ID under which the instance was last updated and the date and time of last update.

DELETE_CONTROL — is used to specify whether or not the instance is to be deleted when the ER construct or repository function it represents is deleted.

6.3.4   The Higher Level Language Submodel

This submodel contains 13 entity types, 26 relationship types, and 2 aggregation types. The name of each construct in this submodel has the prefix HLL_.

The purpose of this submodel is to provide data model definitions for source program data objects. Such model definitions can be shareable among application programs and other interactive tools for describing data to be used by application source programs.

The Supplied ER Model Version 1 Release 1 Higher Level Languages submodel is limited to those model definitions required for the System/370 COBOL support.

The following are relationships between the major submodel constructs and the COBOL external views:

- An HLL_DATA_COLLECTOR entity instance with its subordinate entities and relationships represents a logically related set of COBOL data descriptions.

- An HLL_DATA_ITEM entity instance with its subordinate entities and relationships represents one of the following:

  - COBOL record
  - COBOL group item
  - COBOL elementary item
  - COBOL table
  - COBOL table key
  - COBOL item specifying the object of the OCCURS DEPENDING ON clause

- Physical attributes are available in instances of the HLL_GENERIC_DATA_DEFINITION entity type. There are two ways of accessing these:

  1. If a data item is defined locally within a data structure, the relationship type HLL_ITEM_HAS_GDD should be used.

  2. If the item shares a global data element, the relationship type HLL_DATA_ITEM_BASED_ON_GDE should be used.

- A COBOL data item defined as an array or table is represented by instances of the entity types HLL_DATA_ITEM, HLL_ARRAY_DIMENSION_SPEC, and HLL_COBOL_ARRAY_ITEM.

- COBOL table indexes are represented by attributes of the HLL_COBOL_ARRAY_ITEM entity type.

- A COBOL RENAME subject (i.e., level-66 data item) is represented by an HLL_COBOL_ITEM_66 entity type instance.

- A COBOL Condition Name (i.e., level-88 data item) is represented by an HLL_COBOL_ITEM_88 entity type instance.

In order to facilitate the extension of this submodel to support other languages, the design rationale included the following:

- Instances of the upper-level set of entity types (HLL_DATA_ITEM, HLL_GENERIC_DATA_DEFINITION, and HLL_ARRAY_DIMENSION_SPEC) hold non-language-specific information about a data item.

- Instances of the lower-level set of entity types (HLL_COBOL_DATA_ITEM, HLL_COBOL_ARRAY_ITEM, and the related entity types) hold COBOL-specific information about a data item.

Other design decisions were made to optimize performance characteristics of the current Repository Manager/MVS.

6.4   USE OF THE GLOBAL SUBMODEL FOR OBJECT MODELING

The use of the GLO Submodel Object Control Information structure provides important modeling facilities not directly available in the Repository Manager data modeling formalism. If data for an object is stored in the repository, the aggregation type for that object type must include at least one subordinate entity type. With the techniques given in this section, it is then possible to model the following:

- Simple entities or versions of simple entities as objects

- Relationships between objects

- Composite entities or versions of composite entities as objects

6.4.1   Modeling Simple Entities or Versions of Simple Entities as Objects

The following steps will provide the capability of modeling simple entities or versions of simple entities as objects:

1. The entities or their versions are represented as an entity type.

2. This entity type is given a system-assigned key attribute. Nonkey attributes can be assigned to represent characteristics whose values will be used as object data.

3.   PART, the key attribute of GLO_OBJECT_PART, is used to represent the entities' primary identifying characteristic. This makes it possible for the characteristic's value to become the part names within the four-part names of the object data.

Values of PART are not allowed to exceed 32 characters. If the values of the primary identifying characteristic are longer, then the following should be done:

–   Create a shortened form and assign it to these values.

–   Add a nonkey attribute to the entity type for the entities or versions and assign the full value to this attribute.

4.   A relationship type is created that connects the entity type of GLO_OBJECT_EDITION. The name of this relationship type in the primary direction is OBJECT_HAS_[name of entity type], and the entity type is the target of the relationship type. The cardinality of the relationship type is 1–1.

5.   The construct created is defined as an aggregation type whose root is GLO_OBJECT_EDITION.

The preceding could, for example, be used to model the versions of all programs within a given set of libraries. The versions could be represented by means of an entity type called PROGRAM. Nonkey attributes could be used to indicate the language and length of programs. Suppose that PROGRAM represents several versions of programs called Payroll and Work Order; PART could be used to represent the program name. Now, creating the relationship type OBJECT_HAS_PROGRAM connects PROGRAM to GLO_OBJECT_EDITION. The resulting structure, which allows versions of these programs to be modeled in the repository, is shown in Figure 6-4.

6.4.2   Modeling Relationships Between Objects

Repository Manager does not directly support modeling relationships between objects. However, there are techniques for simulating such associations — specifically, those that allow the following to be modeled:

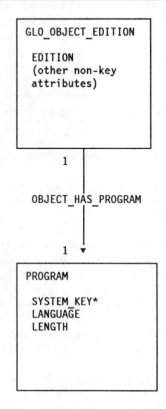

Figure 6-4 Example of an ER Model for modeling simple entities or versions of simple entities as objects.

- Binary relationships between objects
- n-ary relationships between objects
- Characteristics of relationships between objects

6.4.2.1   *Binary Relationships*

The following steps will provide the capability of modeling binary relationships between objects:

1. With the procedure described in the preceding section, the related entities or versions are represented as entity types connected to GLO_OBJECT_EDITION.

2. At this point, all related entities or versions are connected to GLO_OBJECT_EDITION. Some instances of GLO_OBJECT_EDITION will reference an instance or version of one type and others, an instance or version of the other type. To indicate the relationships between the two types, a relationship from GLO_OBJECT_EDITION to itself must be created.

3. The appropriate instance control, controlling, and ordered set properties can now be assigned. Mandatory properties cannot be assigned, as they would apply to all source or target instances, not just selected ones. This property must be implemented with application logic.

4. Two aggregation types, one for each entity type, must be created. The relationship type that connects GLO_OBJECT_EDITION to itself must be added to both aggregation types using the primary direction in one and the inverse direction in the other.

6.4.2.2   *n-ary Relationships*

The following steps will provide the capability of modeling n-ary relationships between objects:

1. Using the procedure in 6.4, 6.4.2.1, the participants in the relationship are modeled as entity types.

2. The participation of each type of participant is represented by a relationship type, as described in 6.4, 6.4.2.1, using GLO_OBJECT_EDITION as both source and target, supplying any required relationship characteristics.

3. Multiple aggregation types are created, one for each entity type created in (1) above. For each aggregation type, GLO_OBJECT_EDITION is the root, and it includes the relationship type created in (2) above that represents its participant. In the aggregation type for the n-ary relationships, all relationship types participating are included.

As an example, consider a ternary relationship type (i.e., an n-ary relationship type where n = 3) involving programs, programmers, and test cases. Figure 6-5 shows the aggregation type for one of the participants, and Figure 6-6 illustrates the aggregation type for the n-ary relationships.

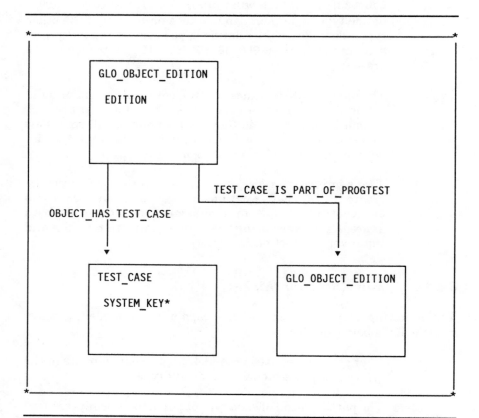

Figure 6-5 Diagram of the aggregation type for the Test Case object.

6.4.2.3   *Characteristics of Relationships*

Characteristics of relationships between objects can be modeled in a manner similar to characteristics of relationships between entities.

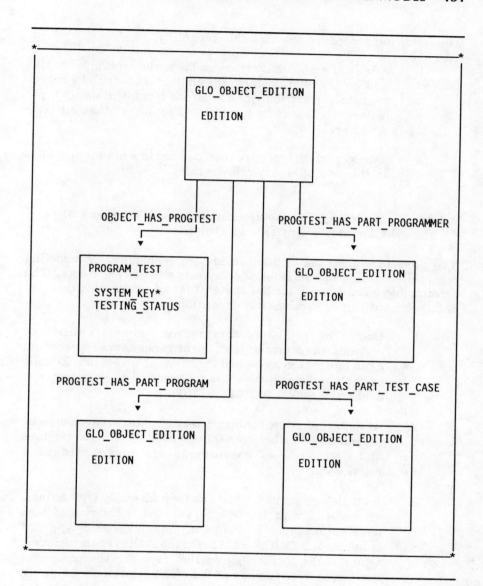

Figure 6-6   Diagram of an aggregation type for the n-ary relationship type object.

The following procedure provides this capability:

1. After setting up entity types, as for modeling simple entities and binary relationships, the characteristic can be represented as an attribute of a separate dependent entity type. This entity type is then connected to the relationship type for the relationships.

2. Two aggregate types are then defined in a manner parallel to the case of binary relationships.

6.4.3   Modeling Composite Entities and Versions of Composite Entities as Objects

The procedure described below provides the capability of modeling composite entities and versions of composite entities as objects. The terminology used here describes the entities of versions within the composite entities or versions as "constituents."

1. Using the procedure for modeling simple entities or versions, the composite entities or versions are represented as an entity type connected to GLO_OBJECT_EDITION. Equally each class of constituents is represented as an entity type connected to GLO_OBJECT_EDITION.

2. As in the procedure for binary relationships between objects, the relationships between the composite entities or versions and each class of constituents are represented as a relationship type.

3. Multiple aggregation types, one for each entity type defined, are created, with GLO_OBJECT_EDITION as the root of each aggregation type. In one path, the relationship type that connects GLO_OBJECT_EDITION to the entity type is included. Other paths to the aggregation type for the composite entities or versions are added. The relationship type (in the primary direction) for the relationships between the composite entities or versions and one class of constituents is included in the path.

In each aggregation type for a class of constituents, one additional path is included. In this path, the relationship type (in the inverse direction) for the relationships between the composite entities or versions is included.

7 TEMPLATES AND TEMPLATE SERVICES

Repository Manager can be used to build tools made up of discrete units called *repository functions*. Each tool is assembled from one or more repository functions.

A repository function is a repository interface construct that provides access to repository services and repository interface data. Each repository function has a set of specifications that identify the data, logic, and services that the repository function requires.

A logical view is repository function-specific; i.e., the view of information and function are defined for each repository function. The logical view contains the specifications of repository functions, and each time a new repository function is defined, its specifications are added to the logical view. These specifications are how a repository function identifies those things in the repository data store that can be accessed through repository services. Additionally, the specifications of a repository function can identify any optional procedural logic to be executed or other repository functions that may be invoked.

Each repository function has access to a subset of the repository data store through its logical data view. This information view is represented by *templates*.

This chapter will discuss templates and the services Repository Manager provides for manipulating them.

7.1 TEMPLATES

Templates are the primary means of communication and the unit of transfer between Repository Manager functions (see 7.3) and Repository Manager. Templates are used for more than just data-base access; they are also used to transfer data from one Repository Manager function the another. Data is carried within fields of templates.

An important characteristic of templates is that they provide functions with program independence of data; i.e., templates will, in general, be shared by many programs.

Templates are structured record buffers, allocated by Repository Manager and provided to Repository Manager applications at execution time. In general, a template is used in one of the following ways:

- To transfer data from one Repository Manager function to another, or from one Repository Manager function to a built-in function, i.e., a function whose actions may take place on a wider basis than template actions. Typically, a built-in function operates on whole template trees rather than on a single template. These built-in functions are part of the Repository Manager logical data services.

- As a work area for a Repository Manager function.

- To transfer data to and from an entity set.

7.1.1 Types of Templates

There are three types of templates:

- *Data templates*

- *Parameter templates*

- *Local work area templates*

7.1.1.1   *Data Templates*

A *data template* is used for transferring data to and from a conceptual view entity type. It contains template control information and structured record buffers. It is allocated by repository services and made available to a repository function when repository services are used to access data. A data template specification can be used by multiple repository functions; such a template is referred to as a "shared" data template.

A template of a function has fields that map to entity attributes. The fields in a function's data template can differ from the entity attributes in the following ways:

- They may be a different data type than that defined for the entity attribute.

- They may exclude some attributes.

- They may have fields that do not map to entity attributes, such as derived fields or local work areas.

Repository Manager will automatically perform the required mapping and data conversions at repository data read and write.

There are several types of data templates:

- *Entity Template*. An entity template maps to a single entity type. It is also possible to have a "dynabind" (or dynamically bound) template that is dynamically bindable to any entity type during execution.

- *Template Tree*. A template tree is a hierarchical data structure of entity templates that is used to specify a logical data view, and therefore it maps to multiple entity types. A template tree consists of a root template that has template connections to subordinate templates. The structure is strictly hierarchical; i.e., every lower-level (subordinate) template has a template connection to one and only one higher-level (parent) template. Every *template connection* corresponds to a conceptual view relationship type and defines the relative positioning between templates in the hierarchy.

- *Arrayed Template.* An arrayed template is an ordered collection of identical entity templates (siblings) identified by a single template name. An individual template in the array is referred to as an element of the array. Each element is represented by a number, or index, starting with 1 for the first element. The number of elements in the array is called the "extent" of the array. Only leaf templates of a template tree may be arrayed.

A template array is specified by establishing a value for the extent attribute of a template. Repository services are provided that operate on the entire array.

7.1.1.2   *Parameter Templates*

Each repository function has a parameter template that is used when the function is invoked. The parameter template has the same name as the repository function, which is created automatically by Repository Manager when it is asked to ADD a repository function specification to a logical view.

A repository function must also have a parameter template specified for each repository function that will be called directly. A special template known as the "universal scheduling template," named DWKPARM, can be used to call any repository function. This template contains a field named DWKNAME. The name of the repository function to be called can be placed in this field, after which a CALL action to the DWKPARM can be issued.

A parameter template is used to pass data between:

- A repository service and a repository function or repository program

- Two repository functions

A data template specification can be used by multiple repository functions; such a template is referred to as a "shared" data template. The fields in a function's parameter template may be different from the fields in the called or calling function's parameter templates.

- Data types may be different.

- Some fields may be excluded.

- Fields may be included that do not map to the called function's parameter template, such as derivation or local work area fields.

Again, Repository Manager will automatically perform the required mapping and data conversions at function initiation and termination.

7.1.1.3 *Local Work Area Templates*

A function template that is not used as a data template or parameter template is referred to as a *local work area template*. A local work area template cannot be shared with another template during execution of a function.

7.1.2 Specification of a Template

The *specification of a template* consists of the following:

- *Name* — the unique identification of the template within the scope of the logical view.

- *Description* — for documentation purposes, a short or long description, or both, of the template (optional).

- *Trigger policies* — constraints on the template to be enforced by repository services at the time the template is used (optional).

- *Template fields* — the identification of the individual data elements included in the template.

The *specification of a template field* consists of the following:

- *Name* — the unique identification of the template field within the scope of the template.

- *Description* — for documentation purposes, a short or long description, or both, of the template field (optional).

- *Characteristics* — the data type and length of the data that will be placed in the template field by repository services.

- *Integrity policies* – The constraints on the template field value, which are enforced by repository services whenever data is placed in the template field by the use of repository services (optional).

- *Derivation policies* — the identification of an algorithm that specifies how the value to be placed in the template field is to be derived (optional).

- *Trigger policies* — the identification of conditions, and a repository function to be initiated when that condition is met, whenever a value is placed in the template field or removed from it by use of repository services (optional).

7.1.3   Components of a Template

A template consists of the following components:

1. The *action code* (ACODE), used to specify the action to be performed.

2. The *action qualifier* (AQUAL), used to modify the scope of the action code.

3. In arrayed templates, the *last occurrence index* (LOI), which is set by Repository Manager to indicate the number of occurrences that have been retrieved.

4. In arrayed templates, the *selector field* (SELECT1), which indicates in which fields an action is to take place. A value of 0 is used if the action pertains to all fields, and the value n designates that the action pertains to the nth field.

5. A two-part *completion code*, consisting of:

    a. A *call return code* (CRC), which is a numerical value, conveys information about the result of the action. This value can be set either by Repository Manager or the Repository Manager application function.

Examples of the meaning of such codes might be "normal," or "call terminating error."

b.   A *call state indicator* (CSI), which is a two-character value to convey additional information about the call return code. Again, this value can be set either by Repository Manager or the Repository Manager application function. A large number of CSI values exist. For example, when the CRC is "normal," the call state indicator might also be "normal," and when the CRC is "call terminating error," the call state indicator might be "invalid parameter." The CSI is also used to report attempted violations to a policy.

6.   *Template fields*, which represent the data content of the template. Each template field consists of the following:

a.   A *field state indicator* (FSI), which is a two-character code set by Repository Manager or a Repository Manager function to convey information about a template field. Examples of the definition of such codes are: "The field has a value assigned to it that was too long for the field, and some significant digits have been lost," or "The field has no value assigned to it."

b.   A *current length value*, which is present only if the field has been defined as being of variable length. It is set by Repository Manager or a Repository Manager function. If the FSI indicates that the field has no value, Repository Manager will ignore the current length value.

c.   A *value*, set by Repository Manager or a Repository Manager function, to communicate the current value of the field.

Like the current length, the contents of the field value are undefined if the FSI indicates that the field is null.

Figure 7-1 gives a diagram showing a template and its fields.

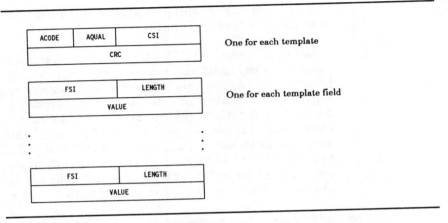

Figure 7-1   Diagram of a template and its fields.

7.1.4   Template Domains

A template's *domain* is the complete, sorted set of entity key attributes available to the current user of the template. Restrictions on the instances in the domain will be based on the tool or the tool user's defined authority.

A root template always has a domain: it is the complete entity set (subject only to authority restrictions). If there are no instances, the domain is empty.

A subordinate template's domain depends on the cursor position of its parent and the instances of the relationship connecting them. If its parent has no cursor position, it can have no domain. Even if its parent has a cursor position, its domain may be empty; this is a valid domain. Retrieval calls may not be issued against a subordinate template that has no domain.

The domain is ordered by the sort sequence of the entity access names.

Consider the Repository Manager entity type PERSON, with instances ALICE, BOB, CAROL, TED, and ZELDA, and also relationship type WIFE, having person as both source and target and having as instances the entity instances BOB and CAROL, TED and ZELDA, and TED and ALICE (Ted having been married twice). The following template has both templates mapping to PERSON and connected by relationship WIFE:

Since TMPL1 is a root template, its domain is always ALICE, BOB, CAROL, TED, and ZELDA. The domain of TMPL2 depends on the cursor position of TMPL1, as shown in Figure 7-2.

TMPL1 position	*TMPL2 position*
BOB	CAROL
CAROL	empty
TED	ZELDA ALICE
ALICE	empty
ZELDA	empty
none	none

Figure 7-2   Example of a domain of a root template and a subordinate template.

Since only instances in the current domain of a template can be retrieved in that template, when TMPL1 is positioned at TED, only ZELDA and ALICE can be retrieved in TMPL2, and when TMPL1 is positioned at CAROL, nothing can be retrieved in TMPL2. TMPL1, however, can always retrieve all PERSON instances.

A *template cursor* is a pointer that keeps track of where a program is positioned within a template's domain. Before any call has been issued against a template, the template has no cursor position. The cursor is set by a successful retrieval and certain add calls; it is destroyed after certain actions. There is no way to query the template cursor position directly; it can be deduced via the application program's processing logic from the sequence of actions that have been performed.

7.1.5 Keyed Retrievals

In Section 7.1.3 the *Action Qualifier* (AQUAL) of a template was addressed. To review, the action qualifier is used to modify the scope of the action that is specified in the action code. For calls that use the KEYED qualifier, key values are specified by being placed in the template key field.

7.1.6 Qualified Retrievals

Retrievals using the QUALIFIED qualifier require that a field in the template contain a *selection expression*. This section discusses this subject.

A selection expression is made up of one or more selection clauses, each one of which returns a true or false result. Each clause consists of two operands and an operator and has the general form:

```
attribute  operator  value
```

where:

Attribute is the name of an attribute of an entity type whose value is to be compared.

If the attribute name contains special characters, i.e., any character other than a letter, a digit, or an underscore, then a delimited string must be used. Attribute names beginning with a digit must be specified using a delimited string.

A delimited string may include any character and is delimited either by the single quote character ('), or the double quote character ("), and must begin and end with the same delimiting character. Two consecutive single quotes (''), and two consecutive double quotes ("") are used to represent a single quote and double quote, respectively, in a delimited string.

The parent key attributes of a dependent entity are referenced by using identifier strings named DWKQnnn, where nnn is a key sequence number beginning with 001 for the first, most distant parent.

Operator specifies the comparison to be made. Comparisons between number and character strings cannot be made.

The following operators can be used:

=	equal
¬=	not equal
>	greater than
<	less than
>=	greater than or equal
<=	less than or equal
¬<	not less than
¬>	not greater than

as well as the operators LIKE and NOT LIKE, which have the same syntax as they have in SQL. These operators indicate a "wildcard" matching pattern. The following two "wildcard characters" are recognized: the character " _ " indicates a single unspecified character, and the character "%" indicates 0 to n unspecified characters.

These operators can best be seen in some examples: LIKE "ABC_EFG" would yield a value of true for "ABCDEFG" and "ABCXEFG", but would yield a value of false for "ABCEFG" and "ABCDEF". LIKE "ABC%EFG" would yield a value of true for "ABCEFG" and "ABCXYZXYZXYZEFG", but would yield a value of false for "ABCXEFGH". NOT LIKE "ABC%EFG" would yield a value of true for "AXCEFG". Note that NOT LIKE is equivalent to NOT(ATTRIBUTE LIKE VALUE). If ATTRIBUTE is null, the result is unknown.

The LIKE and NOT LIKE operators cannot be used for numeric attributes. Care should be taken when these operators are used with attributes that are defined as fixed length, in which case trailing blanks will be significant.

Slightly different rules for these operators apply in the case of mixed single-byte and double-byte character strings.

Value refers to the specification of the value against which the entity attribute value is to be compared. The following two cases can exist:

1.   *Value* can refer to a template field in a function; it will be in the form template.field. Since template field names

can contain only the characters A through Z, 0 through 9, and the underscore character _, the template field name will be put into EBCDIC upper case before use.

If the template is an arrayed template, the array element is specified in the form `template.field(nn)`, where (nn) is the character representation of the integer element identifier.

2. *Value* can be a literal value, i.e., a character or a numeric value. The same conventions for delimited strings that exist for attribute names also apply to values.

Multiple Selection Clauses are connected by the Boolean operators "&" and "|", and the precedence of operators is determined by the bracketing operators "(" and ")". Innermost clauses are evaluated first, and where brackets are omitted, clauses connected by an "&" are evaluated before clauses connected by a "|".

7.1.7 Template Actions

Different template actions exist in Repository Manager, depending on whether a single template, a pair of templates, or an arrayed template is involved.

7.1.7.1 Single Template Actions

Entity, or single template calls, affect instances of the entity mapped to by the template.

For KEYED calls, the key is placed in the key field of the template named in the call.

FIRST

Query an entity instance. The resulting data occupies the template's fields. This action may be qualified as:

KEYED — Query a specific entity instance.

UNQUALIFIED — Query the first instance in the domain.

QUALIFIED — Query the first instance in the domain that satisfies the selection expression in the template's selection field. If there is no selection field or no selection expression, the action is the same as UNQUALIFIED.

NEXT

Query an entity instance. The resulting data occupies the template's fields. This action may be qualified as:

UNQUALIFIED — Query the next instance in the domain following the current cursor position.

QUALIFIED — Query the next instance in the domain following the current cursor position that satisfies the selection expression in the template's selection field. If there is no selection field or no selection expression, the action is the same as UNQUALIFIED.

LAST

Query an entity instance. The resulting data occupies the template's fields. This action may be qualified as:

KEYED — Query a specific entity instance. This is identical to FIRST KEYED.

UNQUALIFIED — Query the last instance in the domain.

QUALIFIED — Query the last instance in the domain that satisfies the selection expression in the template's selection field. If there is no selection field or no selection expression, the action is the same as UNQUALIFIED.

PREVIOUS

Query an entity instance. The resulting data occupies the template's fields. This action may be qualified as:

UNQUALIFIED — Query the instance in the domain preceding the current cursor position.

QUALIFIED — Query the instance in the domain preceding the current cursor position that satisfies the selection expression in the template's selection field. If there is no selection field or no selection expression, the action is the same as UNQUALIFIED.

UPDATE
Updates attributes of a previously retrieved entity instance.

This action may only be qualified as UNQUALIFIED.

ADD
Adds a new entity instance.

This action may only be qualified as KEYED.

DELETE
Deletes a previously retrieved entity instance.

This action may only be qualified as UNQUALIFIED.

Additionally, Repository Manager/MVS has COMMIT and RESTORE operations that affect all entity and relationship instance changes initiated during the function invocation, including called functions. These operations can be requested through any template, whether it maps to an entity or not.

7.1.7.2 Two-Template Actions

Relationship, or two template calls, affect instances of the relationship whose logical source is the entity mapped to key the first template, and whose logical target is the entity mapped to the second template.

ADD
Add the relationship instance whose source is the key of the first template and whose target is the key of the second template.

This action may be qualified as KEYED to add the relationship into the domain of the second template.

DELETE

> Delete the relationship instance whose source is the key of the first template and whose target is the key of the second template.

> This action may only be qualified as UNQUALIFIED.

7.1.7.3   *Arrayed Template Actions*

All template actions for an arrayed template are invoked through its first element.

The entire array may be operated on by setting the SELECT1 field to 0; if it is desired to operate only on the nth template of the array, the SELECT1 field is set to n. In the case of two-template calls (for relationships), the SELECT1 field of the second template is used for this purpose.

The following actions, and their description, apply to arrayed templates.

ADD

> For a one-template array, the action is the same as for a single-element ADD on each element that has a non-null key field.

> In the two-template case, if both templates are arrayed, the action is the same as issuing a two-template ADD on each pair of elements where both elements have non-null keys. If the first template is not arrayed, and the second template is arrayed, the action is the same as issuing a two-template ADD for each non-null element of the target template. The result is a set of relationship instances between the source entity type instance and each non-null element of the target template.

DELETE

> For a one-template array, the action is the same as for a single-element DELETE on each element.

> In the two-template case, if both templates are arrayed, the action is the same as issuing a two-template DELETE on each pair of elements. If the first template is not arrayed, and

the second template is arrayed, the action is the same as issuing a two-template DELETE for each element of the target template. The action deletes each relationship instance between the source entity type instance and each non-null element of the target template.

FIRST

For the primary template in the array, the first element receives the same instance as it would from a single-element call. Succeeding elements receive succeeding instances from the domain until either the template or the domain is exhausted. The LOI field of the first element is set to the number of the last element that received an instance.

For a secondary template in an array, the action is the same as issuing a single-element FIRST on each element whose immediate parent element has a cursor position.

LAST

For the primary template in the array, the first element receives the same instance as it would from a single-element call. Preceding elements receive preceding instances from the domain until either the template or the domain is exhausted. The LOI field of the first element is set to the number of the last element that received an instance.

For a secondary template in an array, the action is the same as issuing a single-element LAST on each element whose immediate parent element has a cursor position.

NEXT

For the primary template in the array, the first element receives the next instance in the domain that follows the latest instance retrieved by the previous retrieval action that operated on the entire array. Succeeding elements receive succeeding instances from the domain until either the template or the domain is exhausted. The LOI field of the first element is set to the number of the last element that received an instance.

For a secondary template in an array, the action is the same as issuing a single-element NEXT on each element that has a cursor position.

PREVIOUS

For the primary template in the array, the first element receives the instance in the domain that precedes the earliest instance retrieved by the previous retrieval action that operated on the entire array. Preceding elements receive preceding instances from the domain until either the template or the domain is exhausted. The LOI field of the first element is set to the number of the first element that received an instance.

For a secondary template in an array, the action is the same as issuing a single-element PREVIOUS on each element that has a cursor position.

UPDATE

The action is the same as issuing a single-element UPDATE on each element that has a template cursor position.

The COMMIT and RESTORE actions, which are available as part of the Repository Manager/MVS API, operate in the same manner as do single-element actions. In each case, the SELECT1 field is ignored.

7.2   REPOSITORY SERVICES

This section will discuss a number of different repository services that are provided for applications programs. Before these services are discussed, we will first deal with the manner in which repository services are invoked.

7.2.1   Repository Service Routine Entry Points

The Repository Manager service routine entry points are invoked directly through standard language program invocation statements for Higher Level Language programs, and by subcommands supplied by Repository Manager for REXX programs.

Service routines use the information they receive in parameter lists and/or templates to select and perform the requested service. These entry points will now be described.

7.2.1.1 OPEN Service

The OPEN service is established through the DWKOP entry point for all *non-integrated functions*. The service establishes the function's environment and establishes addressability to the templates of the requesting function. This service and the CLOSE service are used by functions using what is termed "open/close interaction." This service is not required for *fully integrated functions*, where the templates are passed directly to it by Repository Manager in what is termed *fully integrated interaction*.

An open/close interaction function program must have one function open at a time, and may have more than one open.

The entry point allows subsequent DWKT1 and DWKT2 service requests to be opened to the function.

7.2.1.2 CLOSE Service

The CLOSE service is established through the DWKCL entry point. Repository Manager is called and de-allocates all resources previously allocated by an OPEN service call for the function.

7.2.1.3 INFO Service

The DWKIN service routine is used to query Repository Manager and the operating system. Programs specify a data item to be retrieved and designate a variable into which the result is to be placed.

Information that can be requested is the value of a system-defined variable, such as the name of the function that is currently active or the name of the operating system environment. The current time and date can also be retrieved.

7.2.1.4 DWKT1 and DWKT2 Services

These services provide entry points for repository applications to request Repository Manager services involving templates.

These service routines use information they receive in their parameter list and templates to select and then perform the requested service.

The Repository Manager function must assign appropriate values to the template's action code and action code qualifier fields denoting the service to be performed.

These facilities are initiated through a *user services template*. An action code is specified in the template's ACODE field. This action can be further defined by a qualifier in the template's ACODE field.

The action code VIEWTEMPLATE is used to display a panel. Qualifiers also make the following capabilities available:

- Setting the panel cursor position

- Determining the current cursor position

- Issuing ISPF commands

- Determining user commands entered on the panel command line

- Controlling scrolling in the panel scrollable area

- Parsing action codes on list panels

- Displaying a message on a panel

The action code VIEWMESSAGE is used to specify a message to be displayed on the next panel that will be shown.

The action code MSG2FIELD is used to write a message to a template field.

The action code LOG causes a message to be written to the diagnostic trace file.

The action code *CLEAR* causes the FSI of all template fields mapping to input panel fields to indicate that the field is null.

7.2.1.5   *System Services — Template Actions*

Additional system services on templates cans be invoked through the action codes discussed below.

The action code CALL can be used in either of two ways:

- With a function's parameter template to call that function.

- With the universal scheduling template DWKPARM, in which case, the name of the function to be called must be specified on that template.

An arrayed parameter template can also be used to call a repository function, as would be desirable if a repository function were to be called repetitively with different parameters. The SELECT1 field must be used to identify a single element of the template array for each CALL action. The value placed in the SELECT1 field must be a positive integer no greater than the extent of the template array. The calling parameter values are placed in the element identified by SELECT1; the return codes and output parameter values are returned in this element.

The one-template action BIND can be used to dynamically bind a template to an entity type. The dynabind template that is to be bound dynamically to the entity type must specify the name of the entity type in the template's ENT_NAME field.

A template array can also be bound dynamically to an entity type by using an arrayed dynabind template with a one-template BIND action.

The action code UNBIND can be used to unbind a dynabind template from the entity type to which it is bound.

The two-template action BIND, for templates that map to entity types, can be used to dynamically connect the two specified templates via a relationship type. The template that is the target of the relationship type must contain a template field containing the name of the relationship type. If the target template is already subordinate to another template, the two-template BIND action first deletes the existing connection between the target template and its existing parent and then carries out the normal BIND action.

Templates that can be dynamically connected are:

- A non-arrayed template to an arrayed template.

- An arrayed template to another arrayed template, but only if the extent of the two arrayed templates is the same.

These rules are the same as the ones for building template trees.

The two-template action UNBIND can be used to dynamically delete a connection between two specified templates. Two templates can also be disconnected in the following ways:

- If the source or target template is a dynabind template, by unbinding the template that is the source or the target of the connection.

- Unbinding another template that is the source of the connection.

7.2.1.6   *User Exits*

Repository Manager provides a set of execs as user exit routines, which take control at specified user exit points in Repository Manager. These execs can be modified to set and then reset data set allocations. The following user exits are supported:

DWKEXIT0   Brings up ISPF.

DWKEXIT1: Can be invoked just before Repository Manager starts and can be used to modify any necessary TSO ALLOCATEs, create necessary data sets on TSO, or perform any necessary LIBDEFs in TSO.

DWKEXIT2: Invoked just after Repository Manager terminates. It can be modified in the same manner as DWKEXIT1, especially to undo any LIBDEFs.

DWKEXIT5: Invokes SCRIPT/VS and can be tailored to reflect the name of the SCRIPT command and any other local SCRIPT naming conventions.

7.3   TEMPLATE BUILT-IN FUNCTION SERVICES

A set of built-in functions is available in the Repository Manager CPI that deal with actions on templates. In general, the scope of these built-in functions is wider than template actions, in the sense that they will typically operate on whole template trees rather than on a single template or pair of templates. These functions may also operate on multiple template trees. A root template that is not connected to any other template is considered to be a template tree with a single node.

Built-in functions are invoked through the use of a parameter template. The completion codes are returned in the CRC and CSI fields of the parameter template. The CRC and CSI fields of each template in a template tree will contain the completion codes of the actual data calls performed on the template.

The functions available in Repository Manager for template services will now be discussed.

7.3.1 First Entity Instance (DWKFIRST)

This function gets the first entity instance for each template in the template tree.

A FIRST call is issued to each template. A call with a KEYED action code is issued to all non-null calls.

7.3.2 Next Entity Instance (DWKNEXT)

This function gets the next entity instance in the root template of the template tree and its first set of descendants.

First it issues a call with a NEXT action code to the root template; then calls with FIRST action codes are issued to all subordinate templates. The root template must have a cursor position established on it.

7.3.3 Last Entity Instance (DWKLAST)

This function gets the last entity instance in the root, then in the root template of the template tree, and then issues calls with a LAST action code to each of the subordinates of the root to get the last descendants of the root instance.

A call with a LAST action code is issued to each template, and a KEYED call is issued to all non-null templates.

7.3.4   Previous Entity Instance (DWKPREV)

This function gets the entity instance previous to the current entity instance in the root template.

It issues a call with the action code PREV to the root template, then calls with a LAST action code are made to all subordinate templates in the template tree.

7.3.5   Next Leaf Entity Instance (DWKNBOT)

This function gets the next entity instance in each of the leaf templates of the template tree.

A call with a NEXT action code is issued on all leaves of the template tree. Empty leaves are not operated on. Successive calls to this function retrieve more leaf node instances.

When issued on a template tree with a single template, this function operates the same as DWKNEXT.

7.3.6   Next Descendants (DWKNDEP)

This function gets the next descendants at the bottom of the template tree.

Each branch of the tree is traversed backward from its leaf to the first template found, below the root, that yields an instance with a call with action code NEXT. Calls with an action code of FIRST are then made on all its subordinate templates.

These actions can best be illustrated in the example template tree shown in Figure 7-3.

A call to DWKNDEP will:

1.   Retrieve the next descendants of B from C and D, the next descendant of E from F, and the next descendant of G from H.

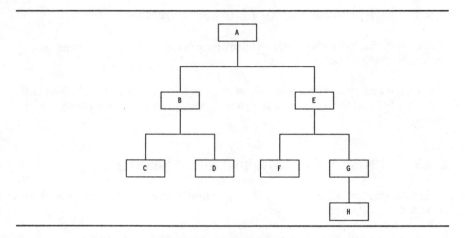

Figure 7-3   Example of a template tree.

2.   If H is empty, a call with action code NEXT on G, and a call with action code FIRST are issued on H.

3.   If F, G, and H are empty, a call with action code NEXT is issued on E, and calls with action code FIRST are done, down the template tree, on F, G, and H.

4.   Then another call to DWKNDEP will do calls with action code NEXT on F and H.

5.   The call cycle repeats until F, G, and H are empty again and another call with action code NEXT is issued on E.

6.   If C and D are empty, a call with action code NEXT is issued on B, and calls with action code FIRST are done on C and D.

7.   Again, the cycle repeats until C and D are empty.

8.   If B, C, D, E, F, and G are all empty, a CSI value indicating that there are no more values is returned. A call with action code NEXT is not issued on the root.

Note that a call with action code NEXT will not be done on E unless F, G, and H are empty.

This function, when issued on a template tree with a single template, operates the same as DWKNEXT.

7.3.7   Previous Descendants (DWKPDEP)

This function gets the previous descendants at the bottom of the template tree. It functions in the same manner as DWKNDEP, except that it issues calls with action codes LAST and PREV in place of calls with action codes FIRST and LAST.

7.3.8   Browse Forward (DWKBRWSF)

This function browses all entity instances in a tree in the forward direction.

This function issues a DWKNDEP and, when informed that no more descendants are found, issues a call with a NEXT action code on the root. When there are no more instances of the root to browse, an appropriate return code is issued.

DWKBRWSF requires that a cursor position be established on the root template.

7.3.9   Browse Backward (DWKBRWSB)

This function browses all entity instances in a tree in a backward direction.

It acts in the same manner as DWKBRWSF, except that it issues calls with action code PREV in place of calls with action code NEXT.

7.3.10   Update Entity Attributes (DWKUPDT)

This function updates attributes of an entity. It operates on every template in a template tree for which the key is not null.

If all keys in a tree are null, or all templates in the tree are empty, appropriate return codes are issued to indicate that no updates were performed.

DWKUPDT requires that a cursor position be established on the root template.

7.3.11   Add Entities and Relationships (DWKADD)

This function adds entities and relationships. A call with an ADD action code is issued to each template for which:

1.   The key is not null.

When an entity type is designated as having system-generated keys, a program is generally not responsible for supplying a key, as the key is generated when the add is done. However, in the case of templates mapping to entities with system-generated keys, the requirements of the DWKADD function are that some key must be supplied if a program wants the entities to be added.

2.   The key is null, but the template's database write derivation policies have been specified for the key, in which case it can be assumed that a value for the key will be supplied.

A call to the *Add Relationships* function DWKADDR is then issued to each non-null template pair.

When errors cause adding entity instances to fail because the entity instances already exist, the errors are ignored and processing continues. The suitable return codes are inserted into the templates.

7.3.12   Add Relationships (DWKADDR)

This function adds relationship instances to each template pair that has non-null source and target keys. Duplicate relationship instances are ignored, and suitable error codes are left in the templates.

The function uses a qualifier of AFTER; hence, if a relationship type is an "ordered set" relationship type, the relationship instance is added just after the current cursor position, i.e., the cursor for the subordinate template that is "pointed at" by the "ordered set" relationship type.

If the function is issued against a template tree in which all templates are null, an appropriate return code is issued.

7.3.13   Delete Entity Instances   (DWKDEL)

This function deletes entity instances and, for that reason, it should be used with caution.

7.3.14   Delete Relationship Instances   (DWKDELR)

This function deletes relationship instances; a call with an action code of DELETE is issued to each non-null template pair.

7.3.15   Commit Database Changes   (DWKCOMMT)

This function is available only in the Repository Manager/MVS API. It commits all database changes made via any template, in all repository functions in use by a single user.

7.3.16   Restore Database   (DWKRESTR)

This function is available only in the Repository Manager/MVS API. It restores the database to the point of the last COMMIT.

7.3.17   Set Template Fields to Null   (DWKNULL)

This function sets to null all template fields in the template tree(s) that map to an entity.

8 REPOSITORY FUNCTIONS

Repository Manager can be used to build tools made up of discrete units called *repository functions*. Each tool is assembled from one or more repository functions.

A repository function is a repository interface construct that provides access to repository services and repository interface data. Each repository function has a set of specifications that identify the data, logic, and services that the repository function requires.

A logical view is repository function-specific; i.e., the view of information and function are defined for each repository function. Each repository function has access to a subset of the repository data store through its *logical data view*. This information view is represented by *templates* and contains the specifications of repository functions. Each time a new repository function is defined, its specifications are added to the logical view. These specifications are how a repository function identifies those things in the repository data store that can be accessed through repository services. Additionally, the specifications of a repository function can identify any optional procedural logic to be executed or other repository functions that may be invoked.

Repository function global specifications define a function to the repository. The specification of a repository function consists of name, function type, description, required locks, templates, policies, procedural logic, function procedures for pending database changes upon initiation and termination, and whether or not the repository function shares resources with its caller.

The repository program containing the procedural logic may be called automatically by repository services when the repository function is executed, or it may be called from the operating system and then open the repository function.

Template information is passed from repository services to the repository program in the repository function parameter template and data template fields. Appropriate program language descriptions of all templates associated with the repository function are included in the application interface header file.

When a template is to be used, its address is specified. Some functions act based on the template type and the action code and details that are filled in the template. The functions that are called are defined (DWKX functions, where X is the rest of the string in the function name) in the Repository Manager CPI or Repository Manager/MVS API. Templates are defined in the repository before template data fields can be instantiated.

The functionality specified for the functions is a close parallel to the functionality available through the dialogs with panel hierarchies, which are discussed in Chapter 9.

8.1 REPOSITORY FUNCTION TYPES

As previously described, there are different types of repository functions. These are:

- *Fully integrated functions*, which are tied to a specific tool program. By calling the repository function, the tool program is invoked. The tool program can then directly access the repository services and data.

- *Non-fully integrated functions*, which are not tied to a specific tool program and cannot be invoked directly. They are opened and closed within a program. When opened it allows the program to use the function's logical data view and panels and establishes addressability. Any program can use one or more non-fully integrated functions to access repository data and services.

- *Methods*, which are another type of repository function; they define the operations that may be invoked on object instances of a particular object type. Once a method is invoked for a specific object instance, Repository Manager:

1. Determines the object type of the specific object instance for which it was invoked.

2. Selects a method implementation based on the method and object type of the specific object instance.

3. Invokes the selected method implementation.

For example, if a business report method has been defined, when this method is invoked, Repository Manager:

1. Selects an appropriate function (method implementation) based upon the data format (object type) in which the data is written.

2. Invokes the selected function to process the data into a report.

- *Method Implementations*, which are the fourth type of repository function. These functions are also associated with object types, and they define which operations are performed on object instances of a particular object type. They are similar to fully integrated functions in that they have a logical data view, tool program, and optional panels and policies. However, they are invoked differently: method implementations are invoked only from methods, but fully integrated functions are called directly.

When an object type is defined, its allowed methods are also defined. Each method maps to a method implementation. For example, assume that SOURCE_PROGRAM has been defined as an object type. Table 8-1 shows the methods and method implementations that might have been defined for this object type.

Table 8-1   Example of methods and method implementations.

Object Type	Allowed Methods	Method Implementations		
SOURCE_PROGRAM	SFCREAT	SFMKCOB	SFMKFOR	SFMKC
	SFEDIT	SFEDCOB	SFEDFOR	SFEDC
	SFDELET	SFDLCOB	SFDLCOB	SFDLC

When a source program is to be created the SFCREAT method is called, that in turn invokes the appropriate method implementation to create a file that will contain a source program. Three different method implementations are shown in the example depending on the language used in the source file, COBOL, FORTRAN, or C. Once a file is created, the SFEDIT method can be called, the contents of the source program file is retrieved, and the appropriate method implementation invokes the editor with the correct format parameters (and possibly a syntax checker) to allow updates to the source program file to be made. If the program is to be deleted, the SFDELET method is called that invokes one of the method implementations to delete the program.

8.2   REPOSITORY MANAGER BUILT-IN FUNCTIONS

Repository services include a collection of built-in functions. They can be used to automate the tasks of creating, populating, and maintaining the repository data store. These repository services can be applied to templates or template trees. There are two types of built-in functions:

1.   Functions that accept input from either a panel interface or a list of parameters.

2.   Functions that accept input only from a list of parameters.

A built-in function is used "interactively" when it uses the panel interface to accept input, and is used "non-interactively" when it accepts input from a list of parameters, i.e., its parameter template.

Built-in functions may be called from application programs to perform database actions on behalf of the calling function. These actions may take place on a wider basis than template actions, typically operating on whole template trees rather than on a single template. The built-in functions make up part of the Repository Manager logical data services.

All of these database functions may operate on multiple template trees. Note that a root template that is not connected to any other template via a relationship is still considered a template tree — it is simply a tree with only one node.

Built-in functions can be invoked through the use of a parameter template. An example of such a template would be the universal scheduling template, DWKPARM. The parameter template must contain the field DWKFNAME as well as any other fields that may be necessary for the built-in function. The program assigns the DWKFNAME field the name of the built-in function it wants called and sets the other parameter template fields to the values it wants.

For data services built-in functions, the TMPLNAME field is the only parameter template field that may be needed. It is optional; if the TMPLNAME field is not specified, the built-in function will operate on all template trees in the function. If a template name is specified in the TMPLNAME field, the built-in function will operate on the template tree or subtree having the named template as its root. If a template array is encountered when a template tree is being operated on, all elements of the template array will be operated on.

In addition to the built-in functions representing services on templates, which were described in the previous chapter, Repository Manager/MVS provides a set of built-in functions which are described below. Those that are also available in the Repository Manager CPI are again marked with an asterisk. It must be cautioned that the descriptions given are by no means complete enough to be used for programming purposes; in particular, the parameter templates are not described, and not all parameters are specified. Neither are CRC and CSI codes discussed. This information is available in the IBM publications listed in the Appendix.

In the description of the built-in functions that follows, the functions are assigned to one of the following types:

- ER Modeling Functions
- Logical View Functions
- Security Functions
- Storage View Functions
- Tool Group Functions
- Utility Functions
- ER Model Maintenance Functions
- Data Services Functions
- System Services Functions

The assignment of these types is intended to be informational only and does not represent a fundamental characteristic of the functions. Functions that are available as part of the Repository CPI are marked with an asterisk. A summary of these functions is given in Table 8-2. In this table it is also shown whether the function can be invoked in both interactive and non-interactive mode or only in non-interactive mode.

Functions shown as being invocable in both the interactive and non-interactive mode may be called from a tool program, either in interactive mode through a panel or in non-interactive mode through its parameter template. The built-in function's display parameter is used to specify the mode. Those shown as being invocable only in the non-interactive mode have no associated panels. Data is passed to or from each non-interactive built-in function through its parameter template.

Additional discussion on invocation of a function in interactive mode will be given in Chapter 9.

8.2.1   ER Modeling Functions

The process of using built-in functions for the definition and maintenance of conceptual view constructs can be summarized in the following manner:

Add a new entity type

- Add the new entity type, key attribute, and owning relationship, if any, using DWKCED, *Define Entity Type* (See 8.2.1.1).

Table 8-2   Summary of functions (Part 1 of 4).

Type	Name	Description	Mode
ER Modeling	DWKCCOL	Maintain collection instances	Interactive/ Non-interactive
	DWKCEAC	Maintain entity attributes	Non-interactive
	DWKCED	Define an entity type	Interactive/ Non-interactive
	DWKCEDP	Create entity type derivation policies	Interactive/ Non-interactive
	DWKCEIP	Create entity type attribute integrity policies	Interactive/ Non-interactive
	DWKCEQ	Query an entity type definition	Non-interactive
	DWKCETP	Create entity type trigger policies	Interactive/ Non-interactive
	DWKCLPQ	Query Repository Manager policies	Non-interactive
	DWKCOE	Maintain object edition instances	Interactive/ Non-interactive
	DWKCOP	Maintain object part instances	Interactive/ Non-interactive
	DWKCOT	Define an object type	Interactive/ Non-interactive
	DWKCOTM	Maintain methods in an object type	Interactive/ Non-interactive
	DWKCRD	Define a relationship type	Interactive/ Non-interactive
	DWKCRIP	Create relationship type integrity policies	Interactive/ Non-interactive
	DWKCRTP	Create relationship type trigger policies	Interactive/ Non-interactive
	DWKUDEP	Return information about a dependent entity	Interactive/ Non-interactive

* Denotes that the function is part of Common Programming Interface

Table 8-2   Summary of functions (Part 2 of 4).

Type	Name	Description	Mode
Logical View	DWKLBND	Bind a function	Non-interactive
	DWKLFTP	Create function trigger policies	Interactive/ Non-interactive
	DWKLPNC	Invoke SDF II panel creation	Non-interactive
	DWKLTDP	Create template field derivation policies	Interactive/ Non-interactive
	DWKLTFC	Maintain template/template field	Non-interactive
	DWKLTFQ	Query template use in a function	Non-interactive
	DWKLTIP	Create template field integrity policies	Interactive/ Non-interactive
	DWKLTTP	Create template trigger policies	Interactive/ Non-interactive
	DWKLTTQ	Query template trees in a function	Non-interactive
	DWKLVT1	Define function	Interactive/ Non-interactive
Security	DWKBSEC	Security profile binding	Non-interactive
Storage View	DWKS2MB	Bind multiple storage views	Non-interactive
	DWKS2MD	Generate DDL for multiple tables	Non-interactive
	DWKS2MM	Map storage view for multiple entity and relationship types	Interactive/ Non-interactive
Tool Group	DWKTGQ	Query members of a tool group	Non-interactive
* Denotes that the function is part of Common Programming Interface			

Table 8-2   Summary of functions (Part 3 of 4).

Type	Name	Description	Mode
Utility	DWKPGM	Call a tool program	Non-interactive
	DWKTEDT	Text annotation function	Non-interactive
	DWKUEDT	Edit a template field	Non-interactive
	DWKUFLT	Retrieve aggregation instance	Non-interactive
	DWKUIAO	Import aggregation instance	Interactive/ Non-interactive
	DWKULCK*	Lock and unlock aggregation instance	Non-interactive
	DWKULD	Batch repository maintenance	Interactive/ Non-interactive
	DWKULST	Build aggregation tree	Non-interactive
	DWKUTDF	Retrieve template definition	Non-interactive
	DWKUTM	Maintain system messages table	Interactive/ Non-interactive
	DWKUTRE	Build template tree	Non-interactive
	DWKUXAO	Export aggregation instance	Interactive/ Non-interactive
ER Model Maintenance	DWKZMLG	Maintain PTF log entries	Interactive/ Non-interactive
	DWKZMPR	Place construct in PTF hold status	Interactive/ Non-interactive
Data Services	DWKADD*	Add entity instances and relationship instances	Non-interactive
	DWKADDR*	Add relationship instances	Non-interactive
	DWKBRWSB*	Browse all entity instances in a tree in a backward direction	Non-interactive
	DWKBRWSF*	Browse all entity instances in a tree in a forward direction	Non-interactive
*	Denotes that the function is part of Common Programming Interface		

Table 8-2   Summary of functions (Part 4 of 4).

Type	Name	Description	Mode
Data Services (cont.)	DWKCOMMT	Commit database changes	Non-interactive
	DWKDEL*	Delete entity instances	Non-interactive
	DWKDELR*	Delete relationship instances	Non-interactive
	DWKFIRST*	Retrieve the first entity instance for each template in the template tree	Non-interactive
	DWKLAST*	Retrieve the last entity instance for each template in the template tree	Non-interactive
	DWKNBOT*	Retrieve the next entity instance in each of the leaf templates	Non-interactive
	DWKNDEP*	Retrieve the next descendant instances at the bottom of the tree	Non-interactive
	DWKNEXT*	Retrieve the next entity instance in the root template of the tree and its first set of descendants	Non-interactive
	DWKPDEP*	Retrieve the previous descendant instances at the bottom of the tree	Non-interactive
	DWKPREV*	Retrieve the entity instance previous to the current entity instance	Non-interactive
	DWKRESTR	Restore database (backout changes)	Non-interactive
	DWKUPDT*	Update entity attribute values	Non-interactive
System Services	DWKNULL*	Set data template fields to the null state	Non-interactive
* Denotes that the function is part of Common Programming Interface			

- Add additional attributes to the entity type, one at a time, using DWKCEAC, *Define Entity Attribute* (See 8.2.1.2).

- Provide long descriptions of the attributes and owning relationships using the update capability of DWKCEAC, *Define Entity Attribute*, and DWKCRD, *Define Relationship Type* (See 8.2.1.3).

- Add trigger, integrity, and derivation policies using DWKCETP, *Create Trigger Policy* (See 8.2.1.4), DWKCEIP, *Create Integrity Policy* (See 8.2.1.5), and DWKCEDP, *Create Derivation Policy* (See 8.2.1.6), respectively.

- Use the BIND command option of DWKCED, *Define Entity Type*, to bind the entity type.

Update an entity type

- Retrieve the entity type definition with the list of attributes using DWKCEQ, *Query Entity Type* (See 8.2.1.7).

- Depending on what changes are required, retrieve, and then update the entity type using DWKCED, *Define Entity Type*. Add, update, or delete entity type attributes using DWKCEAC, *Define Entity Attribute*, or policies using DWKCETP, DWKCEIP, or DWKCEDP.

- Use the BIND command option of DWKCED, *Define Entity Type*, to bind the entity type incorporating the changes.

Delete an entity type

- Use DWKTGQ (See 8.2.5.1), *Query Members of a Tool Group*, to determine what tool groups contain the entity type.

- Use the DELETE command option of DWKCED, *Define Entity Type*, to delete the entity type sequentially from each tool group.

The built-in functions used above are defined as follows:

8.2.1.1   *Define Entity Type* (DWKCED)

This function is used to:

- Add, Delete, Update, Query, or Bind an entity type definition.

- Change the lock status or dependent status of the entity type.

- Modify the long or short description of the entity type.

The *Define Attribute Type* function (DWKCEAC) is used to update the attribute characteristics, their default characteristics, or their description. A *Policy* function (DWKCETP, DWKCEIP, or DWKCEDP) is used to add, update, or delete entity type trigger, integrity, or derivation policies, respectively, as well as their descriptions.

When using DWKCED to *add* a new entity type, all input parameters that do not have a default value must be provided. The owning relationship parameters OWNING RELATIONSHIP TYPE NAME, OWNING RELATIONSHIP TYPE INVERSE NAME, SOURCE NAME, and SOURCE TYPE are not required unless the entity type is dependent. Other owning relationship parameters are optional if the entity type is dependent.

When using DWKCED to *update* an existing entity type, the identity of the key attribute cannot be changed if any instances of the entity types exist. All input parameters that do not have a default value must be provided, even if they have not changed. The owning relationship parameters OWNING RELATIONSHIP TYPE NAME, OWNING RELATIONSHIP TYPE INVERSE NAME, SOURCE NAME, and SOURCE TYPE are not required unless the entity type is dependent. Other owning relationship parameters are optional if the entity type is dependent. The status of an entity type cannot be changed from dependent to non-dependent if any instances of the entity type exist, or if the entity type is used in a function.

Using DWKCED to *delete* an existing entity type will also delete its associated entity attributes and policy definitions. If the entity type has relationships, the relationship type definitions will also be deleted.

This function, as a Repository Manager/MVS API function, has an additional semantic consequence. If the entity type is mapped to the private storage view, then all instances of the entity are also deleted. If the entity type is mapped to a database, the instances of the entity that are in the database are unaffected. These instances can be deleted by the use of database utilities.

DWKCED can be used to *query* an existing entity type. If the name of a tool group is not specified, the function will find a tool group containing the specified entity type and return it in the proper field. The entity definition is returned in the other parameter template fields.

When DWKCED is used to *bind* the specified entity type definition, an execution time Repository Manager control block is generated from the current definition.

8.2.1.2   *Define Entity Attribute* (DWKCEAC)

This function is used to maintain the attributes of an entity type one at a time. It can be used to:

- Add an attribute to an existing entity type.

- Update an attribute of an existing entity type.

- Delete an attribute of an existing entity type. If instances of the entity type exist, the key attribute cannot be deleted.

8.2.1.3   *Define Relationship Type* (DWKCRD)

This function is used to add, update, delete, query, or bind a relationship definition.

When the function (DWKCRD) is used to *add* a relationship type, all input parameters that do not have defaults must be specified. The source and target of the relationship type, each one of which can be either an entity type or a relationship type, must have been previously defined before being used in a relationship type definition.

When the function (DWKCRD) is used to *update* a relationship type, all input parameters that do not have defaults must be specified.

When the function (DWKCRD) is used to *delete* a relationship type, either the primary or inverse relationship type name must be provided. A relationship type cannot be deleted if it is the source or target of a relationship in the conceptual view or is used by a function. A relationship type that is owning can only be deleted by deleting the dependent entity type.

8.2.1.4   *Create Entity Type Trigger Policies* (DWKCETP)

This function is used to add, update, delete, and query trigger policies for a specified entity type.

The ADD command option causes a new trigger policy for an entity type to be added to the repository. The position at which it is entered is after a position specified by an integer in the invocation of the function. If the integer specified is greater than the number of policies existing for the entity type, it is added after all existing policies.

The UPDATE command option is used to modify an existing trigger policy. All parameters that contain a value must be specified, even if they are not changed.

The DELETE command option causes an existing trigger policy to be deleted. The policy is specified by its position in the set of policies.

In each of the above cases the entity type must be rebound to make the changes effective.

The QUERY command option returns a specified trigger policy. The number of policies can be queried using the *Query Policies* function DWKCLPQ (See 8.2.2.1).

The invocation point of the policy must be specified. Allowed values are *Entity Write* and *Entity Read*.

8.2.1.5   *Create Entity Type Integrity Policies* (DWKCEIP)

and

8.2.1.6   *Create Entity Type Derivation Policies* (DWKCEDP)

These functions follow the pattern set by *Create Entity Type Trigger Policies* (DWKCETP) (See 8.2.1.4), except that they deal with integrity or derivation policies.

8.2.1.7   *Query an Entity Type Definition* (DWKCEQ)

This function is used to return the definition of an entity type and its attributes. The name of the entity type must be specified, and a list containing the following is returned:

- The short description of the entity type.

- The name of the key attribute and whether it is system-assigned or user-assigned.

- Whether or not the entity type is dependent and, if so, the name of its owning relationship type.

- Whether or not an instance of the entity type must be locked before Repository Manager allows a user to update or delete the instance.

- The number of trigger policies defined for the entity type.

- A string containing a list of attributes, their short descriptions, default characteristics, and number of integrity and derivation policies defined for each.

This attribute list contains 25 attributes. If the entity type has more than 25 attributes, the name of the next attribute is returned in the NEXTATT parameter. A subsequent request to the DWKCEQ returns the next (up to) 25 attributes, starting with the attribute specified in NEXTATT. The attributes are returned in collating sequence by name.

Other built-in functions are described below.

8.2.1.8 *Define Collection* (DWKCCOL)

This function is used to add, update, query, and delete instances of collections.

When the ADD, UPDATE, or QUERY option in the function is used, there is a significant field in the definition of the collection called *Based-on Collection*. The meaning of this field is that there can be a base collection, which may contain members of a product, an application, or a tool. The collection instance being addressed in the function may contain members related to the base collection. No inheritance from the base collection is maintained. A collection cannot be based on itself; thus, in any series of collection instances related by based-on relationship instances, no collection instance can be repeated and the series cannot form a loop.

Retrieval of a based-on collection name is case-sensitive.

8.2.1.9 *Query Policies* (DWKCLPQ)

This function enables a Repository Manager application to query Repository Manager about policies defined on entity types, relationship types, functions, templates, and template fields. The function returns the number of trigger, integrity, or derivation policies defined on a specific conceptual view or logical view construct at each invocation point in its parameter template.

Options exist to query each of the following:

- *Trigger Policies* on
  - Entity Types
  - Relationship Types
  - Templates
  - Functions

- *Integrity Policies* on
  - Entity Attributes
  - Relationship Types
  - Template Fields

- *Derivation Policies* on
  - Entity Attributes
  - Templates

After determining the number of policies of a given type, a Repository Manager application can query the details of a specified policy or update that policy using the appropriate policy definition function.

The possible invocation points of each policy are prescribed. For example, integrity policies can be invoked at Entity Write for entity types, Relationship Write for relationship types, and Function Initiation and Display Read for functions.

8.2.1.10   *Maintain Object Edition Instances* (DKWCOE)

This function is used to add, update, delete, and query instances of object editions.

An instance of an object edition is dependent on the collection, object type, and object part specified at the time it is created. Hence, an object edition has a four-part name, (collection, object type, object part, and object edition), which must be specified for each action of this function.

In a manner parallel to the function DWKCCOL, *Define Collection* (See 8.2.1.8), a *based-on object instance* is an object instance on which a specified object instance can be based, and the relationship between the two object instances is maintained in the repository. The base object instance may be a member, application, or tool of the same or different collection. If this optional facility is used, the base instance must be specified by its four-part name.

Optional fields referring to a "Host" and a "Workstation" can be specified. However, these are maintained not by Repository Manager but by tools. They are provided for tools to use as appropriate.

The ADD action code locks and adds an object edition, which instantiates a new object instance.

The UPDATE action code locks an existing object and updates its control information — i.e., the attributes of the corresponding GLO_OBJECT_EDITION instance without changing the four-part name. Current information, even if it is not changing, must be supplied.

The DELETE action code locks the object edition and deletes it from the repository. Any ER instances that are dependent on this object edition are also deleted. The individual collection, object type, and object part are not affected by the command.

The QUERY action code causes the specified object instance to be returned. Additionally, in Repository Manager/MVS, a COMMIT and ROLLBACK can be specified, and the authorization of the user to execute the command is checked.

8.2.1.11   *Define Object Part* (DWKCOP)

This function is used to add, update, delete, and query object part instances.

The ADD command option will add a new object part instance to the repository. All mandatory input parameters that do not default values must be provided.

The UPDATE command option is used to lock and update an existing object part instance. All required parameters must be supplied, even if they are not changing.

The DELETE command option is used to lock an object part and to delete it from the repository. An object part that has any object instances associated with it cannot be deleted.

The QUERY command option returns the definition of the specified object part.

8.2.1.12   *Define an Object Type* (DWKCOT)

This function is used to add, update, query, delete, bind, and bindall an object type definition.

In addition to the object type name, short description, and long description, the definition of an object type contains:

- A super object type, that provides inheritance of method – method implementation pairs.

- Method implementations that map to the methods specified for the object type.

- An aggregation type that provides the ability to lock/unlock all of the ER components of an object instance as a single unit rooted in the edition/level entity.

- A set of methods designated for managing instances of the object type.

The ADD command option of the function is used to add an object type definition to the repository. If the object type already exists, the function will add the existing object type to the current or specified tool group. If the specified tool group does not exist, it will be added.

The UPDATE command option of the function can be used to change the short description, super object type, or aggregation. However, the aggregation cannot be changed if the object type is associated with any object edition instances. All template definition fields must be provided, even if they are not changed by the update.

The DELETE command option of the function is used to delete the named object type from the current or specified tool group. If the object type exists in only one tool group, it will be deleted from the repository. An object type can only be deleted if there are no instances defined for it, and if it is not the super object type of any object type. The DELETE option will delete the repository definition of the object type; the bound form of the object type is not affected.

The QUERY option produces the definition of the object type. If the tool group has been specified, the definition of the object type is returned only if the object type is a member of the specified tool group. If the tool group is not specified, then the name of the tool group of which the object type is a member will be returned.

The BIND option uses the added or updated definition of the object type and creates a file that Repository Manager uses to access instances of the object type, lock object instances, and route methods invoked to manipulate instances. The *bound* form of the definition includes the method – method implementation pairs of the definition, as well as the method – method implementation pairs inherited from the object type's super object type.

The BINDALL option binds the object type, and all affected object types in the super object type hierarchy of this object type, into their useable forms. The importance of this option is that it proliferates the changes made to methods of the super object type through its hierarchy.

The AGGREGATION parameter (which is optional for the ADD and UPDATE command options) when present will include in the aggregation all of the ER components that make up comprise the definition of object data, and it has the GLO_OBJECT_EDITION as its root entity. The aggregation is used for locking/unlocking and exporting/importing instances.

8.2.1.13   *Define Methods in an Object Type* (DWKCOTM)

This function is used to add, update, delete, and query the method – method implementation pairs for a given object type. A method added to an object type can either be in addition to or refinement of a method – method implementation pair inherited from a super object type.

The ADD command option will add a new method – method implementation pair to the specified object type. For a given object type, a method may map to exactly one method implementation. All mandatory input parameters that do not default values must be provided.

The UPDATE command option is used to update an existing method implementation for a method in the object type.

The DELETE command option is used to delete a method – method implementation pair from the specified object type.

The QUERY command option returns the method implementation for the specified method.

A significant parameter in the parameter template for this function is the field *Method Implementation*. Two special functions are available that can be specified as the method implementation for any method: *Method Implementation No-op* (DWKNOOP) and *Method Implementation Required* (DWKMIRQ).

DWKNOOP is used in the development of an object hierarchy when it is desired that a method implementation not be inherited from the super object type. DWKMIRQ is used when it is not intended to create instances of the super object type, but it is required that all affected object types in the hierarchy are to be provided a method implementation for a certain method.

8.2.1.14 Create Relationship Type Trigger Policies (DWKCRTP)

This function is used to add, update, delete, and query trigger policies for a specified relationship type. The specification of this function is identical to the function *Create Entity Type Trigger Policies* (DWKCETP) (See 8.2.1.4), except that it deals with relationship types in place of entity types.

8.2.1.15 Create Relationship Type Integrity Policies (DWKCRIP)

This function again follows the pattern set by *Create Entity Type Trigger Policies* (DWKCETP), (See 8.2.1.4), except that it deals with integrity policies.

8.2.1.16 Return Information About a Dependent Entity (DWKUDEP)

This function is used to determine whether a given entity is dependent and, if so, the name of its owning relationship type, the number of qualifying parent entity types, and the names of its parent entity types.

8.2.2 Logical View Functions

The logical view built-in functions described below deal primarily with the maintenance of logical views, including the policies associated with these views.

8.2.2.1 Bind a Function (DWKLBND)

This function is used to bind a specified function definition. In Repository Manager/MVS, it reads the specified definition from the repository and produces the bound form of the function in a file that is read when a tool function is executed It must be moved to a disk to be made available to all users of the function.

8.2.2.2 *Create Function Type Trigger Policies* (DWKLFTP)

This function is used to add, update, delete, and query trigger policies for a specified function. The description of this function is, again, identical to the function *Create Entity Type Trigger Policies* (DWKCETP) (See 8.2.1.4), except that it deals with functions in place of entity types.

8.2.2.3 *Invoke Screen Definition Facility II Panel Creation* (DWKLPNC)

This function is used to invoke Screen Definition Facility II (SDF II) in order to create a panel for a repository function. The fields in the root template, as well as the fields in the subordinate trees in the tree structure are passed to the function. Each panel field is mapped to the corresponding template field. The panel field is preceded on the panel by a constant containing either of the following:

- The abbreviated name of the entity type attribute to which the field maps

- The template field name, if the field does not map to an entity type attribute

The SDF II object library name in which the panel is to be stored must be provided.

8.2.2.4 *Create Template Derivation Policies* (DWKLTDP)

This function again follows the pattern set by *Create Entity Type Trigger Policies* (DWKCETP) (See 8.2.1.4), except that it deals with integrity policies.

8.2.2.5 *Define Template/Field* (DWKLTFC)

This function is used to add, update, delete, or query a template or template field belonging to a function. A template may also be rebuilt by adding to it all the fields needed for that template in order to map to all the attributes of that template's entity type.

When using the ADD command option, the following actions can take place:

- A new template field can be added to a specified template of a function. If the specified template does not exist, it is also added.

- If no field is specified, only the template is added to the function.

When adding a field corresponding to an entity type attribute to a template, any user-supplied data specifications (i.e., Data Type, Data Length, Scale, and Format) take precedence in the definition of the field. If these are not supplied, the data specifications of the corresponding attribute are used. If neither of these cases apply, a one-character field of varying format is created.

Template trigger policies are not created with the DWKLTFC function but, rather, with trigger policy functions. For functions of type *method*, the only valid template is the function parameter template, which may not be mapped to an entity type.

The ADDATTR command option rebuilds a template that maps to an entity type in such a manner that the template will contain fields that map to all the attributes of an entity type, in addition to other fields that existed in the template, prior to the option being invoked, that do not map to the entity type's attributes. This command option eliminates the need to deal with an entity type's attributes one by one.

The UPDATE option allows a template and template field to be updated with information entered. If no template field information is entered, only the template is updated.

Using the DWKLTFC function, only the following *template items* can be updated:

- The short description.

- The entity type mapping to the template, if the template has no fields and does not already map to an entity type.

- The array extent, if the template is the primary template in the array.

- The selection field, which can also be added if the template currently does not have a selection field. In order to insert a selection expression, the field must exist. To delete an existing selection field specification, the parameter can be set to "*"; the field itself will not be removed.

The following *template field items* can be updated:

- The short description of a template field, which can also be added if it does not exist.

- The entity type attribute to which the field maps, but only if the field is not shared by the template in another function. The attribute must exist in the entity type that maps to the template.

- Data specifications (i.e., Data Type, Data Length, Scale, and Format), but only if the field is not shared by the template in another function.

Some specifications for template and template field items are ignored if the function is of type *method*.

When using the DELETE command option, a specified template field is deleted. If no template field is specified, the template is deleted from the function. If a field maps to a an attribute for the template, it cannot be deleted. However, if more than one template field maps to the key attribute, deletion of those fields, except the last remaining key field, is allowed.

The QUERY command option returns the template or field definition in definition form.

8.2.2.6   *Query Template Use in a Function*   (DWKLTFQ)

This function is used to query a template and obtain its description. Specifically, execution of the function will provide the following information:

- The name of the entity type, if there is one, which maps to the template.

- The name of the template's *parent* template, if one exists.

- If the template is arrayed, the array extent of the template.

- The name of the field that is the selection field.

- The short description of the template and of the function.

- A string containing a list of template fields and their characteristics, such as the name of the attribute mapped to the field (if there is one), the name of the entity type containing this attribute, the data type, length, scale, etc.

  This list will contain information of up to 25 template fields. If the template contains more than 25 fields, the name of the next field will be returned in the NEXTFLD field, and a subsequent call to DWKLTFQ will produce the next (up to) 25 fields. The fields are produced in collating sequence by name of the field.

8.2.2.7   *Create Template Field Integrity Policies* (DWKLTIP)

This function again follows the pattern set by *Create Template Field Derivation Policies* (DWKLTDP) (See 8.2.2.5), except that it deals with integrity policies.

8.2.2.8   *Create Template Trigger Policies* (DWKLTTP)

This function operates in a similar manner to *Create Entity Type Trigger Policies* (DWKCETP) (See 8.2.1.4), except that it deals with template trigger policies.

8.2.2.9   *Query Template Trees in a Function* (DWKLTTQ)

This function is used to return information about the contents and structure of template trees in a Repository Manager function. Selective use of this function allows the contents and structure of even complex function templates to be established.

The following options exist:

- *All Templates*. The names of all templates are returned. The templates are presented in tree order, left to right. All children are presented before any siblings. Root templates are returned in collating sequence by name of the template. Templates within trees are associated with a *level number* specifying their level below the root template. Thus, a root template has a level number of 1, immediate children of a root template have a level number of 2, etc.

- *All Root Templates*. This option causes all templates that do not have parents to be returned.

- *Single Template Tree*. This option returns all the templates in a specified template tree or subtree.

- *Immediate Children*. This option returns all the templates that are immediate subordinates of a specified template. The level number is not provided.

- *Parent*. This option causes the name of the template immediately superior to the specified template to be returned.

For the options where multiple templates are returned, a single call will return up to a maximum number of 25; additional templates can be returned by one or more subsequent calls to DWKLTTQ.

8.2.2.10 *Define Function* (DWKLVT1)

This function is used to add, update, delete, query, and bind a function. When using the ADD command option, the global specification, such as name, description, initiation and termination synchronization points, resource sharing, and type of function invocation are specified. Optionally, the function can be bound to make it executable.

The function accepts as input one or more "data trees" that are used to describe the template trees that will be produced for the function. A data tree is represented by one of the following:

- A conceptual view entity type

- A conceptual view entity type followed by one or more conceptual view relationship types

- A conceptual view aggregation type

DWKLVT1 processes the input and builds logical view template trees for the function based on the conceptual view specification in the data trees.

Types of functions that can be added are:

1. *Integrated.* This function is invoked by a Repository Manager CALL action. This type of function is also referred to as *fully integrated.*

2. *Open/Close.* This function is not fully integrated; it can be called by a program that uses the OPEN/CLOSE interface to Repository Manager. It may not be invoked by a Repository Manager CALL action.

3. *Method.* A method is invoked by a Repository Manager CALL action in the same manner as an integrated function. It is used to manage repository objects through a method implementation identified in the object type. When a function of this type is defined, the function's parameter template is created with four fields which make up an object instance four-part name: *collection, object type, object part,* and *object edition.*

4. *Method Implementation.* This type of function is invoked by a Repository Manager CALL to a method. Repository Manager will determine which method implementation to call based on the object's type field specified in the method's parameter template. When a function of this type is defined, the function's parameter template is created with four fields, which make up an object instance four-part name: *collection, object type, object part,* and *object edition.*

The default is integrated.

If the function exists in another tool group, it will be added to the current or specified one. If the specified tool group does not exist, it will be added to the repository.

When using the UPDATE command option, the function must belong to the specified or current tool group. As the current information must be provided even if it does not change, it is desirable to issue a *query* call prior to the UPDATE call. Optionally, the function can be bound to make it executable.

Allowable changes in the type of the function are:

- From method to any other valid type. In this case, the function parameter template for the target function will be the method function parameter template.

- Changing from method implementation to any other valid type (other than method). In this case, the function parameter template for the target function will be the method implementation function parameter template.

- Changing from any valid type to method implementation The four template fields associated with a method implementation parameter will be added to the target function's parameter template.

Changing a function with a valid type to method is not allowed.

When using the QUERY command option, the function definition is returned in a form suitable for modification and subsequent submission for execution. If a tool group has been specified, the definition is returned only if the function is a member of the specified tool group. If a tool group was not specified, the name of the first tool group that contains the function is returned.

When using the DELETE command option, the function is deleted from the specified or current tool group, or from the repository if it is in only one tool group.

8.2.3   Security Functions

Repository Manager/MVS has one security built-in function which, is described below.

8.2.3.1   *Security Profile Binding* (DWKBSEC)

As discussed in Chapter 4, security profiles are files created with Repository Manager that define exactly what repository information a user or group of users can access. Each security profile contains identifiers of groups and individual items of repository definition data.

This function is used to bind security profiles to make them effective after having been defined.

8.2.4   Storage View Functions

The built-in functions of this type deal with the definition and administration of storage views. A brief discussion of storage views will be given prior to discussing these functions.

The *storage view* defines how the repository data is mapped to physical storage controlled by DB2 or MVS itself.

Entity and relationship types can be mapped to MVS physical storage in two ways:

- A mapping to a DB2 storage view
- A mapping into the private storage view

A DB2 storage view is a mapping of repository instance data to tables in the DB2 DBMS. Data contained in DB2 tables, can be shared; additionally, all DB2 facilities in areas such as backup and recovery, security, and optimization are available.

The private storage view, which consists of private MVS partitioned data sets, is generally used when only a small amount of data is required, which is not shared with other users. Such circumstances may arise when it is desired to prototype new applications or tools. By default, entity and relationship types are mapped by Repository Manager to the private storage view. The mapping does not have to be defined by the user unless it is desired to modify the mapping that takes place automatically, to build a DB2 storage view.

Multiple DB2 storage views can be defined. In this way repository data can be partitioned. These partitions can be set up based on the usage of the data or any other criteria.

A limitation is that a single entity type or relationship type can belong to only one storage view per repository user. This limitation creates a problem when it is desired to remap from an old storage view to a new one.

The mapping of entity types and relationship types to a DB2 storage view is strongly influenced by the fact that DB2 is a relational database management system. DB2 runs as one or more subsystems under the MVS operating system. The language used to operate on data in DB2 tables is Structured Query Language (SQL). SQL serves as both the Data Manipulation Language (DML) and the Data Definition Language (DDL).

The primary DB2 *objects* are:

- *Tables*. A table is a group of rows all having the same columns.

- *Indexes*. An index is an ordered set of pointers to the data in a table and is stored in an *index space* separate from the table. Indexes speed up the access to data; the trade-off to this performance improvement is the space occupied by the indexes and the processing required to maintain them.

- *Table Spaces*. A table space contains one or more tables. It can consist of up to 64 VSAM data sets, which can contain, together, up to 64 gigabytes of storage. In Release 1 of Repository Manager, *Simple* and *Segmented* Table Spaces are supported.

- *Storage Groups*. A storage group is used by DB2 to define and manage virtual storage access method (VSAM) data sets that contain the index and table spaces. It is a set of volumes of the same device type.

- *Databases*. A database is a group of tables and their associated indexes and table spaces. A single database might contain the data to support one or several related applications.

Repository entity types and relationship types are mapped to DB2 tables. The general rules for the mapping are:

- An entity type maps to a DB2 table. Each attribute maps to a column of the table. An instance of an entity type, — a set of values of the attributes, — maps to a row of the table. For a dependent entity, the table contains an additional column or columns for the key of the parent of the dependent entity type.

•   A relationship type that is not ordered, and that is not an owning relationship type, maps to a single DB2 table. Each row contains the keys of the entities that define the relationship instance.

If the relationship type connects two non-dependent entity types, the table contains two columns:

–   A column containing the keys of the source entity instances.
–   A column containing the keys of the target entity instances.

If either the source or target, or both, is another relationship type or a dependent entity type, additional columns exist. In each case, enough columns must exist to uniquely define the source or target of instances of the relationship type.

•   An ordered relationship type maps to two DB2 tables. One of these is like the table to which an unordered relationship is mapped, with two additional columns. These columns, as well as the entire second table, contain information required to maintain the order of the entity type instances of either the source or the target, whichever is ordered.

•   An owning relationship type is not mapped to a DB2 table.

8.2.4.1   *Bind Multiple Storage Views* (DWKS2MB)

This function is used to bind multiple storage views identified in a storage view map list in order to make them effective.

8.2.4.2   *Generate DDL for Multiple Tables* (DWKS2MD)

This function is used to generate DB2 Data Definition Language (DDL) for the tables that correspond to the entity types and relationship types named in the storage view map list.

8.2.4.3   *Map Storage View for Multiple Entity and Relationship Types* (DWKS2MM)

This function is used to define storage view mappings for large groups of constructs and to define default storage mappings. Table definitions for constructs named in a storage view map list can be generated, and the constructs can be mapped to table definitions.

8.2.5   Tool Group Functions

One function, which is a Repository Manager CPI function, exists for this type of built-in functions.

8.2.5.1   *Query Members of a Tool Group* (DWKTGQ)

This function is used to:

- Retrieve the names of a defined tool group, or the names of the entity types, relationship types, aggregation types, object types, or functions that are members of the specified tool group.

- Retrieve the names of the tool groups of which a specified entity type, relationship type, aggregation type, object type, or function is a member.

DWKTGQ is called by tool functions and returns the requested information in the fields of its parameter template. The caller supplies the name of the tool group or the name of the member, and the function returns a string that contains a list of up to 25 names. If there are more than 25 names to be returned, the name of the next member is returned in the NEXT_MEM field. A subsequent call will return the next (up to) 25 names starting with the name in the NEXT_MEM field.

The following options exist:

- If the caller does not specify a tool group, the function will return the members of the current tool group and supply the name of the current tool group. The call can also optionally specify an operator and character string to selectively return member names that satisfy this selection criterion.

- A caller can provide the name of a member and its type, and the function will return a list of the tool groups to which the member belongs. If more than 25 names exist, the procedure described above is followed.

In all cases, the list is returned in key sequence, i.e., the tool group name, entity name, etc., depending on the request.

An optional field in the parameter template is used to specify the *selection expression* to be used. The form of this expression is as specified in the discussion on keyed retrievals in Chapter 7.

8.2.6   Utility Functions

Repository Manager provides built-in functions that are utility services a repository function can call. Among these are functions that are used to call other functions, perform lock, unlock, or query lock status of aggregation instances, and deal with text annotation. These functions will now be described.

8.2.6.1   *Call a Tool Program* (DWKPGM)

This is a general utility function that is used to call a tool program that uses a non-fully integrated function. This function may be invoked from a tool program, from the command line of any Repository Manager panel, or by specifying its name on the IRM EXEC. Its parameter template is used to pass information to and from the called tool program; in it, the program name and program type for the program that are to be called are specified. An argument string containing arguments expected by the tool program can also be specified.

This function uses a non-fully integrated function's logical data view and panels, and establishes addressability.

8.2.6.2   *Text Annotation Function* (DWKTEDT)

This function is used to maintain text stored in the repository. Lines of text stored in the repository will be retrieved and placed in a utility file, where a PDF edit session will begin. After changes are completed, the text records will be returned to the repository.

The GET_TEXT command option is used to obtain a copy of annotation text from the repository to be placed in a file.

The PUT_TEXT command option is used to perform the inverse action: placing annotation text into the repository. This option is useful for placing text existing outside the repository into the repository.

The EDIT command option is used to get a copy of the annotation text from the repository, entering edit. At the conclusion of the edit the text is placed back into the repository.

Three Repository Manager-supplied entity types (See Chapter 6) are used to store the text:

• A GLO_TEXT_GROUP entity type instance contains the system-generated key with no other attributes. It serves as an anchor point from all types of related text.

• A GLO_TEXT_TYPE entity type instance, which contains a key attribute value, is used to designate the type of text that is being annotated.

• A GLO_TEXT_LINE entity type instance is used to store an attribute containing the line number key attribute, and another attribute contains the line of text associated with the line number.

Information is passed to and from this function through a parameter template. To provide the text editor capability, it is necessary to specify the text type and action to be performed, such as get text from, put text to, or edit a text file in the repository. It is also necessary to identify the file name, type, and mode for the text file.

8.2.6.3   *Edit a Template Field* (DWKUEDT)

This function is used to invoke the ISPF/PDF preferred editor on a text string. The text string to be edited is received in this function's parameter template, and a temporary file is created. The temporary file is filled with input data and the PDF edit service is invoked.

It is necessary to specify the text format (string or text), maximum length, and actual text string to be edited.

8.2.6.4   *Import Aggregation Instance* (DWKUIAO)

This function imports aggregation instances into the repository. The following process is repeated until all instances in an import file are processed:

1. Determining the aggregation type being imported by reading the export file.

2. Checking the extended definition of the aggregation type. If the definition shows that a repository function is to be called before import and preprocessing is requested, that function is called. If the function call is successful, the function imports an instance from the named import file. If no function is specified, an instance from the named import file is imported. If the aggregation type was not defined on the import system, an instance is imported from the named import file, but no pre- or postprocessing is possible.

3. Checking the extended definition of the aggregation type again. If the definition shows that a repository function is to be called after import and postprocessing is requested, that function is called.

To use this function, among others, the name of the import file, the command to be executed against it, and whether preprocessing is to take place must be specified.

8.2.6.5   *Lock and Unlock Aggregation Instance* (DWKULCK*)

This function is used to:

*   Lock an aggregation instance for the current or specified user ID.

*   Release an aggregation instance lock held by the current or specified user ID.

*   Obtain the lock status of an aggregation instance.

The function also provides the capability to grant or release locks held by another user. This capability must be provided by a repository administrator.

In order for the locking/unlocking to take place, values for the appropriate parameter template fields must first be specified. Some of the required fields are the aggregation type name and the root entity instance key(s).

The LOCK command option is used to request that Repository Manager grant the current or specified user ID a lock (i.e., to increment the lock count) of the lock type specified on the specified aggregation instance. Lock types that can be specified are:

- *NoUpdate*, which prevents another user from obtaining a lock of any other type on the aggregation instance.

- *Update*, which means that the lock holder has an exclusive right to update the aggregation instance.

- *Add*, which means that the lock holder has exclusive right to add or update the aggregation instance.

- *Delete*, which means that the lock holder has exclusive right to delete, add, or update the aggregation instance.

The UNLOCK command option is used to request that Repository Manager release a lock (i.e., to decrement the lock count) held by the current or specified user ID of the lock type specified on the specified aggregation instance.

The CLEAR command option is used to request that Repository Manager release all locks of all types held by the current or specified user ID on the specified aggregation instance.

The QUERY command option is used to return the user IDs of any person(s) holding a lock on the specified aggregation instance. Different types of locks are reported separately.

Repository Manager/MVS has the additional facility of optionally performing a COMMIT action on completion of granting or releasing a lock. This action causes Repository Manager/MVS to store all pending data, including the locks, in the correct files and databases. Other users are not affected until the COMMIT action has been completed. This option is useful when it is desired to lock or unlock several aggregation instances sequentially to ensure that either all or none of the lock or unlock actions are completed.

8.2.6.6   *Batch Repository Maintenance* (DWKULD)

This function is used to process Batch Command Language statements contained in a specified file. These commands can be used to add or delete entity type, relationship type, or conceptual view policy definitions, as well as add, update, or delete entity type and relationship type instances. The Batch Command Language is discussed in some detail in Chapter 10.

8.2.6.7   *Maintain System Messages Table* (DWKUTM)

This function is used to process a sequential input file of messages and to *add*, *delete*, *replace*, or *update* the message definitions in the system messages table, which contains the set of message definitions stored in the repository. The function can also be used to *display* these messages.

The IRM EXEC is used to start this function. The action codes supplied indicate the following options:

- Add the message if it does not already exist. If this option is chosen and the message already exists, an error results.

- Delete the message if it exists. If this option is chosen and the message does not exist, an error results.

- Replace the message if it exists, or add it if it does not exist.

- Update the message if it exists. If this option is chosen and the message does not exist, an error results.

8.2.6.8   *Export Aggregation Instance* (DWKUXAO)

This function is used to export aggregation instances. The following actions are performed:

- Verify that the requested aggregation type exists.

- Write control information to the export file.

- Determine which aggregation instances are to be exported.

All information is passed to and from DWKUXAO via its parameter template. Mandatory fields in the template are: the command that the service is to perform; the aggregation type name whose instances are to be exported; the type of data to export (definitions or instances); etc. Some of the optional fields used to specify are whether to display a panel, the name of the export file to be created, and whether to bypass processing and simply perform a trial run for verification.

Two output files are created by this function. The first one, the *export file*, contains the actual exported data. The second file, the *log file*, contains the instance keys or definition names that are processed by the function. This latter file is also used by the function DWKIAO, *Import Aggregation Instance*. (See 8.2.6.4).

8.2.7   Utility Functions for Querying Repository Data

The following four *utility* built-in functions are used to query repository data:

- Build Aggregation Tree (DWKULST) (See 8.2.7.1)
- Build Template Tree (DWKUTRE) (See 8.2.7.2)
- Retrieve Template Definition (DWKUTDF) (See 8.2.7.3)
- Retrieve Aggregation Instance (DWKUFLT) (See 8.2.7.4)

Specifically, the following capabilities are provided:

- It can be verified that an aggregation type exists (using DWKULST).

- A template tree can be built dynamically from an aggregation type definition (using DWKULST).

- A template tree or subtree can be built dynamically from a list supplied by a calling tool program or function (using DWKUTRE).

- A template definition can be retrieved from the bound form of a repository function (using DWKUTDF).

- A template key field value can be updated (using DWKUTDF).

- A template selection expression can be updated (using DWKUTDF).

- An aggregation instance can be retrieved into a retrieval table (using DWKUFLT).

8.2.7.1   *Build Aggregation Tree* (DWKULST)

This function is used for the following:

- Verify the existence of an aggregation type.

- Build a template tree from the definition of an existing aggregation type.

The aggregation type name is specified to the function, along with a parameter specifying whether it is desired only to verify the existence of the aggregation type or the template tree is to be built.

8.2.7.2   *Build Template Tree* (DWKUTRE)

This function is used for the following:

- Build a template tree dynamically.

- Remove a template tree.

- Add a subtree to an existing template tree.

A parameter passed to the function specifies whether a template tree is to be built, a template tree is to be removed, or the "one call" option is to be used. In this option, a layout is passed to the function; in this layout, which is an array, each element of the array represents one template in the template tree to be built. In each case the required identification definition, such as, template number, parent number, and template name, is also passed to the function.

8.2.7.3   *Retrieve Template Definition* (DWKUTDF)

This function is used for the following purposes:

- Retrieve the definition of a template in a function

- Set template key field values and selection expressions

- Calculate the minimum size of the retrieval table for the function

- List one or more of the following:
    - All templates in a function
    - All root templates in a function
    - All templates in a specified template tree
    - All templates in a specified subtree
    - Template-level information on one template in a function

A parameter is used to indicate to the function which option is being exercised.

8.2.7.4   *Retrieve Aggregation Instance* (DWKUFLT)

This function is used to retrieve one or more aggregation instances of the same aggregation type. The information is retrieved into a retrieval table, as opposed to being retrieved into a template tree.

8.2.8   ER Model Maintenance Functions

ER Model Maintenance built-in functions are provided by Repository Manager/MVS and can be used, when necessary, to perform maintenance of the Repository Manager Supplied Entity-Relationship Model. These functions allow program temporary fixes (PTFs) to be installed against that model.

8.2.8.1   *Maintain PTF Log Entries*   (DWKZMLG)

This function is used for the following:

- Verify a maintenance-level prerequisite that is associated with a product update.

- Record the application of the current product update, which can be used as a service record for future reference.

- Add maintenance log entries while installing a PTF to record the progress of the manual steps involved in the update process.

- Add, update, or delete PTF entries manually using commands. In the normal case, the installation procedure will add the PTF.

8.2.8.2   *Place Construct in PTF Status*   (DWKZMPR)

This function allows the identification of an entity type, relationship type, or aggregation type that may require user intervention during PTF installation.

The entity type, relationship type, or aggregation type is placed in a "hold" status, which means that it is assured that advance notice will be given in the event that the specified construct will be affected by a maintenance update. A command code option can be given to indicate when a PTF hold is to be added, deleted, or queried. When a PTF hold is added, it is required that a reason for the PTF hold be given. This information is returned when the command code for query is given.

Optionally, a COMMIT action on successful completion can be specified.

Built-in functions for Data Services and System Services have been discussed in Chapter 7.

9 PANELS AND DIALOGS

Repository Manager provides a full set of services via an interactive panel interface. One way to create, query, and modify repository definitions and data is through Repository Manager *dialogs*. Dialogs consist of sets of panels on which new data can be entered, existing data can be viewed or modified, and Repository Manager commands can be entered.

9.1 TYPES OF PANELS

There exist different *types of panels*, as follows:

- *Menu panels* — presenting two or more options from which a user selects a single choice.

- *Definition panels* — presenting data entry fields into which the user types data.

- *List panels* — presenting a list of items upon which a user may initiate an action. Different types of list panels are discussed in 9.1.3.

As might be expected, not all Repository Manager panels conform to just one of the types described above. There are panels that display selection options and have data entry fields, and there are panels that have both data entry fields and present a list of items for which actions can be specified. Some predominantly list-type panels have data entry fields within each entry of the displayed list.

Online help is also available on panels. This is a convenient way to get help information at a terminal. Online help presents both a panel overview and a menu from which the required information can be selected. It is specific to a particular panel and explains the following:

- Fields on the panel
- Actions that can be taken on the panel
- Commands that can be entered on the panel

Online help can also be printed.

Repository Manager is *not* case sensitive to action codes, commands, and most names (e.g., names of entity types) that are entered on a panel. On the other hand, Repository Manager *is* case sensitive to the input for fields that contain descriptions, REXX functions, or repository instance values.

9.1.1   Menu Panels

Menu panels present a fixed selection list of enumerated options, generally to perform some task or to move to a more detailed level of service selection within a task category. The choice of a selection may result in some service being attempted at the current panel level or the presentation of a lower-level panel within the current panel tree. The lower level panel may, in turn, require another selection, data entry, or one or more actions on entries within a list.

9.1.2   Definition Panels

Definition panels present one or more data fields into which the user may place data. Generally, these panels are used to specify values required for maintenance or retrieval actions (e.g., initially add or update attributes of an entity or give the name or key of something to be deleted).

9.1.3   List Panels

List panels present lists of repository data items. There are list panels of tool groups, entity types, relationship types, etc.

Action codes on list panels are provided for selecting the processing that is to be performed on an item. List panels that use action codes can function like a secondary menu set in Repository Manager; they allow positioning on the right panel to perform a task. Each list panel that recognizes action codes displays the list of action codes that are valid for the panel. Action codes exist that allow new items to be added to a list, and existing items to be updated or deleted.

List panels that contain more than one panel's worth of data contain a *scrollable area*, within which there is a set of like entries (e.g., attributes types of an entity type.) Frequently, a list panel will accept action codes upon entries in the list (to insert or add a new entry in a list of authorized users, to delete an attribute type from an entity type, etc.).

Most list panels display the total number of items on the list, as well as the number of the first item displayed on the panel, in the upper-right corner of the panel. There is an upper number of items that a specific list panel can track.

Repository Manager list panels fall into the following categories:

- *Action code selection list panels*, which consist of the following three columns:

  - An action column
  - The name of the data item
  - A brief description of the data item

  These list panels allow for adding, updating, and deleting data items, as well as editing descriptions. A desired action is designated by entering a valid action code in the action column next to a name. If necessary, Repository Manager will display another panel on which the specified task can be performed. Each action code selection list panel displays what action codes are valid for that panel.

- *Data entry list panels*, which consist of columns of input fields on which information can be entered.

- *Mixed action code selection/data entry list panels*, which provide the capability to enter data items and specify processing against them.

9.1.4 Commands Issued on Panels

All Repository Managers provide the capability to issue commands on them. Some commands are applicable to specific panels, and others are applicable to all panels. The following list describes all the commands that can be issued on panels; those that are applicable to all panels are marked with an asterisk.

Command	Explanation
ADD	Adds a definition or instance to the repository. For instance data, the command fails if the definition or instance already exists.
BOTTOM	Displays the last full panel of list entries. This command is equivalent to DOWN MAX.
CALL <function>*	Invokes the specified Repository Manager functions. Parameters can be passed to the function.
CALLPGM <program>*	Invokes the specified program using the ISF SELECT PGM service. Parameters can be passed to the program.
CURSOR*	Moves the cursor position to the command line on the panel.
DELETE	Deletes the currently shown definition or instance from the repository.
DOWN	Displays the next panel of data. This command is only applicable to list panels that display a list of data items.
EDIT	Invokes an editor to add, update, or delete a long description of a policy definition.
END*	Processes any action codes or updates the current panel and returns to the invoking panel. EXIT is a valid alias.

Command	Explanation
EMPHASIS*	Displays the panel DWKUECD1, which allows the attributes for the emphasis classes to be changed for the terminal being used.
FIND <item-name>	Redisplays the list with the specified entry as the topmost entry.
FIRST	Displays the first definition within a tool group, or the first instance based on the contents of the first key field on the panel. If the first key field is blank or null, the first instance within the domain is displayed.
HELP*	Invokes Repository Manager help panels.
HELPMSG msgid*	Displays the help text for the specified message ID.
KEYS*	Displays the PF key definitions and Labels panels, on which command-to-PF key mappings can be changed.
LAST	Displays the last definition within a Tool Group, or the last instance based on the contents of the last key field on the panel. If the first key field is blank or null, the last item in the domain is displayed.
LOCATE nnn	Redisplays the list with the entry whose number corresponds to the argument (nnn) as the topmost entry. Deleted entries are deleted before the panel is displayed.
NEXT	Displays the definition or instance following the one currently being displayed.
PDF <command>*	Invokes ISPF/PDF to process the specified command.
PFSHOW <on|off>*	Displays (or suppresses display of) the current PF key settings at the bottom of each panel.
PREVIOUS	Displays the definition or instance prior to the one currently displayed.

Command	Explanation
QUIT*	Leaves the current panel and returns to the invoking panel. CANCEL is a valid alias.
RESTORE	Discards all data entered or changed since the previous COMMIT action. This command is valid only on a limited number of panels.
RETURN*	Returns to the Repository Manager Main Menu. Other rules for the effect of this command exist.
SAVE	Saves all pending data to the database. This command is valid only on a limited number of panels.
SERV*	Displays the panel DWKUSRV1, which provides the system services for tracing and timing, editing files, or changing the currently active security profile. This command is most often used for error processing in a diagnostic trace file.
TOP	Displays the first full panel of list entries. The command is equivalent to UP MAX.
TSO <command>*	Invokes TSO to process the specified command.
UP	Displays the previous panel of data. The command is only applicable to panels that display a list of data items.
UPDATE	Updates definitions or instances in the repository.

As can be seen from some of the above commands, valid commands can be mapped to PF keys. Pressing a PF key that is mapped to a command is equivalent to entering the command explicitly from the Command or Selection line and pressing ENTER.

9.2   PANELS FOR INTERACTIVE BUILT-IN FUNCTIONS

The discussion in Chapter 8 pointed out that certain built-in functions could be used in the interactive mode. The following list shows these functions and the panel identifiers that correspond to them. These panels will be discussed further later in this chapter.

Name	Panel ID	Description
DWKCCOL	DWKCCOL1	Maintain collection instances
DWKCED	DWKCED1	Define an entity type
DWKCEDP	DWKCEDP1 or DWKCEDP2	Create entity type derivation policies
DWKCEIP	DWKCEIP1	Create entity type integrity policies
DWKCETP	DWKCETP1 or DWKCETP2	Create entity type trigger policies
DWKCOE	DWKCOE1	Maintain object edition instances
DWKCOP	DWKCOP1	Maintain object part instances
DWKCOT	DWKCOT1	Define an object type
DWKCOTM	DWKCOTM1	Maintain methods in an object type
DWKCRD	DWKCRD1	Define a relationship type
DWKCRIP	DWKCRIP1	Create relationship type integrity policies
DWKCRTP	DWKCRTP1	Create relationship type trigger policies
DWKUDEP	DWKUDEP1	Return information about a dependent entity
DWKLFTP	DWKLFTP1, DWKLFTP2, DWKLFTP3, or DWKLFTP4	Create function trigger policies
DWKLPNC	SDF II panel	Invoke SDF II panel creation
DWKLTDP	DWKLTDP1, DWKLTDP2, DWKLTDP3, DWKLTDP4, DWKLTDP5, or DWKLTDP6	Create template field derivation policies

Name	Panel ID	Description
DWKLTIP	DWKLTIP1, or DWKLTIP2	Create template field integrity policies
DWKLTTP	DWKLTTP1 or DWKLTTP2	Create template trigger policies
DWKLVT1	DWKLVT11, DWKLVT12, or DWKLVT21	Define function
DWKS2MM	DWKS2MM	Map storage view for multiple entity and relationship types
DWKUIAO	DWKUIAO1	Import aggregation instance
DWKULD	DWKULD1	Batch repository maintenance
DWKUTM	DWKUTM1 or DWKUTMB1	Maintain system messages table
DWKZMLG	DWKZMLG1	Maintain PTF log entries
DWKZMPR	DWKZMPR1	Place construct in PTF hold status

9.3   REPOSITORY MANAGER MAIN SELECTION MENU

To begin a Repository Manager session, IRM is typed on the command line of the host system and the ENTER key is pressed. This displays panel DWK1, the Repository Manager Main Menu panel. Figure 9-1 shows this panel.

DWK1 is the root panel for all Repository Manager panel dialogs, and as this figure shows, it presents the selection options to initiate activities within the following categories:

- Tool Group maintenance or selection

- Conceptual View maintenance

- Logical View maintenance

- Storage View maintenance

```
DWK1                        Repository Manager Main Menu
Tool Group:  USER1

Select one of the tasks by typing the selection number.  Then press ENTER.

    1  Tool Group       Define or select tool group
    2  CV               Define the conceptual view
    3  LV               Define the logical view
    4  SV               Define the storage view

    5  Transfer         Transfer definitions or data
    6  System           System maintenance
    7  Services         Access Repository Manager facilities

    X  Exit             Exit Repository Manager

You may also call a function by entering CALL followed by a function
name on the Selection line.




Selection ===>
 F1=Help       F2=First      F3=End       F4=Add       F5=Delete    F6=Update
 F7=Up         F8=Down       F9=Last      F10=Previous F11=Next     F12=Cursor
```

Figure 9-1   The DWK1 panel.

- Repository data import and export and repository command processing

- Utilities for system maintenance

- Use of selected Repository Manager and Host facilities

Figure 9-2 shows this panel tree. The root panel is named DWK1, and the panels below it are named DWKTG1, DWKCV1, DWKLVM1, etc. The numbers in the tree correspond to the option numbers by which these lower panels are reached.

This Main Menu then presents selection choices for the following:

1.   Tool group definition maintenance or selection (via panel DWKTG1)

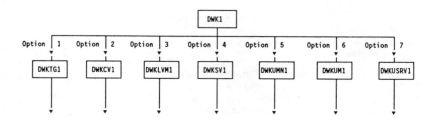

Figure 9-2   First hierarchical level of Repository Manager panels.

2.   Conceptual view definition maintenance (via panel DWKCV1)

3.   Logical view definition maintenance (via panel DWKLVM1)

4.   Storage view definition maintenance (via panel DWKSV1)

5.   Transfer of repository data and processing of repository commands (via panel DWKUMN1)

6.   System maintenance utility (via panel DWKUM1)

7.   Repository Manager and host facilities access (via panel DWKUSRV1)

9.4   TOOL GROUP DIALOGS

The constructs of repository conceptual view and logical view components are organized according to tool groups. A tool group is a collection or grouping of entity types, relationship types, aggregation types, object types, repository functions, and messages that are related.

At definition time, conceptual view and logical view constructs are automatically assigned to the user's currently effective tool group. Tool groups may be established or modified by specifying existing constructs as new members and by deleting existing members.

Within the repository, a tool group definition consists of the following information:

- A tool group name

- A short description of the tool group (optional)

- A long description of the tool group (optional)

- A file type name for the ISPF message library of the tool group

- A file type name for the ISPF panel library of the tool group

- Associations with conceptual view constructs (entity types, relationship types, aggregation types, and object types)

- Associations with logical view constructs (repository functions)

Figure 9-3 presents the hierarchy of panels for the selection or maintenance of tool groups. Note that maintenance within these immediate dialogs can only impact tool group names, descriptions, and file type names. Associations of repository definition constructs with a tool group are accomplished from the dialogs that establish or modify the particular construct definition types.

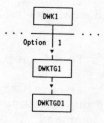

Figure 9-3   Panel hierarchy to display, select, and maintain tool groups.

To initiate a dialog to define a new tool group, modify an existing tool group, delete a tool group, select a tool group as currently effective, or examine tool groups, the control must be at the panel DWKTG1. This is accomplished by selecting option 1 (Define or Select Tool Group) from the Repository Manager Main Menu panel (DWK1).

9.4.1   Defining a Tool Group

One of the fundamental steps involved in using Repository Manager is defining a tool group. To accomplish this, the following steps are followed:

1.   In panel DWKTG1, an I in the *Action* field of a list entry is used to initiate an insertion action. This will bring up the Define a Tool Group panel (DWKTGD1).

2.   In panel DWKTGD1, a name for the new tool group in the *Tool Group* field and a description in the *Description* field is provided. If desired, the ISPF message filetype and ISPF panel filetype may also be provided, and a long description may be entered by using the EDIT command. The EDIT command will result in the display of an ISPF/PDF preferred editor panel into which a long description may be entered. The ADD command is issued to add the new tool group. Use of the END command from DWKTGD1 returns processing to the List Tool Groups (DWKTG1) panel.

Once a tool group is defined, the definition of an ER model may be provided to the repository within the tool group. After the basic components of an ER model definition are established, function definitions can be specified within the tool group for the logical view.

9.4.2   Maintaining a Tool Group Definition

The short description, ISPF message file type and ISPF panel file type fields of an existing a tool group definition may be modified from panel DWKTGD1 using the UPDATE command. To display DWKTGD1 from DWKTG1 to modify an existing tool group, an S is used in the *Action* field of the tool group to be modified. Modification of the long description (via the ISPF/PDF preferred editor) may be initiated from either panel DWKTG1 or panel DWKTGD1 by the EDIT command.

9.4.3   Deleting a Tool Group

A tool group can be deleted only if all its conceptual view and logical view component members belong to at least some other tool group(s). To delete a tool group definition, one of the following is performed:

- From panel DWKTG1, D is entered into the *Action* field of the tool group to be deleted.

- From panel DWKTGD1, a name for the tool group in the *Tool Group* field is entered, and the DELETE command is issued.

9.4.4   Making a Tool Group Currently Effective

To make a tool group currently effective, one of the following is performed:

- From panel DWKTG1, the C action code is entered into the corresponding *Action* field for the tool group to be made currently effective.

- From panel DWKTGD1, the CURRENT command is used to make the tool group whose name is displayed in the *Tool Group* field currently effective.

9.4.5   Tool Group Maintenance and Selection Panels

The following panels are used for tool group maintenance and selection dialogs.

List Tool Groups (DWKTG1) lists the names and descriptions of defined tool groups. Accepts the following actions on a tool group:

- Make currently effective (one tool group only).

- Select for definition display and/or modification (via panel DWKTGD1).

- Initiate the insertion (addition) of a new tool group definition (via panel DWKTGD1).

- Directly delete, provided that each member of the group belongs to at least one other tool group.

- Generate a report on the conceptual view of one or more selected tool groups.

- Invoke the editor to add, modify, delete, or simply display the optional long description of the selected tool group (via panels of the ISPF/PDF preferred editor).

Define a Tool Group (DWKTGD1) accepts the addition, modification, or deletion of a specified tool group. May also be used to invoke the editor to maintain the tool group's long description (via panels of the ISPF/PDF preferred editor), to display a tool group definition, or to select a tool group as currently effective.

9.5   CONCEPTUAL VIEW DISPLAY AND MAINTENANCE DIALOGS

The information contained in a repository to support business and information processing activities must be modeled in the repository. Conceptual view dialogs provide a means to establish, maintain, examine, and test models within the repository.

Models are represented with the following basic constructs:

- Entity type definitions reflecting classes of things about which information is stored in the repository. These definitions include locking characteristics, trigger policies, and specifications of the associated attribute types along with their associated derivation and integrity policies.

- Relationship type definitions that associate instances of entity types with entity types, entity types with relationship types, and relationship types with relationship types. These definitions include instance control, controlling semantics, mandatory existence, and ordering characteristics for instantiation. They also include integrity and trigger policies.

More complex model definition construct types are formed from the basic constructs. These include:

- Aggregation types, which are collections of interrelated entity types, along with associated template names and processing options, and conditions for instance exporting, importing, locking, and unlocking.

- Object type definitions specifying aggregation types with associated method – method implementation pairs dictating the operations that are allowed to be performed on instances of the types.

Figure 9-4 presents the upper-level hierarchy of panels for conceptual view display and maintenance. To initiate a conceptual view dialog, option 2 (Define the Conceptual View) is selected from the Repository Manager Main Menu panel, DWK1. This results in the display of the Define Conceptual View panel, DWKCV1, from which options may be selected to display or maintain any of the conceptual view construct types, display or maintain any instances of the defined types, and validate entity type definitions, relationship type definitions, and their instances.

Define Conceptual View (DWKCV1) is used to designate options for the following actions to be performed:

1. List Entity Types (via panel DWKCEL1).

2. Define an Entity Type (via panel DWKCED1).

3. List Relationship Types (via panel DWKCRL1).

4. Define a Relationship Type (via panel DWKCRD1).

5. List Aggregation Types (via panel DWKCAL1).

6. Define an Aggregation Type (via panel DWKCAD1).

7. List Object Types (via panel DWKCOTL1).

8. Define an Object Type (via panel DWKCOT1).

9. Display or maintain Entity, Relationship, or Object Instance (via panel DWKCOCM1).

10. Validate Entity/Relationship Types (via panel DWKCVM1).

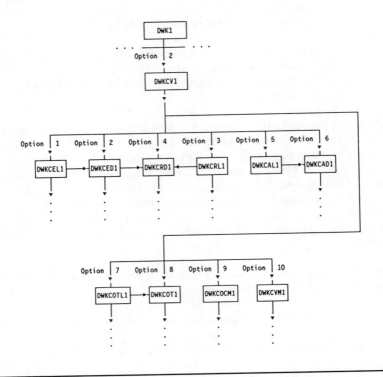

Figure 9-4 First hierarchical level of conceptual view panels.

9.5.1 Defining and Listing Entity Types and Relationship Types

Within the repository, an entity type definition consists of the following information:

- An entity type name.

- A short description of the entity type (optional).

- A long description of the entity type (optional).

- Whether an update lock must be obtained on instances of the entity type before updates or deletes can be accomplished.

- Whether the entity type is dependent and, if so, the name of the owning relationship type.

- A set of entity attribute type definitions, including one for the key attribute of the entity type. Each attribute type definition consists of the following:

  - An entity attribute type name.

  - Characteristics of the attribute type including data type (character, fixed binary, or decimal), length, scale, and system assigned key attributes, as appropriate.

  - A short description of the attribute type (optional).

  - A long description of the attribute type (optional).

  - Derivation policy definitions associated with the reading or writing of a nonkey attribute of an instance of the entity type. Each derivation policy definition consists of an optional description, a derivation expression, and a derivation condition.

  - Integrity policy definitions associated with writing an attribute of an instance of the entity type. Each integrity policy definition consists of an optional description, an acceptance condition, and an optional message to display upon rejection.

- Trigger policy definitions associated with the reading or writing of instances of the entity type. Each trigger policy definition consists of an optional description, a trigger condition, a repository function name to invoke, and a list of parameters to pass to the function.

Within the repository, a relationship type definition consists of the following information:

- A primary relationship type name.

- An inverse name of the relationship type.

- A short description of the relationship type (optional).

- A long description of the relationship type (optional).

- Name and type of the construct (entity type or relationship type) that is the source of the primary direction of the relationship type.

- Name and type of the construct (entity type or relationship type) that is the target of the primary direction of the relationship type.

- Properties of the relationship type, including instance control and whether its instances are controlling, mandatory, or ordered.

- Integrity policy definitions associated with writing an instance of the relationship type. Each integrity policy definition consists of an optional description, an acceptance condition, and an optional message to display upon rejection.

- Trigger policy definitions associated with writing instances of the relationship type. Each trigger policy definition consists of an optional description, a trigger condition, a repository function name to invoke, and a list of parameters to pass to the function.

Figure 9-5 presents this panel hierarchy.

The panels in the hierarchy perform the functions described below.

9.5.1.1 *Listing Entity Types*

List Entity Types (DWKCEL1) lists, for the current tool group, the entity types and their short descriptions. The following actions may be performed or initiated upon entries in the list:

- Invoke the ISPF/PDF preferred editor to display or maintain the optional long description.

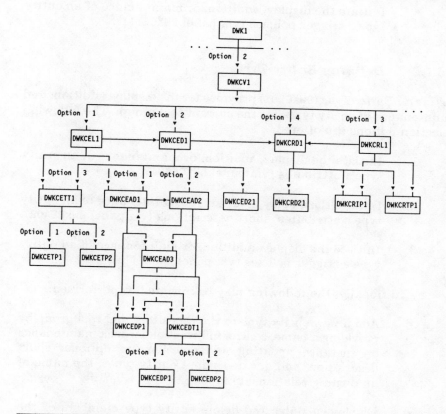

Figure 9-5   Panel hierarchy to define and maintain entity and relationship types.

- Directly delete an entity type definition from the tool group.

- Generate a report listing all entity types or selected entity types in the current tool group.

- Bind an entity type definition.

- Initiate the display, addition, or maintenance of an entity type (via panel DWKCED1).

- Initiate the display, addition, or maintenance of an entity type's attributes (via panel DWKCEAD1).

- Initiate the display, addition, or maintenance of an entity type's trigger policies (via panel DWKCETT1).

9.5.1.2   Defining Entity Types

Define an Entity Type (DWKCED1) provides for the display, addition, and maintenance of entity types for the current tool group. The following selection options are offered:

1. Initiate the display, addition, or maintenance of an entity type's attributes (via panel DWKCEAD1).

2. Initiate the display, addition, or maintenance of an entity type's attributes' short descriptions (via panel DWKCEAD2).

3. Initiate the display, addition, or maintenance of an entity type's trigger policies (via panel DWKCETT1).

Additionally, the following may be initiated or performed:

- Add a new entity type to the repository and tool group by providing a name, control information for lock maintenance on instance updating and deletion, an optional short description, and, for dependent entity types, the name of an owning relationship type.

- Display, update, and delete entity type members of the current tool group.

- Add an entity type that is not a member of the current tool group but is a member of one or more tool groups (via panel DWKCED21).

- For a dependent entity type being added or having its owning relationship type updated, add the controlling relationship type definition (via panel DWKCRD1).

- Invoke the ISPF/PDF preferred editor to display or maintain the optional long description.

- Bind the entity type definition.

Define Entity Attributes (DWKCEAD1) provides for the following capabilities:

- Invoke the ISPF/PDF preferred editor to display or maintain the optional long description.

- Initiate the display, addition, and maintenance of attribute integrity policies (via panel DWKCEIP1).

- Initiate the display, addition, and maintenance of nonkey attribute derivation policies (via panel DWKCEDT1).

Describe Entity Attributes (DWKCEAD2) is used to:

- Invoke the ISPF/PDF preferred editor to display or maintain the optional long description.

- Initiate the display, addition, and maintenance of attribute integrity policies (via panel DWKCEIP1).

- Initiate the display, addition, and maintenance of nonkey attribute derivation policies (via panel DWKCEDT1).

Add Entity Attributes (DWKCEAD3) is used for the following:

- Invoke the ISPF/PDF preferred editor to display or maintain the optional long description.

- Initiate the display, addition, and maintenance of attribute integrity policies (via panel DWKCEIP1).

- Initiate the display, addition, and maintenance of nonkey attribute derivation policies (via panel DWKCEDT1).

Entity in Another Tool Group (DWKCED21) displays the name and short description of an entity type that is not a member of the current tool group but is a member of one or more tool groups. May optionally add the displayed entity type to the current tool group.

9.5.1.3   *Defining, Maintaining, and Displaying Entity Type Trigger Policies*

Select Entity Trigger Policy Type (DWKCETT1) initiates the display, addition, modification, or deletion of trigger policies for entity types. Selection choices are presented for the following:

1. Entity write trigger policies (via panel DWKCETP1).

2. Entity read trigger policies (via panel DWKCETP2).

Create Entity Write Trigger Policies (DWKCETP1) provides for the display, addition, modification, and deletion of an entity write trigger policy. For the initial specification or modification of policy description, policy condition, or function parameter fields, the ISPF/PDF preferred editor panel may be invoked to allow multi-line input.

Create Entity Read Trigger Policies (DWKCETP2) provides for the display, addition, modification, and deletion of an entity read trigger policy. For the initial specification or modification of policy description, policy condition, or function parameter fields, the ISPF/PDF preferred editor panel may be invoked to allow multi-line input.

9.5.1.4   *Defining, Maintaining, and Displaying Entity Type Derivation Policies*

Select Entity Attribute Derivation Policy Type (DWKCEDT1) initiates the display, addition, modification, or deletion of derivation policies for nonkey attributes of entity types. Selection choices are presented for the following:

1. Entity write derivation policies (via panel DWKCEDP1).

2. Entity read derivation policies (via panel DWKCEDP2).

Create Entity Write Derivation Policies (DWKCEDP1) provides for the display, addition, modification, and deletion of an entity write derivation policy. For the initial specification or modification of policy description, policy condition, or attribute derivation fields, the ISPF/PDF preferred editor panel may be invoked to allow multi-line input.

Create Entity Read Derivation Policies (DWKCEDP2) provides for the display, addition, modification, and deletion of an entity read derivation policy. For the initial specification or modification of policy description, policy condition, or attribute derivation fields, the ISPF/PDF preferred editor panel may be invoked to allow multi-line input.

9.5.1.5 *Defining, Maintaining, and Displaying Entity Type Integrity Policies*

Create Entity Attribute Write Integrity Policies (DWKCEIP1) provides for the display, addition, modification, and deletion of an entity attribute write integrity policy. For the initial specification or modification of policy description, attribute acceptance condition, or message display fields, the ISPF/PDF preferred editor panel may be invoked to allow multi-line input.

9.5.1.6 *Listing Relationship Types*

List Relationship Types (DWKCRL1) lists, for the current tool group, the relationship types and their short descriptions. The following actions may be performed or initiated upon entries in the list:

- Invoke the ISPF/PDF preferred editor to display or maintain the optional long description.

- Directly delete a relationship type definition from the tool group.

- Generate a report listing all or selected relationship types in the current tool group.

- Bind a relationship type definition.

- Initiate the display, addition, or maintenance of a relationship type (via panel DWKCRD1).

- Initiate the display, addition, or maintenance of a relationship type's integrity policies (via panel DWKCRIP1).

- Initiate the display, addition, or maintenance of a relationship type's trigger policies (via panel DWKCRTP1).

9.5.1.7   Defining, Maintaining, and Displaying Relationship Types

Define a Relationship Type (DWKCRD1) provides for the display, addition, and maintenance of relationship types for the current tool group. The following may be initiated or performed:

- Add a new relationship type to the repository and tool group by providing a primary and inverse name, source and target construct name, source and target construct type identification, and instance and semantic control information, and an optional short description.

- Display, update, or delete a relationship type member of the current tool group.

- Add a relationship type that is not a member of the current tool group but is a member of one or more tool groups (via panel DWKCRD21).

- Invoke the ISPF/PDF preferred editor to display or maintain the optional long description.

- Initiate the display, addition, or maintenance of a relationship type's integrity policies (via panel DWKCRIP1).

- Initiate the display, addition, or maintenance of a relationship type's trigger policies (via panel DWKCRTP1).

- Bind a relationship type definition.

9.5.1.8   Defining, Maintaining, and Displaying Relationship Type Integrity Policies

Create Relationship Write Integrity Policies (DWKCRIP1) provides for the display, addition, modification, and deletion of a relationship write integrity policy. For the initial specification or modification of policy description, relationship acceptance condition, or message display fields, the ISPF/PDF preferred editor panel may be invoked to allow multi-line input.

9.5.1.9   *Defining, Maintaining, and Displaying Relationship Type Trigger Policies*

Create Relationship Write Trigger Policies: (DWKCRTP1) provides for the display, addition, modification, and deletion of a relationship write trigger policy. For the initial specification or modification of policy description, policy condition, or function parameter fields, the ISPF/PDF preferred editor panel may be invoked to allow multi-line input.

9.5.2   Defining and Listing Aggregation Types

Within the repository, an aggregation type definition consists of the following information:

- An aggregation type name.

- The name of the entity type that is the root of the aggregation type.

- A short description of the aggregation type (optional).

- A long description of the aggregation type (optional).

- The elements of the aggregation type consisting of the names of parent relationship types and their associated target entity types.

- The names of the templates assigned to the aggregation type elements.

- The special processing options assigned to aggregation type elements for the exporting, importing, locking, and unlocking of aggregation type instances.

- The extended definitions specifying repository functions to invoke whenever an instance of the aggregation type is exported, imported, locked, or unlocked.

Figure 9-6 shows the panel tree used to list or define aggregation types.

The meaning of the panels is as follows:

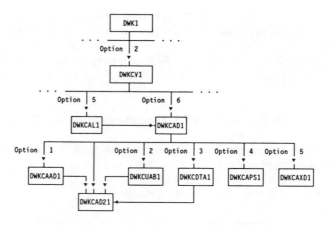

Figure 9-6   Panel hierarchy to list or define aggregation types.

List Aggregation Types (DWKCAL1) lists, for the current tool group, the assigned aggregation types and their short descriptions. The following actions may be performed or initiated upon entries in the list:

*   Initiate the display, addition, or maintenance of an aggregation type (via panel DWKCAD1).

*   Invoke the ISPF/PDF preferred editor to display or maintain the optional long description.

*   Directly delete an aggregation type definition from the tool group.

*   Generate a report listing all or selected aggregation types in the current tool group.

*   Initiate the display, addition, or maintenance of an aggregation type (via panel DWKCAD1).

Define an Aggregation Type (DWKCAD1) provides for the display, addition, modification, or deletion of an aggregation type definition. Selection options are presented to perform the following:

1.   Automatically build an aggregation type based on a specified root entity type (via panel DWKCAAD1).

2.   Manually build or modify an aggregation type (via panel DWKCUAB1).

3.   Define templates for the aggregation type (via panel DWKCDTA1).

4.   Select processing specifications for importing, exporting, and locking instances of the type (via panel DWKCAPS).

5.   Extend definition to include additional processing when exporting, importing, locking, or unlocking instances of this type (via panel DWKCAXD1).

6.   Edit long description of the aggregation type (via the ISPF/PDF preferred editor).

Additionally, action can be initiated to add an aggregation type that is not a member of the current tool group but is a member of one or more tool groups (via panel DWKCAD21).

Automatically Build an Aggregation Type (DWKCAAD1) automatically adds new or updated aggregation elements to the root entity type specified on DWKCAD1. The additions or updates are specified as the names of the relationship types the aggregation type is to include. If ambiguities are encountered using primary relationship type names, the Repository Manager attempts to build the aggregation type using inverse names, as appropriate. Additionally, action can be initiated to add an aggregation type that is not a member of the current tool group but is a member of one or more tool groups (via panel DWKCAD21).

Manually Build Aggregation Type (DWKCUAB1) displays and accepts additions, modifications, and deletions to the aggregation path elements of an aggregation type specified in DWKCAD1. Each displayed path element includes the level within the aggregation hierarchy, parent relationship type, target entity type, and associated import, lock, and unlock processing selections. Updates are specified in the form of the parent relationship type names. Additionally, action can be initiated to add an aggregation type that is not a member of the current tool group but is a member of one or more tool groups (via panel DWKCAD21).

Aggregation in Another Tool Group (DWKCAD21) displays the name and short description of an aggregation type that is not a member of the current tool group but is a member of one or more tool groups. May optionally add the displayed aggregation type to the current tool group.

Define Templates for Aggregation (DWKCDTA1) is used to define, modify, delete, or display template name assignments to path elements of the specified aggregation type. Template names may be specified, or the Repository Manager will generate default template names. Each displayed path element includes the level within the aggregation hierarchy, parent relationship type, target entity type, and assigned template name. Additionally, action can be initiated to add an aggregation type that is not a member of the current tool group but is a member of one or more tool groups (via panel DWKCAD21).

Specify Aggregation Processing (DWKCAPS1) is used to display and maintain special processing options on aggregation instance elements of the specified type whenever importing, locking, or unlocking.

Extend Aggregation Definition (DWKCAXD1) is used to display and maintain aggregation type definition extensions to invoke a repository function whenever an instance of the aggregation type is exported, imported, locked, or unlocked. Function invocations may be specified for immediately prior to the object action initiation, immediately following successful completion of the object action, or immediately following unsuccessful completion of the object action. Parameters to be passed to the function can be the aggregation name, aggregation key(s), return code from the completed object action, and a command field specified within the definition. Additionally this panel may be used to assign a default member name to be used for the export file whenever instances of the aggregation type are exported from the repository.

9.5.3   Defining and Listing Object Types

Within the repository, an object type definition consists of the following information:

- An object type name

- The aggregation type associated with the object type

- A short description of the object type (optional)

- A long description of the object type (optional)

- The owner of the object type (optional)

- The supertype of the object type (optional)

- Associations of method – method implementation pairs, where each association is expressed by the following:

    – Name of a repository method function

    – Indicator of method intent, signifying the lock level requirement for instances of the object type

    – Description of the method (optional)

    – Name of a repository method implementation function

    – Description of the method implementation (optional)

Figure 9-7 shows the panel hierarchy to list or define object types.

List Object Types (DWKCOTL1) lists, for the current tool group, the object types and their short descriptions. The following actions may be performed or initiated upon entries in the list:

- Initiate the display, addition, or maintenance of an object type (via panel DWKCOT1).

- Initiate the display, addition, or maintenance of an object type's assignment of method – method implementation pairs (via panel DWKCOTM1).

- Initiate the display, addition, or maintenance of a relationship type's trigger policies (via panel DWKCRTP1).

- Directly delete an object type definition from the tool group.

- Invoke the ISPF/PDF preferred editor to display or maintain the optional long description.

- Bind an object type definition.

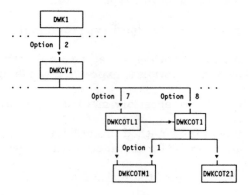

Figure 9-7   Panel hierarchy to list or define object types.

Define an Object Type (DWKCOT1) provides for the display, addition, and maintenance of an object type for the current tool group. The following may be initiated or performed:

- Add a new object type to the repository and tool group by providing an object type name and the name of the associated aggregation type, and, optionally, an owner name, a supertype name, and a short description.

- Display, update, or delete an object type member of the current tool group.

- Add an object type that is not a member of the current tool group but is a member of one or more tool groups (via panel DWKCOT21).

- Initiate the display, addition, or maintenance of an object type's method – method implementation assignments (via panel DWKCOTM1).

- Invoke the ISPF/PDF preferred editor to display or maintain the optional long description.

- Bind an object type or bind an object type and all of its subtypes.

Maintain Methods in an Object Type (DWKCOTM1) provides for the display, addition, update, or deletion of method – method implementation pair assignments associated with an object type for the current tool group.

Object Type in Another Tool Group (DWKCOT21) displays the name and short description of an object type that is not a member of the current tool group but is a member of one or more tool groups. May optionally add the displayed object type to the current tool group.

9.5.4   Maintaining Instances

The panel hierarchy for maintenance of instances of entity, relationship, or object types is shown in Figure 9-8.

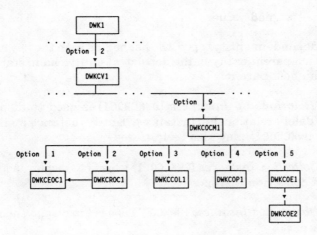

Figure 9-8   Panel hierarchy to maintain instances of entity, relationship, or object types.

The panels in this hierarchy are the following:

Entity/Relationship/Object Instance Menu (DWKCOCM1) presents an option selection to display or maintain:

1.   Entity instances

2.   Relationship instances

3.   Collection instances

4.   Part instances

5.   Object edition instances

Maintain Entity Instances (DWKCEOC1) is used to display, add, update, or delete entity instances. For a specified entity type, a list of the applicable attribute types is displayed. Each entry consists of

- Attribute type name

- Default length

- Data type

- Assigned value

For dependent entity types, the list begins with the key attributes for each parent entity in the dependent entity chain, starting with the highest parent.

Maintain Relationship Instances (DWKCROC1) is used to display, add, update, or delete relationship instances. Entity instance maintenance (via panel DWKCEOC1) may also be initiated.

Maintain Collection Instances (DWKCCOL1) is used to display, add, update, or delete a collection instance.

Maintain Object Part Instances (DWKCOP1) is used to display, add, update, or delete a part.

Maintain Object Edition Instances (DWKCOE1) is used to display, add, update, or delete control information of object edition instances. Object instance status maintenance (via panel DWKCOE2) may also be initiated.

Maintain Object Instance Status (DWKCOE2) is used to display, add, update, or delete status and location information of object edition instances. Note that location can be an aggregation instance within the repository or an alternate data store outside the repository.

9.5.5   Validating Conceptual View Definitions and Associated Bound Structures

The panel hierarchy for the validation of conceptual view definitions and associated bound structures is shown in Figure 9-9.

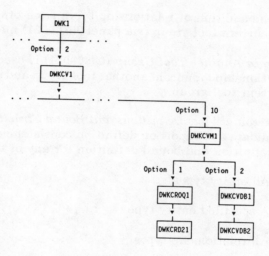

Figure 9-9   Panel hierarchy to validate entity or relationship types.

The panels in this hierarchy are the following:

Validate Entity/Relationship Types (DWKCVM1), which allows a selection to validate existing relationship instances (via panel DWKCROQ1) or to validate entity and relationship type definitions along with the consistency of their bound forms (via panel DWKCVDB1).

Validate Relationship Instances (DWKCROQ1) is used to validate whether instances of a specified relationship type satisfy actual or proposed semantic constraints, and if the instances are complete. The validation process, optionally, will report on

- Whether or not any instances exist.

- Whether or not all instances meet the mandatory specification.

- Whether or not all instances meet the cardinality specifications.

- Whether or not any dangling instances exist (i.e., a relationship without a source or a target) and, optionally, delete all dangling instances.

Also, the addition of relationship types from other tool groups to the current tool group (via panel DWKCRD21) may be initiated.

Relationship in Another Tool Group (DWKCRD21) is used to display an existing relationship type from another tool group and selectively add it to the current tool group.

Validate Conceptual View Definitions and Bound Structures (DWKCVDB1) is used to validate and report on definition consistencies between the repository definition and bound definition for any of the following:

- All entity types

- A specified entity type

- All relationship types

- A specified relationship type

- All entity and relationship types

Validate Conceptual View Definitions and Bound Structures (DWKCVDB2) is used to display inconsistencies between the repository definition and the bound definition for a specific entity type or relationship type specified on panel DWKCVDB1.

9.6 LOGICAL VIEW MAINTENANCE DIALOGS

The panel hierarchy for maintenance of logical views is shown in Figure 9-10.

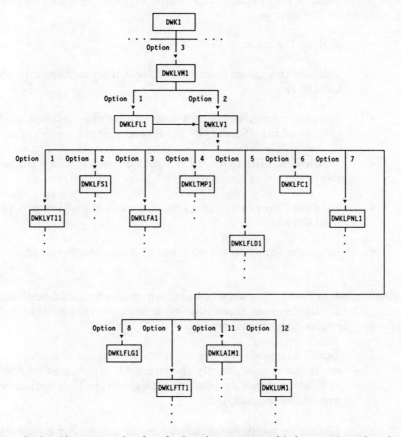

Note: Option 10 on DWKLV1 invokes the function DWKLBND to bind a repository function.

Figure 9-10   First level hierarchy of panels for logical view maintenance.

The panels in this hierarchy are the following:

Define Logical View (DWKLVM1) is used to select an option for defining or modifying a repository function, or an option to list existing functions in the current tool group.

List Functions (DWKLFL1) lists repository fully integrated, non-fully integrated, method, and method implementation functions of the currently effective tool group. The following actions may be selected for entries in the list:

- Delete function.

- Initiate the generation of a report on a function (via panel DWKLUM1).

- Initiate modification of a function's long description (via panels of the ISPF/PDF preferred editor).

- Initiate modification of a function definition (via panel DWKLVM1).

- Initiate the creation of a new function definition (via panel DWKLVM1).

- Invoke a function (applicable to fully integrated functions only).

Define Function (DWKLV1) is used to select an option to initiate definition, modification, display, or reporting of a repository function. The following actions can be performed:

1. Build a repository function to validate a portion of the conceptual view, verify the function input, and create the validation function (via panel DWKLVT11). This option is not applicable to methods.

2. Define or modify the global specifications for a repository function (via panel DWKLFS1).

3. Display and maintain aggregations for a repository function (not applicable to methods), where each aggregation type within the function corresponds to a template tree for the function (via panel DWKLFA1).

4. Define or modify templates for a fully integrated, non-fully integrated, or method implementation repository function (via panel DWKLTMP1). For a function of type *method*, the *Define or Modify Template* field (via panel DWKLFLD3) is used.

5. Define connections between predefined templates of the repository to form template trees for the function (via panel DWKLFC1). This option is not applicable to methods.

6. Maintain and design panel layout for an interactive repository function (via panel DWKLPNL1). This option is not applicable to methods.

7. Specify the program that contains the procedural logic for a repository function (via panel DWKLFLG1). This option is not applicable to methods or non-fully integrated functions.

8. Define trigger policies for a repository function (via panel DWKLFTT1).

9. Invoke the function DWKLBND to bind a repository function into an executable form (via Option 10).

10. Create an application interface macro for the repository function (via panel DWKLAIM1). For more information about application interface macros, see 9.6.11. This option is not applicable to methods.

11. Generate a repository function report, delete a repository function description, delete template tree connections, copy the data view of a repository function, or copy templates (via panel DWKLUM1).

9.6.1 Building a Fully Integrated Function to Validate Some Part of the Logical View

The panel hierarchy used for building a fully integrated function, which can be used to validate some part of a logical view, is shown in Figure 9-11.

The panels in this hierarchy are the following:

Build Validation Logical View (DWKLVT11) is used to create or modify a repository function definition by specifying the name, description, panel requirements, and template tree definitions. Additionally, the selection may be made to build or modify a data tree (via panel DWKLVT12) and to display the template tree, change it, or bind the repository function into an executable form (via panel DWKLVT21).

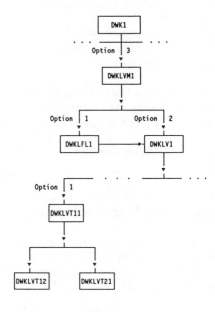

Figure 9-11   Panel hierarchy for maintenance of a logical view validation function.

Conceptual view definitions must be defined before template trees can be defined.

Modify Validation Logical View (DWKLVT12) is used to create or modify repository function data trees by specifying aggregation types, entity types, and relationship types.

Verify Validation Logical View (DWKLVT21) performs verification and displays template trees defined for the function. It accepts the BIND command to make the repository function executable, generates a panel if requested, and commits the repository function definition to the repository. It also allows the source template of a relationship type to be changed.

9.6.2   Defining Global Specifications of a Function

The panel hierarchy for defining global specifications of a function consists of choosing option 2 from the panel DWKLV1. The following two panels are available in this hierarchy:

Define a Function's Global Specifications (DWKLFS1) is used to specify the name of a repository function and to define its global specifications such as name, description, type, and processing options. Also allows query, update, and deletion of repository functions in the current tool group, including the editing of the function's short and long descriptions.

Function in Another Tool Group (DWKLFS21) is used to include a function from another tool group into the current tool group.

9.6.3   Maintaining Aggregation Types for a Function

The panel hierarchy for maintaining aggregation types for a function is shown in Figure 9-11, Figure 9-12. The panels in this hierarchy and their use are:

Maintain Aggregations for Function (DWKLFA1) is used to display and maintain the list of aggregation types for a repository function. Aggregation types and their corresponding template trees may be deleted directly. Additionally, the following may be initiated:

- Display and maintain the template tree for an aggregation type (via panel DWKLDTT1).
- Add aggregation types to the repository function (via panel DWKLFA2).

Add Aggregations for Function (DWKLFA2) is used to add aggregation types to a repository function. Additionally, the display and maintenance of the template tree associated with an aggregation type can be initiated (via panel DWKLDTT1).

Display Function Template Tree (DWKLDT11) is used to display the template tree of a specified name for a specified repository function. Additionally, it initiates the display of and maintenance on template fields for a specific template within the tree.

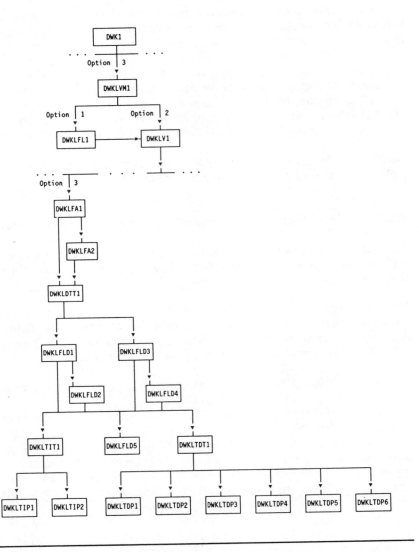

Figure 9-12   Panel hierarchy for maintenance of the aggregation types of a function.

Maintain Template Fields (DWKLFLD1) displays and maintains fields of a template that maps to an entity type. Fields that map to an entity type can also be maintained. Previously defined fields may be directly updated or deleted. If the template has no defined fields, all the attribute types of the entity type may be mapped to template fields. Additionally, the following may be initiated:

- Define new template fields (via panel DWKLFLD2).

- Specify or modify of initial value for a template field (via panel DWKLFLD5).

- Define integrity policies for a template field (via panel DWKLTIT1).

- Definition of derivation policies for a template field (via panel DWKLTDT1).

Add Template Fields (DWKLFLD2) is used to add new fields to a template that maps to an entity type. Additionally, the following may be initiated:

- Specify or modify initial value for a template field (via panel DWKLFLD5).

- Define integrity policies for a template field (via panel DWKLTIT1).

- Define derivation policies for a template field (via panel DWKLTDT1).

Maintain Template Fields (DWKLFLD3) displays and maintains fields of a template that does not map to an entity type. Previously defined fields may be directly updated or deleted. Additionally, the following may be initiated:

- Define new template fields (via panel DWKLFLD4).

- Specify or modify initial value for a template field (via panel DWKLFLD5).

- Define integrity policies for a template field (via panel DWKLTIT1).

- Define derivation policies for a template field (via panel DWKLTDT1).

Add Template Fields (DWKLFLD4) is used to add new fields to a template that does not map to an entity type. Additionally, the following may be initiated:

- Specify or modify initial value for a template field (via panel DWKLFLD5).

- Define integrity policies for a template field (via panel DWKLTIT1).

- Define derivation policies for a template field (via panel DWKLTDT1).

Select Template Field Integrity Type (DWKLTIT1) is used to select the type of integrity policy to be defined for the template field. The options are for policies that process:

1. After a command is entered on a panel (via panel DWKLTIP1)

2. When a function is called (via panel DWKLTIP2)

Create Display Read Integrity Policies (DWKLTIP1) is used to establish, display, update, or delete integrity policy definitions for policies to be processed when a function invokes user services to read data from the terminal (i.e., after a user enters a command on a panel).

Create Function Initiation Integrity Policies (DWKLTIP2) is used to establish, display, update, or delete derivation policy definitions for policies to be processed when a function is called.

Initialize Template Field (DWKLFLD5) is used to establish, display, or modify an initial value for a template field. (Applicable only to fields in nonshared templates). Shared templates are discussed in 7.1.1.1.

Select Template Field Derivation Type (DWKLTDT1) is used to select derivation policy type to be defined for the template field. The options are for policies that process when a function:

1. Is called or opened (via panel DWKLTDP1).

2. Returns to its caller (via panel DWKLTDP2).

3.   Invokes user services to write data to the terminal (via panel DWKLTDP3).

4.   Invokes user services to read data from the terminal (via panel DWKLTDP4).

5.   Issues a one-template database add or update call (via panel DWKLTDP5).

6.   Issues a database retrieval call (via panel DWKLTDP6).

Create Function Initiation Derivation Policies (DWKLTDP1) is used to establish, display, update, or delete derivation policy definitions for policies to be processed when a function is called or opened.

Create Function Termination Derivation Policies (DWKLTDP2) is used to establish, display, update, or delete derivation policy definitions for policies to be processed when a function returns to its caller.

Create Display Write Derivation Policies (DWKLTDP3) is used to establish, display, update, or delete derivation policy definitions for policies to be processed when a function invokes user services to write data to the terminal before the panel is displayed.

Create Display Read Derivation Policies (DWKLTDP4) is used to establish, display, update, or delete derivation policy definitions for policies to be processed when a function invokes user services to read data from the terminal (i.e., after a user enters a command on a panel).

Create Template Write Derivation Policies (DWKLTDP5) is used to establish, display, update, or delete derivation policy definitions for policies to be processed when a function issues a one-template database add or update call.

Create Template Read Derivation Policies (DWKLTDP6) is used to establish, display, update, or delete derivation policy definitions for policies to be processed when a function issues a database retrieval call.

9.6.4   Defining Repository Function Templates

The panel hierarchy used to define repository function templates is shown in Figure 9-13.

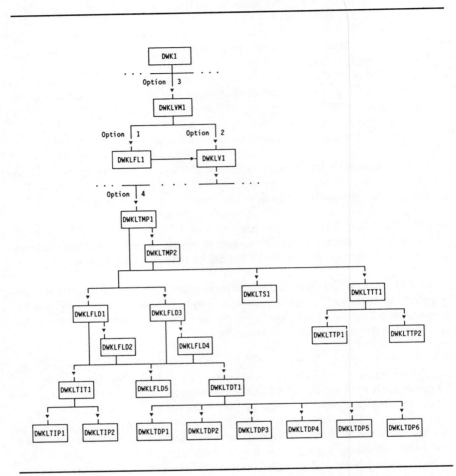

Figure 9-13 Panel hierarchy for defining and maintaining non-method function templates.

Maintain Function Templates (DWKLTMP1) is used to define and maintain templates for a repository function. The following may be performed from this panel:

- Generate a list of templates belonging to the selected repository function. Entries in this list may be acted upon for maintenance or display.

- Delete a template from the list for the repository function.

- Initiate the addition of a new template for the repository function (via panel DWKLTMP2).

- Modify fields of a template in the list for the repository function (via panel DWKLFLD1 for a template that maps to an entity type or panel DWKLFLD3 for a template that does not map to an entity type).

- Initiate modification of the specifications of a template in the list for the repository function (via panel DWKLTS1).

- Initiate the modification of trigger policies of a template in the list for the repository function (via panel DWKLTTT1).

- Invoke the editor to enter or modify the description of a template in the list for the repository function.

Maintain Template Fields (DWKLFLD1) is used to define or maintain template fields from a displayed list of fields for a template that maps to an entity type.

Define Template Fields (DWKLFLD2) is used to define new template fields.

Initial Value of Template Field (DWKLFLD5) is used to display, specify, or modify an initial value for a template field.

Derivation Policies for a Template Field (DWKLTDT1) is used to initiate the display, definition, or modification of derivation policies for a template field.

Integrity Policies for a Template Field (DWKLTIT1) is used to initiate the display, definition, or modification of integrity policies for a template field.

9.6.5   Defining Template Fields for Methods

The panel hierarchy for this dialog is very similar to the one for defining template fields for repository functions (See 9.6.4). It will not be discussed here.

9.6.6 Defining Template Trees for Functions

The panel hierarchy for this dialog introduces the following new panel:

Maintain Function Connections (DWKLFC1), which is used to define and maintain connections between predefined templates of the repository to form template trees for the function. This dialog is not applicable to methods.

9.6.7 Designing and Maintaining Panel Layouts for Interactive Functions

The panel hierarchy for the design and maintenance of panel layouts for interactive functions is shown in Figure 9-14.

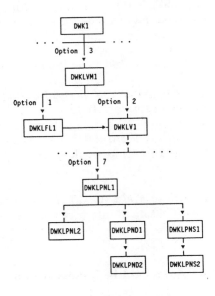

Figure 9-14 Panel hierarchy for design and maintenance of panel layouts.

Maintain Function Panels (DWKLPNL1) is used to maintain and design the panel layout for an interactive repository function. This panel cannot be used for methods.

Add Panels to Function (DWKLPNL2) is used to add panels to a function.

Map Scrollable Panel Fields (DWKLPND1) allows for scrollable panel fields to be mapped to template fields.

Add Scrollable Panel Fields (DWKLPND2) provides the ability to add scrollable panel fields to template fields.

Map Scalar Panel Fields to Template Fields (DWKLPNS1) is used to map a scalar panel field to a template field.

Add Scalar Panel Fields to Template Fields (DWKLPNS2) is used to add a scalar panel field to a template field.

9.6.8   Specifying the Program for a Function

The panel hierarchy used to specify the program containing the procedural logic for a repository function is shown in Figure 9-15.

Specify Program Containing a Function's Logic (DWKLFLG1) is used to specify the program name that contains the procedural logic for a repository function and program language. Additionally, an indicator of the function's template location may be specified.

9.6.9   Defining Trigger Policies for a Function

The panel hierarchy used to specify trigger policies for a function is shown in Figure 9-16.

Select Function Trigger Policy Type (DWKLFTT1) initiates the definition maintenance of trigger policies for a repository function. Allowable selections are for trigger policies that execute when a function:

- Is called (via panel DWKLFTP1).

- Returns to the caller (via panel DWKLFTP2).

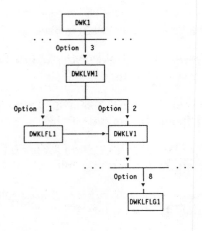

Figure 9-15   Panel hierarchy for specifying a program for a function.

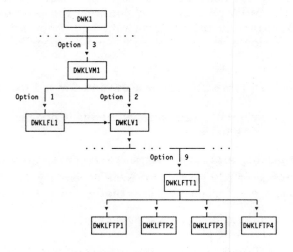

Figure 9-16   Panel hierarchy for defining trigger policies for a function.

- Invokes user services to present data to the user (via panel DWKLFTP3).

- Invokes user services to read data from the user's panel (via panel DWKLFTP4).

The following panels are used in this hierarchy:

Create Function Initiation Trigger Policies (DWKLFTP1) is used to define or maintain the definition of a trigger policy that executes when a function is called.

Create Function Termination Trigger Policies (DWKLFTP2) is used to define or maintain the definition of a trigger policy that executes when a function returns to the caller.

Create Display Write Trigger Policies (DWKLFTP3) is used to define or maintain the definition of a trigger policy that executes when a function invokes user services to present data to the user.

Create Display Read Trigger Policies (DWKLFTP4) is used to define or maintain the definition of a trigger policy that executes when a function invokes user services to read data from the user's panel.

9.6.10   Binding a Repository Function

Option 10 is selected on panel DWKLV1 (See 9.6) to bind the selected function into an executable form. This option causes the logical view built-in function DWKLBND to be invoked.

9.6.11   Creating an Application Interface Macro for a Function

In the panel hierarchy used in the creation of an Application Interface Macro (AIM), the following panels are used

Create an Application Interface Macro (DWKLAIM1) is used to establish an application interface macro for the repository function (not applicable to methods). An AIM is a macro in the language of the tool program that provides the interface to Repository Manager . It is created from the bound version of the repository function rather than from the logical view definition of the function.   The AIM contains all the data declarations required for a program to access all the templates in the function. It is used for all supported programming languages other than REXX.

Resolve Duplicate Application Interface Macro (DWKLAIM2) is used if an attempt is made to create an AIM that already exists at the current user level. The following options are given:

1.   Delete the pre-existing AIM and proceed with the creation of the new AIM.

2.   Keep the pre-existing AIM at the current user level and terminate the attempt to create the new AIM.

Figure 9-17 contains a code fragment illustrating the COBOL template structure generated in the AIM for an arrayed template named MODULE and a non-arrayed template named PROGMMER.

The following comments apply to this code fragment:

•   The 01-level identifier for the arrayed template structure consists of a template name and the suffix -DMY. This is followed by a 10-level identifier that does not include the suffix. The 10-level identifier is used for setting and retrieving template field values from a template structure, and also in calls to Repository Manager service routines on arrayed template.

•   The 01-level identifier for non-arrayed templates is the same as the template name and is used in all operations on the template.

9.6.12   Miscellaneous Utilities for Repository Function Maintenance

Miscellaneous utilities can be invoked from a panel hierarchy containing the following panels:

Report, Delete, or Copy Functions and Templates (DWKLUM1) initiates report generation or selected maintenance actions as follows:

•   Generate a repository function report of one of the following forms:

```
01 MODULE-DMY.
   10 MODULE OCCURS 10 TIMES
      20 ACODE        PIC X.
      20 AQUAL        PIC X.
      20 CSI          PIC XX.
      20 CRC          PIC S9(9) USAGE COMP-4.
      20 FILLER       PIC X(8).
      20 LOI          PIC S9(4) USAGE COMP-4.
      20 SELECT1      PIC S9(4) USAGE COMP-4.
      20 NAME.
         30 FSI       PIC XX.
         30 LEN       PIC S9(4) USAGE COMP-4.
         30 VAL       PIC X(8).
      20 LANGUAGE.
         30 FSI       PIC XX.
         30 LEN       PIC S9(4) USAGE COMP-4.
         30 VAL       PIC X(10)
      20 DWK-SIZE.
         30 FSI       PIC XX.
         30 VAL       PIC S9(6) USAGE COMP-3

01 PROGMMER.
   20 ACODE          PIC X.
   20 AQUAL          PIC X.
   20 CSI            PIC XX.
   20 CRC            PIC S9(9) USAGE COMP-4.
   20 FILLER         PIC X(8).
   20 IDNUMBER.
      30 FSI         PIC XX.
      30 VAL         PIC S9(9) USAGE COMP-3.
      30 FILLER      PIC X.
   20 NAME.
      30 FSI         PIC XX.
      30 LEN         PIC S9(4) USAGE COMP-4.
      30 VAL         PIC X(20).
   20 DWK-POSITION.
      30 FSI         PIC XX.
      30 LEN         PIC S9(4) USAGE COMP-4.
      30 VAL         PIC X(10).
```

Figure 9-17   Example of a COBOL template structure generated in an AIM.

- Complete report including template connection report and panel report

- Template connection report

- Panel report

• Delete a repository function description.

• Delete a repository function's relationship connections.

• Initiate copying the entire data view (templates, connections, and policies) or a single template of a repository function (via panel DWKLCDV1).

Note that deletions do not affect any existing bound form of a function. When deleting a repository function's relationship connections, any connections that belong to more than one tool group are left intact. The connections are removed only from the current function definition.

Copy Function's Logical Data View (DWKLCDV1) allows copying of the logical data view of one repository function to another and allows copying and renaming of a single template within a repository function.

When the logical data view is copied, the target repository function is added to the current tool group and will have the same global specifications as the source function. All templates in the source function will also appear in the target function. Of note is that the parameter template of the target function will have the name of the target function.

When copying a single template within a repository function, the function must belong to the current tool group. The target template will have the same specifications and policies as the source. The only exception is that if the source template is arrayed, the target will not be arrayed.

9.7   STORAGE VIEW DISPLAY AND MAINTENANCE DIALOGS

An extensive number of panel hierarchies exist for mapping to the storage view and administration of this view. These dialogs will not be discussed at the same level of detail as previous dialogs in this chapter.

The creation of DB2 storage views consists of two phases:

> The *Definition Phase*, which takes place with the Repository Manager. Here occur the generation of DB2 Object Descriptions and mappings, SQL CREATE statements, and access modules (DB2 application programs).

> The *Postprocessing Phase*, which takes place under DB2. Here SQL statements are executed, creating DB2 objects and DB2 applications and load modules.

The following steps take place in the *Definition Phase*:

1. The storage view, DB2 subsystem (MVS subsystem name for the DB2 DBMS being used), and DB2 plan (same as the application plan name used by DB2) are identified.

2. Optionally, descriptions of DB2 objects and associations among DB2 objects are defined. DB2 objects include:

    -   Tables
    -   Indexes
    -   Databases
    -   Storage groups
    -   Table spaces
    -   Volumes
    -   VSAM catalogs

3. Optionally, parameter defaults for tables and indexes are modified. Such parameters control the definition, naming, and association characteristics of DB2 tables and indexes.

4. Mappings of conceptual view constructs (entity and relationship types) to storage view objects are established.

5. Optionally, the DB2 object descriptions created by the Repository Manager in step 4 are modified and additional DB2 objects are defined if desired.

6. DB2 object descriptions in the repository are validated and the SQL statements used to create the associated DB2 objects are generated.

7.   A Repository Bind is performed that binds the storage view to generate the assembler programs with embedded SQL that are used to access the DB2 objects.

The following steps take place in the *Postprocessing Phase*:

1.   The DB2 objects described in the definition phase, which are needed for the storage, are generated by executing the SQL statements that were also generated in the definition phase.

2.   A DB2 application plan and load module is produced. Standard DB2 application preparation steps are used and applied to the assembler access modules generated by Repository Manager.

At the end of these steps, a DB2 storage view will have been created.

9.7.1   First-Level Panel Hierarchy for Storage View Maintenance

All panel hierarchies dealing with a storage view originate from the first level panel hierarchy, shown in Figure 9-18.

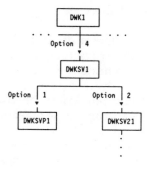

Figure 9-18   First level panel hierarchy for storage view administration.

In this panel hierarchy:

Define Storage View (DWKSV1) is the main menu selection for storage view maintenance facilities. The following options can be selected:

1.   Map or remap entity types and relationship types to the private storage view (via panel DWKSVP1).

2.   Map entity types and relationship types to DB2 tables (via panel DWKSV21).

9.7.2   Mapping Entity Types and Relationship Types to the Private View

Option 1 from DWKSV1 allows entity types and relationship types to be mapped to the private storage view via the following panel:

Bind to the Private Storage View (DWKSVP1) remaps a specified entity type or specified relationship type to the private storage view. The options available are:

1.   Bind an entity type.

2.   Bind a relationship type.

When a private storage view is used, entity and relationship instances are stored in MVS data sets instead of DB2 tables. The use of a private view storage use is appropriate for prototyping a new application, tool, or ER model. In such cases, the amount of data will be small, the data is not to be shared, and the comprehensive features of the DB2 database management system are not needed.

Repository Manager automatically maps entity and relationship types to the private storage view until the mapping and binding processes have been performed, creating the DB2 storage view for the constructs. The panel DWKSVP1 is available for cases where the entity and relationship types have been mapped to a DB2 storage view and the mapping needs to be changed back to a private storage view.

9.7.3   Defining Mappings from the Conceptual View to the Storage View

Option 2 from DWKSV1 leads to the panel DWKSV21. This panel and its descendants offer the following capabilities:

Define DB2 Storage View (DWKSV21) presents a menu selection for DB2 storage view maintenance. The available options are:

1.   Storage View — define and/or select a storage view name (via panel DWKS2V1).

2.   Map — map the conceptual view to the DB2 storage view (via panel DWKS2MP1).

3.   Maintain — maintain the DB2 object descriptions in the repository (via panel DWKS2OT1).

4.   Bind — bind the storage view creating an application plan (a control structure that DB2 uses when it processes SQL statements during application execution).

Panels at lower levels are the following:

Specify DB2 Storage View (DWKS2SV1) is used to display and maintain storage view name definitions and to select the current storage view. Storage views are named or selected as current by specifying the DB2 storage view name, DB2 subsystem name, and DB2 plan name.

Map Conceptual View to DB2 Storage View (DWKS2MP1) initiates the mapping of entity and relationship types to DB2 tables. Available options are:

1.   Map an entity type and create a DB2 table (via panel DWKS2ME1).

2.   Map an entity type to an existing DB2 table (via panel DWKS2ME1).

3.   Map a relationship type and create a DB2 table (via panel DWKS2MR1).

4.   Map constructs in a file (via panel DWKS2MM1), where the entity and relationship types are listed in the SVMAPLST file (an MVS data set).

Map Entity Type to DB2 Table (DWKS2ME1) is used to add, delete, or update entity type mapping definitions. Add or update actions map an entity type to a DB2 table and map each entity attribute to a table column.

Map Relationship Type to DB2 Table (DWKS2MR1) is used to add, delete, or update relationship type mapping definitions. Add or update actions map a relationship type to one DB2 table for an unordered relationship type and to two DB2 tables (primary and secondary) for an ordered relationship type.

Process Storage View Map List (DWKS2MM1) is used to add, delete, or update entity type and relationship type constructs listed in the SVMAPLST file. The file can contain the following:

- Storage view records that select a storage view, name the DB2 subsystem, and name the DB2 application plan.

- Parameter records that change table and index parameters.

- Construct records that list the entity types and relationship types to be mapped.

Select DB2 Object Type (DWKS20T1) specifies first filter criteria (DB2 object type) for the list of DB2 objects to be operated upon and whose descriptions are stored in the repository.

A large number of additional DB2 object maintenance panels exist. They are used depending upon the object type selected and the function to be performed. These panels are not listed here.

9.8   DIALOGS FOR DATA TRANSFERS AND BATCH MAINTENANCE COMMAND PROCESSING

A set of panels in a panel hierarchy can be accessed by selecting option 5 from the DWK1 root panels. These panels correspond to the functionality of the batch commands, which will be discussed in Chapter 10.

9.9   SYSTEM MAINTENANCE DIALOGS

A set of panels in a panel hierarchy can be accessed by selecting option 6 from the DWK1 root panel. These panels are used for system maintenance tasks.

Select System Maintenance Utility (DWKUM1) is a menu panel used to select from the following options:

1.   Maintain system tables (via panel DWKUT1).

2.   Maintain system security (via panel DWKSECM1).

3.   Maintain tuning parameters (via panel DWKUTUN1).

4.   Maintain the IBM-supplied Information Model with Program Temporary Fixes (PTFs) (via panel DWKZMUT1).

9.9.1   Maintaining System Messages

The following panels are available:

• Maintain System Messages (DWKUTM1)

• Bind System Messages (DWKUTB1)

• Generate Message Reports (DWKUTR1)

Panels lower in the hierarchy allow further options for these tasks to be specified. These panels are not listed here.

9.9.2   Security Administration

A set of panels in a panel hierarchy, accessed by selecting option 2 from the DWKUM1 panel, are used for security administration.

Security Maintenance Menu (DWKSECM1) provides an option for selection of the following security maintenance tasks:

1.   Maintain security object groups (via panel DWKSEC22).

2. Maintain security profiles (via panel DWKSEC11).

3. Specify authorized users for security profiles (via panel DWKSEC00).

4. Maintain the Authorized User List (via panel DWKSEC33).

5. Bind security profile (via panels DWKSECM1, DWKSEC11, DWKSEC22, or DWKSEC66).

6. Create reports for security profiles (via panel DWKSECR1).

Panels lower in the panel hierarchy are:

Maintain Security Object Groups (DWKSEC22) is used to define and maintain security object groups.

Maintain Security Objects (DWKSEC55) is used to define security objects and assign security objects to a security object group.

Maintain Security Access and Conditions (DWKSEC77) is used to assign access level and (optionally) a condition to express special circumstances under which Repository Manager grants access.

Maintain Security Profiles (DWKSSEC11) is used to define and maintain security profiles, including the assignment of default access levels to security objects not explicitly included in profiles.

Security Profile Group Maintenance (DWKSEC66) is used to add or delete security object groups to or from a security profile.

Specify Authorized Users for Security Profiles (DWKSEC00) is used to assign users to a security profile.

Maintain Authorized User List (DWKSEC33) is used to add or delete user IDs on the Authorized User List, which is the master list of all user IDs that can be assigned to specific security profiles.

Create Security Reports (DWKSECR1) is used to generate reports about security object groups, security profiles, or assigned users. Media may be online display or hard copy.

9.9.3   Modifying Tuning Parameters

The following panel can be used to maintain tuning parameters:

Maintain Tuning Parameters (DWKUNTUN1) is used to modify the values of the tuning parameters supplied by the Repository Manager. The available parameters consist of:

- General parameters for private storage view and DB2 update concurrency and specification of the number of DB2 rows to read at a time, based upon ranges of bytes in a row.

- Table parameters for automated creation naming and name qualifications for table space database and DB2 table space.

- Index parameters for automated creation naming, automated VSAM data set defining, naming, and access control for the index.

9.9.4   Program Temporary Fix Data Model Maintenance

A set of panels in a panel hierarchy, accessed by selecting option 4 from the DWKUM1 panel, are used for maintenance of the Supplied ER Model with Program Temporary Fixes (PTFs).

These panels are:

Model Maintenance Menu (DWKZMUT1) is a menu panel used for selection from the following options:

1.   Place construct in PTF hold status (via panel DWKZMPR1).

2.   List PTFs (via panel DWKZMPF1).

3.   Maintain PTF log entries (via panel DWKZMLG1).

4.   Install a model PTF (via panel DWKZMLS1).

Lower-level panels are:

Place Construct in PTF Hold (DWKZMPR1) is used to add to or remove from PTF hold status, model constructs (entity types, relationship types and aggregation types).

Add Construct in PTF Hold (DWKZMPR2) is used to specify model constructs to be added to PTF hold status.

List PTFs (DWKZMPF1) is used to produce a list of PTFs, by product identification, PTF identifications, description, and status. Additionally, a PTF and its log entries may be deleted, and manual updating of a PTF's log entries may be initiated.

Maintain PTF Log Entries (DWKZMLG1) is used to display and update the log entries for a specified PTF. Additionally, may initiate the addition of a new log entry for the PTF.

Add PTF Log Entries (DWKZMLG2) is used to add a PTF log entry to manually record the progress for an identified PTF.

Model PTF Installation List (DWKZMLS1) is used to create a display of all received PTFs, their status, and description. Different options can be specified, which are not given here.

9.10   SPECIAL REPOSITORY MANAGER AND HOST FACILITIES ACCESS DIALOGS

These dialogs, which are not shown in detail here, provide the following capabilities:

- Select system services with the following options:

    - Edit a specified file (via the ISPF edit service).
    - Tool trace or timer facility selection.
    - Specify and manipulate system timers.
    - Query or change the active security profile.
    - Maintain emphasis class definitions.
    - Query or maintain locks on objects or aggregations.

- Maintain Aggregation Instance Locks. The following actions can be specified:

    - Edit root entity key value(s).
    - Obtain a lock of the type specified.
    - Remove one lock from aggregation instance.

- Remove all locks from aggregation instance.
- Query lock holders.

- Enter Aggregation Key Values For Lock.

- Aggregation Instance Lock Query.

- Select Trace/Timer Facility.

- Specify System Timers.

- Emphasis Class Selection. The attributes that can be selected are:

  - Code
  - Color
  - Intensity
  - Highlighting
  - Pad

- Emphasis Class Update.

10 BATCH COMMAND LANGUAGE

Repository Manager/MVS provides the facilities of a Batch Repository Maintenance Command Language, which is a set of commands that can be used to:

- Add and delete entity type or relationship type definitions.

- Add and delete repository-wide derivation, integrity, and trigger policies.

- Add, update, and delete entity or relationship instances.

This facility is important when large amounts of information are to be added to, deleted from, or updated in the repository, and it is more efficient from an operational view to run these operations in a batch mode.

At the time of this writing this facility is also used for loading information from an IBM DB/DC Data Dictionary by the Dictionary Migration Tool (DMT), in order to transfer this information to the repository. This tool can be used for this purpose for migration from other dictionaries, however, the required extract and format functions are not supplied by IBM. Thus use of the Batch Command Language for this purpose was a strong motivation for its development. The interface can also be used for a number of other applications.

This facility is invoked through the panel DWKULD1 (Batch Repository Maintenance). Options exist on this panel for the following purposes:

- The commands can be processed as a trial run, i.e., no permanent changes are made to the repository.

- It can be indicated in which add/update mode Repository Manager should process ADD ENTITY command statements, i.e., whether only new definitions should be added or existing definitions should be updated.

- The name of the audit log in which Repository Manager records the results of processing the commands can be specified.

- The file name containing the maintenance commands to be processed can be specified.

10.1   COMMAND LANGUAGE CHARACTERISTICS

Command language statements must obey a number of language conventions. Among these are:

- Each command must start with a new line and must end with a semicolon. A command can start at any place on a line and can span multiple lines, but can only be broken into lines at a place where a blank occurs.

- Operands must be separated by one or more blanks.

- Each comment must begin with a "/*" and end with a "*/".

- Double-byte character set (DBCS) data is allowed in all places where it is supported by Repository Manager.

- Delimited strings are used in a manner consistent with their usage in other parts of Repository Manager.

- A keyword or value must be represented by a delimited string if the keyword contains any of the following characters:

)	right parenthesis
(	left parenthesis
:	colon
	blank
;	semicolon
,	comma
|	solid vertical bar
=	equal sign
'	single quote
"	double quote
/	right slash
*	asterisk

- A keyword value that does not fit on a single line must be represented by a delimited string; it can be broken at any point into segments that must begin and end with an escape character. The terminating escape character of each segment, except the last, must be followed by a solid vertical bar. The last segment must be followed by a semicolon if it is at the end of the command.

10.2   LIST OF BATCH LANGUAGE COMMANDS

Following is the list of *Batch Language Commands* that are supported by Repository Manager/MVS. It must again be pointed out that these are S/370 Application Programming Interface (API) commands and are currently not part of the Repository Manager Common Programming Interface (CPI).

Built-In Functions

    FORMAT
    TEXT

Type Definition Commands

    Entity Type Commands
        Add Entity Type
        Delete Entity Type

Entity Attribute Commands
   Add Entity Attribute
   Delete Entity Attribute

Relationship Type Commands
   Add Relationship Type
   Delete Relationship Type

Trigger Policy Commands
   Add Trigger Policy
   Delete Trigger Policy

Derivation Policy Commands
   Add Derivation Policy
   Delete Derivation Policy

Integrity Policy Commands
   Add Integrity Policy
   Delete Integrity Policy

Instance Commands

Entity Instance Commands
   Add Entity
   Merge Entity
   Refresh Entity
   Replace Entity
   Delete Entity

Relationship Instance Commands
   Add Relationship
   Delete Relationship

Checkpoint Command

These commands will be discussed in the rest of this chapter.

10.3   BUILT-IN FUNCTIONS

Repository Manager provides the following two command language built-in functions:

FORMAT
> This built-in function formats a specified *text string* into one or more lines, with each line, except possibly the last line, containing 72 characters.

RECORDS
> This built-in function formats specified *text strings* into one line for each string, allowing control over the formatting of the text. The function outputs several lines of text for editing and is able to break the lines in the manner desired.

10.4   TYPE DEFINITION COMMANDS

Commands exist that deal either with types or instances of types; this section will discuss those that operate on types.

10.4.1   Entity Type Commands

Commands are available that allow entity types to be added and deleted; modifications to existing entity types are not allowed, as such actions could lead to potential discrepancies between entity type definitions and instances of these types.

10.4.1.1   Add Entity Type

The ADD ENTTYPE (or A ENTTYPE) command adds the specified entity type definition to the repository. If the entity type definition already exists in any tool group, the command adds the entity type to the current or specified tool group and does not change the existing definition; otherwise, it adds the entity type definition to the repository and to the specified or current tool group.

The following *keywords* are used to specify parameters of the command for the case of a *non-dependent* entity type:

> SDESC specifies the short description of an entity type or key attribute. The description applies to the last name specified before the keyword.

> DESC (optionally) specifies the long description of an entity type or key attribute. The FORMAT or RECORDS built-in function must

be used to specify the long description. FORMAT will produce the description as a single paragraph; RECORDS allows control over where each line ends.

TOOLGROUP (optionally) names the tool group to which the entity type definition is added. If not specified, the definition will be added to the current tool group.

LOCK (optionally) specifies whether or not a lock must be obtained before instances can be updated or deleted.

KEYATTR names the key attribute of the entity type.

DATATYPE is required and must designate one of the following: a character string, a decimal number, or a fixed length binary number.

KEYTYPE (optionally) designates whether the key is system-generated or user-specified.

In the case of a *dependent* entity type, the following apply:

SDESC and DESC can be associated with the owning relationship type.

DEPENDENT, for which the default is NO, must be specified as YES.

OWNINGREL specifies the name of the owning relationship type in the primary direction.

INVERSEREL specifies the name of the owning relationship type in the inverse direction.

SOURCE names the source of the owning relationship type.

SRCTYPE specifies whether the source of the owning relationship type is an entity type or a relationship type.

INSTANCE optionally specifies whether the owning relationship type is 1–1 or 1–M. The latter is the default.

MANDATORY (optionally) allows the specification of the mandatory property for the owning relationship type. Options are that it is mandatory for both the source and the target or only for the target.

CONTROLLING (optionally) allows the specification of the controlling property for the owning relationship type. Options are that it is controlling for both the source and the target or only for the target.

10.4.1.2   Delete Entity Type

The DELETE ENTTYPE (or D ENTTYPE) command deletes the specified entity type definition from the current or specified tool group. The optional keyword TOOLGROUP allows the specification of the tool group from which the definition is to be deleted; if not specified, the command will delete the entity type definition from the current tool group.

10.4.2   Entity Type Attribute Commands

This section presents commands that operate on attributes of entity types.

10.4.2.1   Add Entity Type Attribute

The ADD ATTR (or A ATTR) command can be used to add nonkey attributes to an entity type. If the attribute already exists for the entity type, Repository Manager will not process the command

In addition to the keywords specifying the name of the attribute type and the name of the entity type, keywords that apply to this command are SDESC, DESC, and DATATYPE, specifying the short description, description, and data type, respectively.

10.4.2.2   Delete Entity Type Attribute

The DELETE ATTR (or D ATTR) command is used to delete an existing non-key attribute from an entity type definition. Only the attribute name and entity type name are specified.

10.4.3 Relationship Type Commands

This section presents commands that operate on relationship types; they are similar to the commands that operate on entity types.

10.4.3.1 Add Relationship Type

The ADD RELTYPE (or A RELTYPE) command can be used to add a relationship type definition. If the relationship type definition already exists in any tool group in the repository, the current definition is added to the specified or current tool group. The existing definition is not changed.

The following keywords are used to specify parameters for the relationship type definition:

INVERSEREL specifies the name of the inverse relationship type.

SDECR, DESC, and TOOLGROUP have the same characteristics as for entity type definitions.

SOURCE names the source of the relationship type being added.

TARGET names the target of the relationship type being added.

SRCTYPE and TRGTYPE specify whether the source and the target, respectively, are an entity type or a relationship type.

INSTANCE (optionally) allows the specification of the instance control property of the relationship type. Allowable values are 1-1, 1-M, M-1, and M-M. The last one is the default.

MANDATORY (optionally) specifies the mandatory property of the relationship type. Possible options are:

> Mandatory for both source and target
> Mandatory for the source
> Mandatory for the target
> Not mandatory (the default)

CONTROLLING is as above, but specifies the controlling property of the relationship type.

ORDERING (optionally) allows the specification of whether the relationship type is:

> Ordered in the inverse direction
> Ordered in the prime direction
> Not ordered (the default)

10.4.3.2 Delete Relationship Type

The DELETE RELTYPE (or D RELTYPE) command is used to delete a relationship type. If the TOOLGROUP parameter is present, the relationship type will be deleted from the specified tool group. Otherwise, it will be deleted from the current tool group.

10.4.4   Trigger Policy Commands

Commands are available to add and delete trigger policies on entity types or relationship types.

10.4.4.1 Add Trigger Policy

The ADD TRIGPOL (or A TRIGPOL) command is used to add a trigger policy either to an entity type named by the keyword ENTTYPE or to a relationship type named by the keyword RELTYPE.

The following keywords are used in the command:

POLTYPE is required when adding a trigger policy for an entity type; it indicates whether the policy is invoked when an entity instance is read from the repository or an entity instance or relationship instance is written to the repository.

POSITION indicates after which existing trigger policy the new policy will be inserted. If the parameter is not specified, the new policy will be added at the end.

DESC (optionally) specifies the description associated with the trigger policy.

COND is used to name a REXX function that specifies the conditions for invoking the trigger policy.

FUNCTION names the function that is called when the trigger policy is invoked.

PARMS is used to specify the parameters that are passed to the above function.

10.4.4.2   Delete Trigger Policy

The DELETE TRIGPOL (or D TRIGPOL) command is used to delete a trigger policy either from an entity type named by the keyword ENTTYPE or from a relationship type named by the keyword RELTYPE.

In addition to these parameters, only the parameter specified by POSITION needs to be supplied.

10.4.5   Derivation Policy Commands

Commands are available that allow derivation policies to be added or deleted.

10.4.5.1   Add Derivation Policy

The ADD DERVPOL (or A DERVPOL) command is used to add a derivation policy to an entity type named by the keyword ENTTYPE.

The keywords used in the command are similar to those used for trigger policies. The major differences are:

- The command does not apply to relationship types.

- The keyword ATTR is used to specify the attribute of the entity type to which the derivation policy applies.

- The keyword DERVEXP is used to specify a REXX function used to derive the value of the field.

10.4.5.2   *Delete Derivation Policy*

The DELETE DERVPOL (or D DERVPOL) command is used to delete a derivation policy from an entity type named by the keyword ENTTYPE.

In addition to these parameters, the parameters specified by ATTR, POLTYPE, and POSITION need to be supplied.

10.4.6   Integrity Policy Commands

This section discusses commands that are used to add or delete integrity policies on entity types or relationship types.

10.4.6.1   *Add Integrity Policy*

The ADD INTGPOL (or A INTGPOL) command is used to add an integrity policy either to an entity type named by the keyword ENTTYPE or to a relationship type named by the keyword RELTYPE.

The keywords ENTTYPE, RELTYPE, ATTR, POSITION, and DESC are used similarly fashion to those used in the previous policy commands. Other keywords used:

> COND specifies a required parameter representing a REXX function that is used to determine if the field is valid.

> MSGID is used to specify the ID of the message Repository Manager issues if the field is invalid.

10.4.6.2   *Delete Integrity Policy*

The DELETE INTGPOL (or D INTGPOL) command is used to delete an integrity policy either from an entity type named by the keyword ENTTYPE or from a relationship type named by the keyword RELTYPE.

In addition to these parameters, only the parameter specified by POSITION needs to be supplied.

10.5   INSTANCE COMMANDS

This section presents instance commands that operate on instances
of entity types or relationship types.

10.5.1   Entity Type Instance Commands

These commands exert considerably more control over the actions that
can be performed on instances of entity types than on the types
themselves. These options are presented in this section.

10.5.1.1   Add Entity

The ADD ENTITY (or A ENT or A E) is used to add a specified entity type
instance.

The instance to be added is specified by a value of one of the key
attributes of the entity. If the instance is an instance of a dependent
entity type, the correct sequence of all parent key names and key values
must be specified.

The key value of an entity type instance can be either:

- The value of a user-assigned key.

- A placeholder value for a system-assigned key. This
  placeholder has the form DWKKEY*identifier*, where
  identifier is a character string with 1 to 26 characters.

Optionally, one or up to 99 values of attributes can be specified by
clauses of the form attribute-name = value.

In the following entity instance commands, entity instances are specified
as above.

10.5.1.2   Merge Entity

The MERGE ENTITY (or M ENT or M E) command has the following effect:

- If the specified entity instance exists, the command updates the specified attributes and does not change other existing attributes.

- If the specified entity instance does not exist, the command adds the entity and the specified attribute values and sets all other attribute values to null.

10.5.1.3   Refresh Entity

The REFRESH ENTITY (or R ENT or R E) command has the following effect:

- If the entity instance exists, the command updates the specified attribute values and sets all other attribute values to null.

- If the entity instance does not exist, the command adds the entity with the specified attribute values and sets all other attributes values to null.

10.5.1.4   Replace Entity

The REPLACE ENTITY (or REP ENT or REP E) command has the following effect:

- If the entity instance exists, the command deletes the existing entity instance and any associated relationship instances and adds a new entity instance with the specified attribute values.

- If the entity instance does not exist, the command adds the specified entity instance and all specified attribute values.

10.5.1.5   Delete Entity

The DELETE ENTITY (or D ENT or D E) command deletes the specified entity instance.

10.5.2   Relationship Type Instance Commands

Instances of relationship types can be added or deleted with the commands presented here.

10.5.2.1   Add Relationship

The ADD RELATIONSHIP (or A REL or A R) command adds a new instance of the relationship type specified. If the source or target instance is also a relationship, the additional relationship(s) are also added if they do not exist.

A *Source* or *Target* parameter is used to specify the source or target for the relationship instance. The value can be specified either to be an entity instance or a relationship instance. The same rules for specifying an instance as used before apply.

10.5.2.2   Delete Relationship

The DELETE RELATIONSHIP (or D REL or D R) command deletes a specified relationship instance. The relationship instance is specified as above.

The method of specification of a relationship instance is quite general, as can be seen in the example shown in Figure 10-1.

10.6   CHECKPOINT COMMAND

The CHECKPOINT command is provided to specify when Repository Manager should save or discard changes made to the repository while processing batch commands.

If a trial run has been requested, Repository Manager discards all changes made to the repository since it began processing the current batch commands or since processing the last checkpoint command. If a trial run has not been requested, Repository Manager saves all changes. In addition, Repository Manager binds all entity type and relationship type definitions processed.

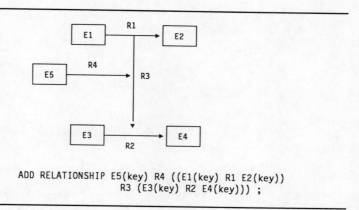

```
ADD RELATIONSHIP E5(key) R4 ((E1(key) R1 E2(key))
                   R3 (E3(key) R2 E4(key))) ;
```

Figure 10-1   Example of adding a relationship instance.

11 THE INFORMATION RESOURCE DICTIONARY SYSTEM

This chapter deals with developments in the standards arena that are related to Repository Manager. They are discussed here from two points of view: that they provide information on developments in the repository systems area, and that they provide additional information on the positioning of the Repository Manager/MVS program product.

In March 1990, IBM proposed to Technical Committee X3H4 an IRDS Services Interface, which is based on Repository Manager. This statement needs a great deal of explanation.

What is Technical Committee X3H4? It is a technical committee reporting to the Accredited Standards Committee X3 on Information Processing Systems. X3, which operates under the procedures of the American National Standards Institute, has a number of technical committees on a variety of subjects, each of which is charged with developing standards on the particular area of information processing assigned to it. IRDS is an acronym for Information Resource Dictionary System, and this particular area is assigned to a technical committee whose name is X3H4 (every technical committee that belongs to X3 has a designator that starts with X3 — for example, X3H2, which is the committee on Database Languages responsible for SQL).

11.1   BACKGROUND OF THE IRDS STANDARD

X3H4 began its work in late 1980 with the goal of developing a standard in the area of dictionary systems. The name Information Resource Dictionary System was chosen to convey the concept that the standard would be a system that not only could be used in connection with the typical data processing environment at which most dictionary systems of that time were aimed, but would provide for the management and control of all information resources.

The initial target was to produce three basic capabilities:

- A command language with hard syntax that could be used in both batch and interactive environments.

- A "panel interface" aimed at the interactive environment, which would be useable by both novice and experienced users.

- A generalized file format that could be used to transport some or all of the contents of one IRDS to another IRDS, even if the two IRDSs were developed by different vendors and operated on different platforms.

Standards development is, under the best of circumstances, a very slow process. The progression of the IRDS standard was even slower than most, in large part because of the committee's desire to progress the standard not only as an American National Standard, but also as an International Standard. This goal was not met.

The standard for an IRDS Command Language and Panel Interface became an American National Standard (ANSI X3.138-1988) in October 1988. It was subsequently adopted as a Federal Information Processing Standard (FIPS 156) in April 1989. A proposed standard entitled "IRDS Export/Import File Format" has recently undergone public review and is currently being processed for adoption as an American National Standard. It will most likely also become a Federal Information Processing Standard.

When the work on the IRDS standard was begun, the emphasis was primarily on developing a tool for Data Administrators and Database Administrators. This purpose could be served by a system which was basically passive, i.e., a documentation aid. An interface was included that allows the IRDS to be called from a program written in a language that includes a "CALL" facility; this interface, however, is not very robust and suffers from the serious disadvantage that programs written to access the IRDS are not transportable from one IRDS implementation to another.

11.2   THE IRDS SERVICES INTERFACE

The development of more formalized and powerful software engineering techniques in the middle 1980s caused the X3H4 committee to reevaluate the scope of the IRDS standards it would develop. The general opinion was that there was a need for the standards under development at that time, but that, in addition, there was a need for a more powerful programmatic interface to the IRDS. The name chosen for this new project was "IRDS Services Interface."

The projected scope for this interface was that it should be "functionally equivalent" to the IRDS Command Language and Panel Interface, which means that it should use the same basic data structures, and that its functionality should be completely parallel to those other interfaces. Specifically, the IRDS Services Interface should allow external programs to populate, access, and maintain the contents of the IRDS dictionary and its schema. This would then allow the IRDS to be actively used as a database of information resource descriptions including: applications, programs, files, databases, data elements, networks, hardware devices, documents, etc. These descriptions could be accessed by a variety of software tools, such as compilers, database administration tools, data administration tools, CASE tools, and application development systems.

An interesting sidelight is that the committee felt, correctly, that one of the prime targets for using the Services Interface, was vendors who would be planning to implement an IRDS Command Language or Panel Interface. The availability of a Services Interface would simplify such a task, and it would be easier to maintain configuration control over such implementations.

It should not be totally surprising that the above sounds very much like a description of Repository Manager; this similarity only reinforces the recognition of the need for tools of this type.

There are substantial differences in some of the fundamental concepts used by the IRDS and Repository Manager. These will be discussed in the next section. On the other hand, given the closely parallel uses, there are also many similarities between the two. It is thus reasonable that IBM should have submitted a proposal for an IRDS Services Interface to the X3H4 committee that, to a large extent, is based on the Repository Manager Common Programming Interface (CPI). As a requirement of a standard, the implementation of this IRDS Services Interface does not require Repository Manager; it can be implemented on any other platform and does not even require the availability of DB2 or any other relational database management system.

The status of this proposal is the following: in early 1991, the committee voted to forward the proposal for public review, and it is expected that it will shortly be available as such.

In order not to be misleading, it must be emphasized that the IRDS Services Interface does not bring the IRDS under the umbrella of the Repository Manager. If and when there should be an implementation of the Services Interface on a platform on which Repository Manager exists, it can be expected that a great deal of the underlying code will be shared by the two systems. On the other hand, the repository managed by Repository Manager and the IRDS database will most likely be two separate repositories, unless, of course, some way is found to map from one to the other. The technology required to manage this mapping is, at present, hardly available and certainly not mature.

The IRDS Services Interface submitted by IBM is based on the use of templates and template trees to access and maintain information stored in the IRDS database. The functionality required for this template interface is very similar to that in Repository Manager. Some of the underlying concepts are different due to the differences in the IRDS data model. A possible proof of the strength of the underlying concepts in Repository Manager is its ability to model the IRDS concepts are foreign to it.

11.3 COMPARISON OF REPOSITORY MANAGER AND THE IRDS

As stated before, the motivation behind the specification of the IRDS was in the area of data administration and database administration; this explains why many of the features of the IRDS are similar to those found in a more traditional data dictionary system. Since the motivation of Repository Manager was basically different — its primary emphasis was on providing an environment oriented toward tools —

it is of interest to compare some of the differences between IRDS and Repository Manager and to examine the reasoning for the differences.

In terms of complexity and sophistication, as well as size, there is no question that Repository Manager represents a radically different kind of system. However, as will be discussed in Sections 11.3.6.4 and 11.3.6.5, basic facilities available in the IRDS in the area of Life Cycle Management and Versioning are not present in Repository Manager.

11.3.1   Views

Repository Manager allows for three distinct views: conceptual, logical, and storage. The IRDS Command Language and Panel Interface specification deals primarily with a conceptual view. The proposed IRDS Services Interface, which is in the form of templates very similar to those used by Repository Manager, presents a logical view similar to the Repository Manager logical view. Since the IRDS does not specify an implementation (this being left to the implementor), no storage view is specified by the standard, but would presumably be supplied by the developer. This matches the fact that the Repository Manager storage view discussed in this book is specific to Repository Manager/MVS.

The IRDS also uses a different concept of views, which should not be confused with the above. An IRD schema view, or an IRD view, consists of a Life Cycle Phase (see 11.3.6.5) together with the types in it that are available to a user.

11.3.2   Data Model

Both Repository Manager and the IRDS use an Entity-Relationship model in their conceptual view. The IRDS model is relatively simple, and the Repository Manager is considerably more complex. Facilities in the latter that do not exist in the former are numerous, among them:

- Policies for entity types and relationship types
- Relationship types capable of having one or two relationship types as members
- Constraints on instances of relationship types
- Aggregation types
- Object interface, including object types, methods, and method implementations

The above facilities provide the means to construct models that are considerably more complex and contain more semantic richness than what is available in the IRDS.

11.3.3   Information Model

As discussed in Chapter 6, the role of the IBM-Supplied ER Model is central to the function Repository Manager is to provide. The IRDS does not have any information model in this sense; there is supplied (in the form of an optional module of the standard) an information model called the "Basic Functional IRD Schema." The role of this IRD Schema is, however, totally different from that of the Supplied ER Model; it is merely intended to supply a "starter set" of entity types and relationship types, along with their attributes. The availability of these, which in a very minimal way describe a traditional data processing environment, is intended to let an enterprise use the IRDS at a very early time after its installation. By way of comparison, the use of Repository Manager is intended to be preceded by a, perhaps lengthy, period of enterprise modeling.

11.3.4   Entity Naming

The major difference in this area is that the IRDS requires that the name of an instance of an entity type be unique in the entire IRDS dictionary, whereas Repository Manager only requires uniqueness within type (i.e., two instances of the same type cannot have the same name, but two instances of different types can have the same name).

The reason for the naming uniqueness in the IRDS was user-friendliness; it was argued that if users knew the name of an entity, they would not have to know its type in order to find it in the dictionary. In a certain way, there is some justification to this reasoning, but it is becoming more and more apparent that the solution adopted by Repository Manager is the better one. IBM argued before the X3H4 Committee that it was unreasonable not to allow a program entity in the IMS environment not to have the same name as its PSB. Other instances in the IRDS environment itself also exist where it would be convenient to have an aggregate for the same name as its root entity.

Both systems have a facility whereby the name of an instance of a specified entity type can have its name generated by the system; however, the intent of providing this facility in the two systems is quite different. In Repository Manager, the name is a key that can be concatenated with other keys. In the IRDS, this feature is considered to be a convenience, whereby entity type instances can be entered into the dictionary prior to the time their real name has been decided on. In such a case,the entity is entered and assigned a name by the IRDS, and the intent is that this name will later be changed.

11.3.5   Relationship Types

The IRDS is much more limited in its ability to model relationship types. It is restricted to binary relationship types, with both members (source and target) being entity types. An n-ary relationship type can be modeled by decomposing it into a series of binary relationship types. This, however, has the disadvantage that, from the user's point of view, intermediate constructs have to be built that generally lack conceptual meaning.

11.3.6   Attributes

It is in the area of attributes (which in the IRDS are referred to as "attribute types") that the IRDS data model has considerably more flexibility in its native modeling capability. This flexibility exists in several areas.

11.3.6.1   Attributes on Relationship Types

The IRDS data model recognizes attributes, as well as attribute groups, on relationship types. There is no need, as there is in the Repository Manager data model, to portray these as dependent entities.

11.3.6.2   Attribute Groups

As above, The IRDS data model recognizes attribute groups, and there is no need to model them as dependent entities.

11.3.6.3   Multivalued Attributes and Attribute Groups

Again, the IRDS allows these constructs to be modeled in a natural fashion without any need to resort to auxiliary constructs. Additionally, the maximum value of the number of occurrences can be specified and is enforced by the system.

11.3.6.4   *Versioning*

Versioning is provided in the IRDS to allow more than one entity type instance or entity type to exist with the same name; these are distinguished by their *version identifier*. In the IRD (the dictionary), the version identifier consists of the concatenation of an optional *variation name* and a *revision number*. The purpose of the variation name is to allow the same name to be assigned to two distinct entity type instances, such as a 5-digit ZIP code and a 9-digit ZIP code. Revision numbers are assigned in an increasing sequence so that progress of an instance can be tracked. In the IRD Schema, a similar arrangement exists, except that variation names are not used.

The *edition number* in the object interface of Repository Manager has a similar meaning; however, it only applies to aggregates, and its use appears to be more suitable for configuration management than for tracking progress of an instance in the Life Cycle.

The manner in which version identifiers are used is related to Life Cycle Management in the IRDS, which will be discussed next.

11.3.6.5   *Life Cycle Management*

The IRDS offers similar, but slightly different, facilities for Life Cycle Management in both the IRD and the IRD Schema. Both of these Life Cycle phases are available in the system, and the general rule is that every entity type instance, as well as every entity type itself (both with their version identifier), exists in exactly one Life Cycle phase. An overview of IRDS Life Cycle Management will now be given.

In the IRD Schema, there are exactly three Life Cycle phases — UNCONTROLLED, CONTROLLED, and ARCHIVED — where an installation has the option to change these names to others that may better reflect local usage. The meaning of these IRD Schema Life Cycle phases (this name is chosen to differentiate them from IRD Life Cycle phases) is as follows:

- An entity type (or some other construct that is also subject to Life Cycle Management control) can be added, subject to the proper permission being available, only to the

UNCONTROLLED IRD Schema Life Cycle phase. It can be modified or deleted subject to permissions.

- Entity types are allowed to migrate between these Life Cycle phases, subject to restrictions that will be described later.

- The meaning of the CONTROLLED IRD Schema Life Cycle phase is that an entity type must be in this Life Cycle phase in order to be instantiated. Any such entity type cannot be modified or deleted. If it needs modifying, it must first be moved to the UNCONTROLLED IRD Schema Life Cycle phase.

- An entity type in the ARCHIVED IRD Schema Life Cycle phase can be thought of as having been a component of a production system in the past, but now superseded or no longer needed. Any such entity type can be deleted, but cannot be modified.

In the IRD Schema, there is a way of designating which relationship types are considered to be significant for Life Cycle Management. This dependency is named "Life Cycle Phase Sensitivity." The rules for moving an entity type into the CONTROLLED IRD Schema Life Cycle phase are simply that it cannot be moved unless all other entity types on which it already depends via a sensitive relationship type are in the CONTROLLED IRD Schema Life Cycle phase.

In the dictionary, a similar situation exists, except that here there can be any number of IRD Life Cycle phases, as determined by the installation, similar to the UNCONTROLLED IRD Schema Life Cycle phase, each with a distinct name assigned by the installation. The meaning assigned to the CONTROLLED Life Cycle phase is that there reside the definitions of applications in production. UNCONTROLLED Life Cycle phases can correspond to activities like development or testing. They can also be set up to provide a partition for an individual project or for specific activities of a project. Since access control can be maintained on a Life Cycle phase, this mechanism provides good separation between teams working on different activities.

There is complete freedom to move an entity from one of these UNCONTROLLED IRD Life Cycle phases to another, subject to the user having access to both of them. A similar rule exists with moving an entity type instance from an UNCONTROLLED Life Cycle phase to the CONTROLLED Life Cycle phase. This is in recognition, for instance, that it would be undesirable to consider a program to be in a production status as long as a module it used was still under development.

Even though Repository Manager contains a substantially wider range of facilities in other areas, it falls short of the IRDS in this important control domain. It can be expected that tools will be made available in AD/Cycle that deal with Life Cycle Management. Since there are many different methodologies and techniques for dealing with this problem, it will be difficult to maintain a consistent underlying structure among tools.

12   REPOSITORIES AND OPEN SYSTEMS ARCHITECTURE

There is no question that Repository Manager/MVS is a very powerful system that can be used to great advantage, nor is there any doubt that it will be a potent influence in the information systems environment. As to whether Repository Manager/MVS, or, perhaps more precisely the current release of this program product, is the ultimate repository system, the answer is probably no. Subsequent releases will undoubtedly introduce new features, but there are questions, discussed later in this chapter, of how Repository Manager will function in an environment containing non-IBM platforms. Of longer-range concern is whether the modeling capability of Repository Manager is sufficiently general to allow it to evolve into what in Section 12.3.3 is called a meta-repository.

Information processing in the 1990s is turning more and more toward what is referred to as "Open Systems Architecture." By this is meant that there is a movement towards establishing networks of hetero-geneous platforms, possibly running heterogeneous software systems using different protocols. From a user perspective, it is necessary that these networks appear as a single homogeneous system. The magnitude of the problems facing the information processing community is such that the move toward Open Systems Architecture is not a "luxury" but a requirement that must be satisfied.

Repository Manager, as part of SAA, shows some future promise in enabling such an integration in an entirely IBM environment. There is no doubt that there will be implementations of Repository Manager on other SAA platforms. Even if Repository Manager/MVS does not at present address the distributed environment, we can only assume that this will come in time. However, the problem lies in the fact that the environments that require an Open Systems capability are not all-IBM environments, and it is doubtful that the Repository Manager technology is sufficiently robust to deal with heterogeneous environments.

Standards, both on the national and international level, play an important part in reaching the Open Systems goal. This is due to the fact that interfaces are a key element in achieving this goal and that much of the concern of standards is to define interfaces. One problem with standards is that their development is time-consuming and slow, making the danger that new technology will overtake a standard under development ever-present.

12.1   REPOSITORY STANDARDS

Among Repository standards currently under development are the following:

- IRDS, as an International Standards Organization (ISO) project, is currently in the last stages of becoming an international standard. The international project ISO IRDS1 and ANSI IRDS1 are not compatible, which is not necessarily a desirable state of affairs.

  IRDS2, in the U.S., to be developed by Technical Committee X3H4, is intended to be the successor to the current IRDS. There is also an understanding that ISO will embark on a new IRDS2 project and that the result of this project will be identical to the U.S. IRDS2 project. This is another way of saying that the conclusion of the U.S. IRDS2 project will be delayed until it is fully accepted by the corresponding ISO group. Estimates of when this new standard will be available vary substantially; considering the extensive review cycles required, a well-informed guess puts this time at a minimum of five years. This standard will then be developed jointly by U.S. and international bodies.

- A Repository standard is being developed by the European Computer Manufacturers Association (ECMA), which is intended to enable integration of tools. The name of this standard is Portable Common Tool Environment (PCTE), and IBM, as well as Digital Equipment Corporation and other U.S. manufacturers, have announced their intention to support PCTE.

- A significant development along similar but somewhat different lines is taking place under the aegis of a U.S. organization named IPO (IGES PDES Organization), which works with ISO Technical Committee 184. The meaning of these acronyms is as follows: IGES is a graphics standard concerned with a neutral format for matters such as engineering drafting and mechanical 3D drawings; PDES is an acronym for Product Data Exchange for STEP. STEP is an acronym for Standard for the Exchange of Product Model Data, which is a soon-to-be international standard. STEP at this point is a joint U.S – European effort reporting to ISO.

  The problem being tackled here is that different specification languages and methodologies use different constructs, and that there is a need for a common model that can be used for converting from one set of constructs to another. The effort has culminated in the STEP Unification Meta-Model (SUMM); this is not a repository model in itself, but the technology developed has important consequences for achieving model unification in a repository environment.

- A new work item undertaken by the X3 Technical Committee X3T2, Data Interchange, in cooperation with ISO is the development of a conceptual schema language. This effort does not include the specification of a repository; however, it is to be expected that the actual definition of an enterprise conceptual schema will ultimately be stored in a repository. It is in this sense that the constructs defined in the conceptual schema language will have an effect on future directions of repository standards.

- CASE tool vendors have formed an organization, under the auspices of the Electronics Industry Association, named CASE Data Interchange Format (CDIF) to develop an interchange format for meta-data shared by CASE tools

12.2 DIGITAL EQUIPMENT CORPORATION REPOSITORY

One of IBM's strongest competitors in providing a repository environment is Digital Equipment Corporation (DEC), which has announced an integrated CASE tools environment named *Cohesion*. Among the strategic components of Cohesion is *CDD/Repository*, a new version of DEC's *CDD/Plus* dictionary product. CDD/Repository implements a tool services interface named *A Tool Integration Standard* (ATIS), which is based on a definition jointly developed by DEC and Atherton Technologies. This interface is strongly object-oriented. In this architecture, CDD/Plus provides an Entity-Relationship interface to CDD/Repository, with ATIS providing an Object-Oriented interface. It should be pointed out that in spite of ATIS being called a "standard," it is not a standard in the sense of a "Standard" in the standards arena.

DEC has positioned Cohesion as part of its Network Application System architecture. This architecture is intended to include not only the DEC VAX/VMS and Ultrix environments but also MS-DOS, OS/2, and the Macintosh operating systems.

DEC, in cooperation with tool builders and selected customers, is developing an Information Model that will take the same role in the DEC environment that IBM's Supplied ER Model takes in the Repository Manager environment. At this point, a comparison of these models cannot be made.

It is also of interest and potential significance that DEC has submitted ATIS to Technical Committee X3H4 as a Base Document for IRDS2. Both X3H4 and the ISO IRDS effort have decided to modify the system by adding to it a template-based interface similar to what is available in the IRDS Services Interface. It is too early to speculate on how well these two approaches can be made to fit together.

12.3 INTEGRATION OF SYSTEMS

Integration of heterogeneous systems has always been a serious problem. This integration is important in the confines of a single large enterprise, where there is a need to provide access to a set of heterogeneous platforms. Yet this problem is relatively minor compared to this same problem involving a set of different and independent enterprises.

In this section, a series of architectures will be presented, all of which, in some sense or another, are aimed at providing integration and unification of multiple heterogeneous systems.

12.3.1   The Pre-Repository Architecture

Architectures that provide integration of multiple systems existed before the idea of a repository being incorporated in them. A conceptualization of such an architecture is shown in Figure 12-1. It is clear that, with sufficient effort, integration of the systems can be achieved. The integration takes place through the definition of a sufficient number of protocols, but this is such a weak case of an Open Systems Architecture that it should not be called that. The mere fact that a way has been provided for systems to communicate with each other does not create an Open Systems Architecture; i.e., communication alone does not mean integration.

12.3.2   The Repository Architectures

An improvement can be expected if a repository is added to the configuration used above. There are two ways this can be done, which appear to be quite similar but have different impacts on an implementation. One configuration is shown in Figure 12-2; here a repository has been attached to one of the systems in the network. This is approximately how the initial release of Repository Manager/MVS would appear, at least until some way of distributing the repository is provided.

The other configuration is shown in Figure 12-3. Here, the repository capability is provided by a dedicated Repository Server. From an implementation point of view, this configuration is simpler because it concentrates this capability onto a single platform, which does not have to perform any other actions, allows more flexibility in the implementation of this Repository Server, and, conceivably, allows the architecture to be customized since only a single set of functions have to be performed. This configuration has been used successfully in some prototype work for the U.S. Air Force on query systems in a heterogeneous DBMS environment on heterogeneous platforms.

Either of these configurations provides for a good measure of integration at a certain cost. In either case, the limits of integration are the extent to which the repository system is able to describe the constructs that exist on the other systems in the network. In the configuration shown

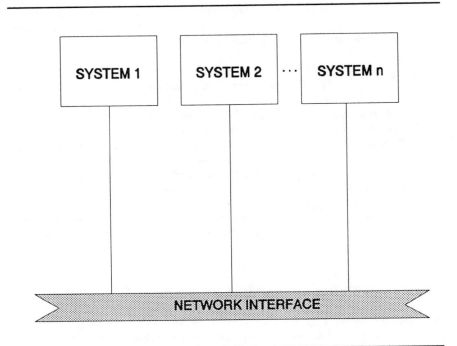

Figure 12-1   A network without a repository.

in Figure 12-2, it appears that Repository Manager/MVS will be able to integrate the network in a satisfactory manner, but probably only as long as the other systems in the network are IBM platforms. In order for AD/Cycle and Repository Manager to perform the required functions in a heterogeneous environment there is a requirement for cross-compilers to non-IBM platforms — it is doubtful that these will ever exist.

12.3.3   The Post-Repository Architecture

Unfortunately, this problem will become more complicated. The more attention being paid to repository technology, the more different the ideas as to what such a system should be. Some of the arguments take on an almost religious fanaticism, as is the case sometimes on the subject of other methodologies. Standards work notwithstanding, it

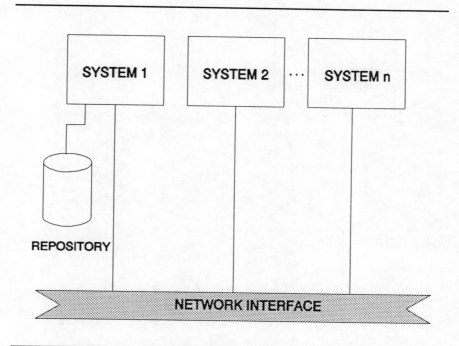

Figure 12-2   A network with a repository.

is more than just unlikely that there will ever be a single "universal" (if not galactic) repository system that will be used by all enterprises. The consequence is that, even if all participants agree to use a repository-based approach, the various repositories, and the constructs and information models peculiar to them, will not be able to inter-communicate as closely as the Open Systems Architecture will require. It is possible to develop technology to unify these approaches, but this has not been done to date. This is the situation that will result in the configuration shown in Figure 12-4.

It almost seems that the problem has come full circle and that repositories will not provide the solution that is required. Fortunately, this is not the case. The problem has now been transformed, and the solution is what is referred to as a *meta-repository*. A conceptual configuration of a network with a meta-repository is shown in Figure 12-5. The function of the meta-repository is to mediate between

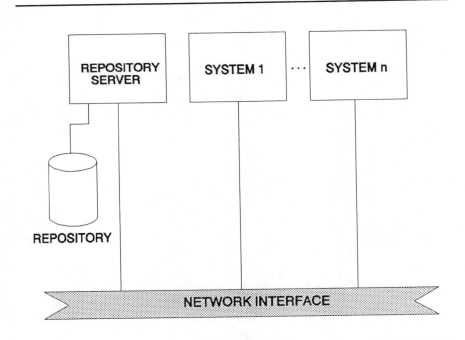

Figure 12-3   A network with a repository server.

the various repositories. Each repository would be able to continue performing local functions, but for purposes of communicating with other platforms, it would use the services of the meta-repository to translate the constructs from its local repository to those of the target repository. This approach does not guarantee absolute universality; sufficient intelligence will have to be built into the meta-repository to allow it to understand all the other repositories.

12.4   COMPUTER INTEGRATED MANUFACTURING

Integration of heterogeneous systems is an important problem in what is referred to as *Computer Integrated Manufacturing* (CIM). In addition to the many functions involved in a single enterprise, the manufacture of any complex system involves a multitude of different enterprises; typical roles required will include subsystem designers, subcontractors

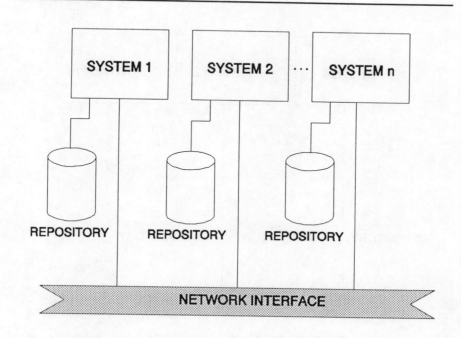

Figure 12-4   A network with many repositories.

(of several tiers), parts suppliers, maintenance personnel, etc. The scope of these is not necessarily within a single country, particularly in Europe where activities generally cross national boundaries.

Current practices in this area are often referred to as *islands of automation* because many areas are supported by stand-alone applications processes that cannot communicate with each other. Within each activity, there may be independent systems, each one executing its own set of subactivities.

This problem has been well recognized not only by manufacturers but also by government agencies which see this problem as one of the most serious and costly. It is generally recognized that the solution to the problem will involve repository technology, as repositories will enable different activities to work cooperatively.

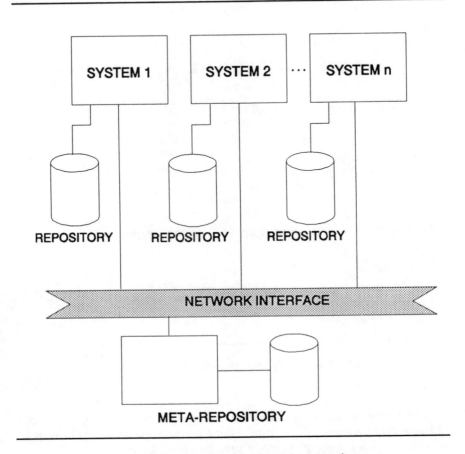

Figure 12-5   A network with a meta-repository.

IBM and DEC, as well as others have been active in CIM, not only because it is a fertile ground for marketing products but also interestingly enough, because they need it for their own operations. Similar in scope to IBM's Repository Manager in SAA is IBM's new suite of products, Computer Integrated Manufacturing Communications and Data Facility (CIM CDF), which is intended to unify manufacturing application systems executing on selected IBM platforms.

The two major efforts aimed at providing enterprise integration exist in the CIM area; one of these is in this country, and the other one in Europe. These will now be discussed.

12.4.1   CALS

Computer-aided Acquisition and Logistics Support (CALS) is a joint-services effort undertaken by the Department of Defense. It consists of a number of separate initiatives aimed at streamlining all the phases of the logistics process. This process, even for a single system (e.g., a new weapons system) normally involves a large number of contractors, sometimes as many as 1,500. CALS is intended to enable sharing of data not only among the contractors but also between contractors and involved government agencies. The current focus of CALS has been on sharing data associated with product definition, and among members of production teams. The problem of Enterprise Integration is receiving a substantial amount of attention.

CALS is also having a significant effect on the private sector by itself, where corporations not involved in government contracts are requiring that the same guidelines be followed by their contractors. There is also substantial interest in Europe in these activities.

Emphasis on different initiatives within CALS has been assigned to individual services. Enterprise Integration has been assigned to the Air Force, and it can be expected that work relating to repository technology will be sponsored.

12.4.2   CIM-OSA

This section describes a similar effort aimed at providing a framework for integration in the Computer Integrated Manufacturing field taking place in Europe. A consortium known as European Strategic Programme for Research and Development in Information Technologies (ESPRIT) is the sponsor of a program called *Open Systems Architecture for Computer Integrated Manufacturing* (CIM-OSA). Responsibility for the program has been delegated to a project team named AMICE (a reverse acronym for European Computer Integration Manufacturing Architecture), which addresses the problem area of Computer Integrated Manufacturing systems design and implementation. It has wide European participation; among its members are Aerospatiale of France, British Aerospace, International Computers Ltd., Siemens, and

Volkswagen AG, as well as IBM Germany and the German subsidiary of Digital Equipment Corporation. Other participants are from Belgium, Denmark, and Italy.

The work done to date is highly complex; in the description that follows some simplifications are introduced, but they do not affect the understanding of the effort.

The broad objectives of the effort are to develop a CIM Open Systems Architecture that can be applied across a broad spectrum of applications and industries and that can be made to encompass new technologies as they evolve. The following summarizes the main objectives of the project:

- Enabling fast, economic utilization of advanced technologies

- Ensuring long-range, evolutionary CIM implementation and growth

- Enabling and supporting independent development of CIM building blocks

The aim of CIM-OSA, then, is to provide an extensive conceptual framework, adaptable to concrete situations, that will allow CIM users to evolve in an open and decentralized way, suppliers to aim for well-defined targets in the development of new products, and developers and implementors to provide migration paths from existing applications to more integrated environments.

An overall CIM-OSA Framework has been established; its conceptual completeness and general applicability have been verified by a number of case studies. The main concepts of the CIM-OSA Framework, which are described in the following sections, form a three-dimensional structure, — i.e., the levels of CIM-OSA Architecture (Section 12.4.2.1), Modeling Levels (Section 12.4.2.2), and Views (Section 12.4.2.3) are the three axes of this construct.

12.4.2.1 CIM-OSA Architecture

CIM-OSA Architecture is an important concept. Two such architectures are defined: The Reference Architecture, which contains generic industry models, and the Particular Architecture, which contains models that are mapped from the Reference Architecture and intended to apply to a specific enterprise. These architectures are further refined into levels.

- The *Reference Architecture* consists of two levels: the Generic Level, which contains generic constructs common to all industries, and the Partial Level, which particularizes these constructs to specific industries.

- The *Particular Architecture* consists of only one level, the Particular Level. CIM-OSA provides a set of guidelines for creating the contents of a Particular Architecture from that of a Reference Architecture. To ease the definition of these guidelines, the creation process has been decomposed into three dimensions:

  - Instantiation, which corresponds to the Architecture axis

  - Derivation, which corresponds to the Modeling (See 12.4.2.2) axis

  - Generation, which corresponds to the View (See 12.4.2.3) axis

  These creation processes are then applied between all levels and views of the architecture.

12.4.2.2   CIM-OSA Modeling Levels

The *CIM-OSA Modeling Levels* allow modeling of both user and CIM system aspects of the enterprise. Three such levels have been defined.

- The *Enterprise Modeling Level* enables the gathering of business requirements of a particular enterprise. Different aspects (See Views in 12.4.2.3) can be established in order to isolate these from requirements, and the requirements can be optimized (e.g., by simulation) according to criteria defined by the user.

- The *Intermediate Modeling Level* allows the requirements, once they have been optimized and logically restructured, to be included in a single model. This model provides a nonredundant and system-oriented description of the business requirements. This level provides isolation between the Enterprise Modeling Level and the Implementation Modeling Level, which is discussed below.

The Intermediate Modeling View is created by making technological choices about the enterprise requirements, expressed in the set of Enterprise Level Views, can be provided in an optimal manner, which may require logically restructuring these requirements to remove redundancy. This derivation process generates four Intermediate Modeling Level Views from the Enterprise Modeling Level Views. These are:

- Function View, a logical grouping of Business Processes

- Information View, a logical grouping of information

- Resource View, a logical grouping of resources

- Organization View, a logical grouping of responsibilities

Current efforts have concentrated on the Intermediate Modeling Information View. The *Conceptual Schema* is the major construct used in the Information View at this modeling level. In this sense, parallel to repositories, this view contains only meta-data and is referred to in CIM-OSA as a *meta-model*.

The main inputs to the creation of a Particular Intermediate Information View are the Particular Enterprise Model and the Reference Architecture constructs for the Information View.

• The *Implementation Modeling Level* enables the translation of the Intermediate Modeling Level contents into a complete system description. This description specifies all the selected components to be included in the CIM system, together with other relevant information such as flow of action and responsibilities.

The contents of the Implementation Model are shown in Figure 12-6. The concept of the Integrating Infrastructure, which is of importance in CIM-OSA, will be discussed in Section 12.4.2.4.

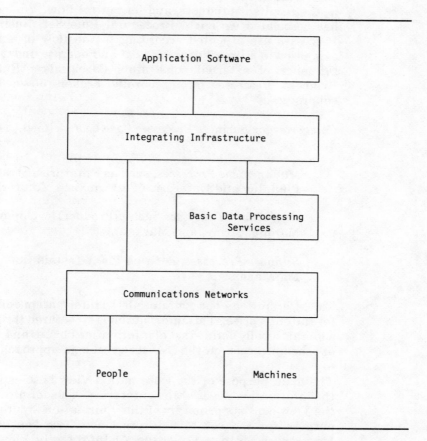

Figure 12-6   Contents of the Implementation Model.

12.4.2.3   CIM-OSA Views

Four different *CIM-OSA Views* have been identified to allow independent modeling and optimization activities to take place.

- The *Function View* is the representation of the enterprise operation in terms of a set of structured Business Processes. Each Business Process is defined by the events that trigger it, the results it produces, and its control flow. An event has associated with it a Procedural Rule Set; Business Processes are executed according to the flow of action expressed in a Procedural Rule Set and operate under the influence of external constraints (Declarative Rules). Business Processes are generally broken down into subprocesses.

  Categories for Business Processes have been defined. These are:

  - *Management Processes*, such as Enterprise Strategy Planning and Enterprise Performance Monitoring.

  - *Operational Processes*, such as Product Development, Manufacturing, and Marketing.

  - *Support Processes*, such as Plant Installation, and Maintenance.

- The *Information View* contains all the information defined for the enterprise. This information is structured through a hierarchically defined set of information classes and a set of schemas based on the ISO three-schema approach.

  The main purpose of the Information View is to capture the information needs of the enterprise. The definition of the View consists primarily of the information inputs and outputs for the set of enterprise activities beneath a hierarchy of Business Processes. An Information View can be generated either for a selection of enterprise activities within a Business Process or for all the enterprise activities.

  - Business Processes tend to range from management to research, and from sales to quality assurance. Current AMICE efforts have been limited to the development of information class structures related to the manufacturing area, and four classes have been defined that are of interest to the user. These are: Product Information, Manufacturing Planning and Control Information, Shop Floor Information, and

Basic Information (e.g., company standards and guidelines, and descriptions valid for the entire enterprise).

–   An *Information Item* is the lowest-level element in any information class. Details about an information item are specified as attributes of the information item.

• The *Resource View* contains all relevant information on enterprise resources; it is structured using a hierarchical concept of cells that are used to group resources.

• The *Organization View* contains all relevant information on enterprise responsibilities; it is also structured using a hierarchical concept of cells that are used to organize responsibilities according to enterprise requirements. This View is considered particularly important by CIM-OSA, as it allows gathering the different responsibilities in the enterprise for function, information, and resources. A multidimensional hierarchy can be used for this purpose.

12.4.2.4   *Integrating Infrastructure*

A major factor preventing the realization of CIM systems today is the lack of an Integrated Environment for them. In CIM-OSA terms, this environment is realized by the *Integrating Infrastructure*. Such an infrastructure serves more than one role:

• It provides common support services to all and should do so at a price lower than an individual user can provide them at, and at a price that is justifiable.

• It coordinates the use of resources.

Problems exist with this concept that will have to be addressed in the future. Among these are:

• Business-oriented services must be implemented by each enterprise according to the manner in which the enterprise conducts its business.

- Information services are mostly based on proprietary technology (e.g., DBMS). They rarely operate in a multivendor environment and tend to be incompatible with each other.

- The infrastructure is vulnerable to changes in technology which must be hidden from the users of the services.

CIM-OSA addresses these problems by specifying a set of services that will control and integrate the definitions in a particular implementation model and the resources performing these functions. This will be achieved by adhering to a set of architectural principles and well-defined protocols.

The services provided by the Integrating Infrastructure are layered in the following manner:

- System-wide Business Process Management Services
- System-wide Information Management Services
- System-wide Exchange Services
- System-wide Front End Services

Communications are in accordance with the Basic Reference Model for Open System Interconnection (ISO 7498). CIM-OSA introduces a generic construct at Layer 7 of this Reference Model called *Functional Entity*. The Functional Entity is an active element that can communicate with other Functional Entities.

In the CIM-OSA Environments (See Section 12.4.2.5) all active elements are Functional Entities, and the whole environment is modeled as a network of Functional Entities. This approach to providing an abstract description uses an Object-Oriented paradigm, and Functional Entities can be considered as Objects. In this sense, Functional Entities are typed.

A Functional Entity can act as a requestor, responder, or both. Communication between two cooperating Functional Entities uses a mechanism referred to as *Transactions*. A Transaction includes three operations:

- Sending a request data unit from the requestor to the responder.

- Action by the responder on the request.

- Sending a response data unit from the responder to the requestor.

In the above, the data units are structured types called *Protocol Data Units*. The entirety of Protocol Data Units agreed to between two partners together with the transaction-oriented interaction rule is called a *Transaction Protocol*. Three categories of protocols have been defined:

- *Access Protocols* between different types of services of the CIM-OSA Integrating Infrastructure.

- *Agent Protocols* between the same types of services of the CIM-OSA Integrating Infrastructure.

- *External Protocols* between the services of the CIM-OSA Integrating Infrastructure and the Functional Entities external to the CIM-OSA Integrating Infrastructure.

12.4.2.5 *CIM-OSA Environments*

To provide the required Business Integration, Application Integration, and Physical Integration, CIM-OSA offers an integrated environment that is subdivided into two parts:

- The *Integrated Enterprise Engineering Environment*, which is intended to provide support for the design and modification of the enterprise system.

- The *Integrated Enterprise Operational Environment*, which is intended to provide ongoing support for the execution of the Business Processes contained in the released Implementation Model.

The CIM-OSA Integrating Infrastructure is common to both the Engineering and Operational environments.

12.4.2.6 *Projected Future CIM-OSA Activities*

The AMICE team will continue to refine the CIM-OSA architecture in the next phase of the project. Tasks to be undertaken include the following:

- Completion of the Functional Standards for the Integrating Infrastructure by definition of protocols

- Creation of generic definitions of the inputs/outputs for enterprise activities

Additionally, a concerted effort will be made to convert CIM-OSA into a set of European national standards in the member countries, leading to it becoming the European standard for Computer Integrated Manufacturing.

12.4.2.7   *CIM-OSA and Repositories*

The goals pursued by CIM-OSA and repository technologies are parallel. In each case, an enterprise model is to be constructed that can be used for enterprise integration. However, the methodology employed by the two technologies is quite dissimilar.

The modeling effort in CIM-OSA is driven by the definition of processes that can be used to achieve integration. Data modeling is almost relegated to a background role, since that once the processes have been defined, data modeling occurs in the form of specifying the inputs and outputs (and in some cases, the internal data stores) of these processes. These definitions eventually become part of an Information View, which is the CIM-OSA equivalent of a repository.

Repository-driven modeling, such as takes place with Repository Manager, takes a totally different approach toward achieving the goal of enterprise integration. Here, the primary emphasis is on describing the enterprise in terms of data structures. Once this has been achieved, powerful mechanisms are available that allow the required functionality that expresses the processes of the enterprise to be defined and constructed.

There is no universally accepted opinion as to which approach yields better results. However, some way will have to be found to make the two approaches coexist, since true integration across enterprises will require the ability to span enterprises that use such different methodologies.

APPENDIX

The following **IBM Publications** on AD/Cycle and Repository Manager/MVS are available:

G520-6626	IBM AD/Cycle: Blueprint for a More Productive Future
G320-9841	IBM AD/Cycle: Product Positioning
G320-6707	Getting Started – Planning for IBM's AD/Cycle
GC26-4641	DevelopMate General Information
GC26-4670	Workstation Interactive Test Tool: General Information
GC26-4671	Software Analysis Test Tool: General Information
G520-6657	IBM Languages: Powerful Programming Language Solutions for Tomorrow's Application Development
GC26-4341	Systems Application Architecture: An Overview
GC26-4531	SAA AD/Cycle Concepts
G520-6654	AD/Cycle Tools Design – Digest
SC26-4684	SAA CPI Repository Reference
GC26-4608	Repository Manager/MVS: General Information
SC26-4612	Repository Manager/MVS: Guide for Users and Administrators

SC26-4613	Repository Manager/MVS: Installation
SC26-4619	Repository Manager/MVS: Repository Modeling Guide
SC26-4620	Repository Manager/MVS: Repository Modeling Reference
SC26-4616	Repository Manager/MVS: Storage View Administration
SC26-4615	Repository Manager/MVS: Security Administration
SC26-4621	Repository Manager/MVS: Programming Guide
SC26-4622	Repository Manager/MVS: Programming Reference
GC26-4734	Repository Manager/MVS: Licensed Program Specifications
GC26-4830	Repository Manager/MVS: Supplied Entity-Relationship Model Definition
SC26-4571	Dictionary Model Transformer: User's Guide
SC26-4579	Query Management Facility: Accessing Repository Data
GG24-3510	Repository Manager/MVS Release 1 Early Experiences (Red Book)

INDEX

A

Action code 160, 164, 173, 174, 176-181, 184, 199, 200, 227, 228, 237
Action qualifier 160, 164
AD/Cycle 1, 5, 6, 29, 31-33, 32, 34-41, 44, 124, 133, 312, 318, 333
Aggregation type 50, 51, 73, 74, 92, 93, 115, 119, 128, 132, 139, 146, 147,
    149-153, 201, 208, 214, 217, 218, 220-223, 239, 249, 250-252, 254, 260,
    263
Aggregation type 92, 129, 249
AIM 273-275, 324
AIX 12
Alias 114
American National Standards Institute 303
Anchor entity types 138, 142, 143, 142
API 21, 62, 171, 181, 184, 194, 289
Application Development/Cycle *see* AD/Cycle
Application Interface Macro *see* AIM
Arrayed template 67, 158, 166, 169, 174, 274
Attribute 129, 293, 309
Attribute 48, 51, 54, 55, 57, 69, 75, 76, 79, 81, 85, 86, 88, 89, 92-96, 98,
    101-103, 102-104, 107-110, 112-116, 125, 131, 135, 137, 138, 142, 146,
    147, 152, 157, 158, 164-166, 188, 189, 192-195, 197, 204-207, 212, 216,
    227, 238, 241, 245, 246, 247, 256, 265, 281, 290-293, 296, 298, 299, 309

E